LLEWE

2 0

Witches' Spell-A-Day Almanac

Holidays & Lore   Spells & Recipes
Rituals & Meditations

Copyright 2010 Llewellyn Worldwide Ltd.
Editing: Ed Day; Design: Michael Fallon
Cover Design: Lisa Novak; Background Photo: © PhotoDisc
Monthly Introductions by Ember Grant; Interior Art: © 2005, Terry Miura (illustrations: pp. 11, 31, 51, 73, 93, 113, 131, 151, 173, 193, 213, 233);
© 2005 Eris Klein (holiday and day icons)

You can order Llewellyn books and annuals from *New Worlds*,
Llewellyn's catalog. To request a free copy of the catalog, call toll-free
1-877-NEW WRLD, or visit our website at http://subscriptions.llewellyn.com

ISBN: 978-0-7387-1136-2
Llewellyn is a registered trademark of Llewellyn Worldwide Ltd.
2143 Wooddale Drive
Woodbury, MN 55125

Table of Contents

About the Authors

Chandra Alexandre is an initiated Tantrika and hereditary Witch. The founder and executive director of SHARANYA (www.sharanya .org), Chandra has worked to help those in the West seeking to embrace the ancient (yet living) embodied and goddess-centered spiritual traditions of India. Chandra holds a Ph.D. in philosophy and religion, and an MBA in sustainable management.

Elizabeth Barrette has been involved with the Pagan community for more than twenty years. She served as the managing editor of *PanGaia* for eight years and the Dean of Studies at the Grey School of Wizardry for four. She lives in central Illinois and enjoys gardening for wildlife and stone magic. Visit her LiveJournal "The Wordsmith's Forge" at http://ysabetwordsmith.livejournal.com.

Castiel is a Green Witch who embraced Neopaganism in 1993 and has been a member of the Elder Grove of the Coven of the Tangled Pines, Tangled Woods Tradition of Witchcraft, since 2006. She has a master's in Theological Studies from the Vanderbilt Divinity School and is pursuing professional studies in massage therapy and herbalism. She lives in her East Nashville, Tennessee, cottage with her husband and eight nonhuman children.

Dallas Jennifer Cobb has made a magical life in a waterfront village on the shore of Lake Ontario. She teaches Pilates, works in a library, and writes to finance long hours spent with her daughter. She regularly writes for Llewellyn almanacs and wrote two novels with support from National Novel Writing Month (www.NaNoWriMo.org). Contact her at: jennifer.cobb@live.com.

Raven Digitalis is a Neopagan priest of the "disciplined eclectic" shadow magick tradition Opus Aima Obscuræ, and is a radio and club deejay. He is the author of *Goth Craft: The Magickal Side of Dark*

Culture. With his Priestess Estha, Raven holds community gatherings, tarot readings, and a variety of ritual services. The two also operate the metaphysical business Twigs and Brews.

Ellen Dugan, a.k.a. "The Garden Witch," is an award-winning author and a psychic-clairvoyant. She has been a practicing Witch for more than twenty-four years. Ellen has written many books, including *Garden Witchery*, *Cottage Witchery*, and *How to Enchant a Man.* www.ellendugan.com.

Abel R. Gomez is a freelance writer who also performs, sings, leads rituals, goes to school, and worships Maa Kali in the San Francisco Bay Area. His magick is aimed at uncovering the beauty of the Earth for use as a tool of transformation and deep healing. An active member of the Reclaiming community of Witches, he also studies Shakta Tantra.

Ember Grant, a freelance writer, poet, and regular contributor to Llewellyn's annuals, wrote the monthly introductions as well as many spells. She lives in Missouri with her husband of thirteen years and their two feline companions.

James Kambos is a regular contributor to Llewellyn annuals whose spellcrafting spark began when he watched his grandmother create spells based on Greek folk magic. When not writing, he paints in the American primitive style. He calls the beautiful Appalachian hill country of southern Ohio home.

Sharynne MacLeod NicMhacha is a Celtic priestess, writer, teacher, and bard of Scottish, Irish, and Welsh ancestry, a direct descendant of "Fairy Clan" MacLeod. She trained in Celtic studies at Harvard and has also studied with a number of indigenous shamans. She is also a professional singer and musician (The Moors) and author (*Queen of the Night*). www.mobiusbandwidth.com.

Paniteowl is lives in the foothills of the Appalachians in northeast Pennsylvania where she and her husband are developing a private retreat for spiritual awarenes. She is co-coordinator of two annual events in Virginia known as the Gathering of the Tribes. She is founder and elder high priestess of the Mystic Wicca tradition.

Susan Pesznecker lives in Oregon and teaches writing at Portland State University and Clackamas Community College. She also teaches online courses in magick through the Grey School of Wizardry.

Diana Rajchel lives in Minneapolis, where she engages with the city spirit daily. A full-time writer, artist, and priestess, she enjoys the world around her and connects to the spiritual through her creative efforts. You can learn more about her and find her blogs at http://dianarajchel.com.

Laurel Reufner has been a solitary Pagan and writer for over a decade. Southeastern Ohio has always been home, where she lives with her wonderful husband and two adorable heathens, er, daughters, and her best friend Kate. She blogs at www.trylsmeanderings.blogspot.com.

Tess Whitehurst is an advocate of self-love, self-expression, and personal freedom. She's also the author of *Magical Housekeeping*, a columnist for *NewWitch* magazine, an intuitive counselor, and a feng shui practitioner. Her website, www.tesswhitehurst.com, and free monthly e-newsletter, *Good* Energy*, include simple rituals, meditations, and musings for everyday magical living.

A Note on Magic and Spells

The spells in the *Witches' Spell-A-Day Almanac* evoke every-day magic designed to improve our lives and homes. You needn't be an expert on magic to follow these simple rites and spells; as you will see if you use these spells through the year, magic, once mastered, is easy to perform. The only advanced technique required of you is the art of visualization.

Visualization is an act of controlled imagination. If you can call up in your mind a picture of your best friend's face or a flag flapping in the breeze, you can visualize. In magic, visualizations are used to direct and control magical energies. Basically, the spellcaster creates a visual image of the spell's desired goal, whether it be perfect health, a safe house, or a protected pet.

Visualization is the basis of all good spells, and as such it is a tool that should be properly used. Visualization must be real in the mind of the spellcaster so that it allows him or her to raise, concentrate, and send forth energy to accomplish the spell.

Perhaps when visualizing you'll find that you're doing every-thing right, but you don't feel anything. This is common, for we haven't been trained to acknowledge—let alone utilize—our magical abilities. Keep practicing, however, for your spells can "take" even if you're not the most experienced natural magician.

You will notice also that many spells in this collection have a some-what "light" tone. They are seemingly fun and frivolous, filled with rhyme and colloquial speech. This is not to diminish the serious-ness of the purpose, but rather to create a relaxed atmosphere for the practitioner. Lightness of spirit helps focus energy; rhyme and common language help the spellcaster remember the words and train the mind where it is needed. The intent of this magic is indeed very serious at times, and magic is never to be trifled with.

Even when your spells are effective, magic won't usually sparkle before your very eyes. The test of magic's success is time, not imme-diate eye-popping results. But you can feel magic's energy for your-

self by rubbing your palms together briskly for ten seconds, then holding them a few inches apart. Sense the energy passing through them, the warm tingle in your palms. This is the power raised and used in magic. It comes from within and is perfectly natural.

Effective magic is often the result of small consistent efforts, which can be as simple as taking advantage of the day's energy to start something new or to banish a negative force in your life. For long-term goals related to health, wealth, or relationships, this could mean storing that energy in a stone, oil, talisman, or another manner so you may draw on it in the future.

Among the features of the *Witches' Spell-A-Day Almanac* are an easy-to-use "book of days" format; new spells specifically tailored for each day of the year (and its particular magical, astrological, and historical energies); and additional tips and lore for various days throughout the year—including color correspondences based on planetary influences, obscure and forgotten holidays and festivals, and an incense-of-the-day to help you waft magical energies from the ether into your space.

In creating this product, we were inspired by the ancient almanac traditions and the layout of the classic nineteenth-century almanac *Chamber's Book of Days*, which is subtitled *A Miscellany of Popular Antiquities in Connection with the Calendar*. As you will see, our fifteen authors this year made history a theme of their spells, and we hope that by knowing something of the magic of past years we may make our current year all the better.

Enjoy your days, and have a magical year!

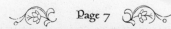

Spells at a Glance by Date and Category *

	Health	Protection	Money/ Success	Love and Relation- ships	Travel and Communi- cation	Home and Garden	Earth/ World
Jan.	6, 11, 12, 14, 31	13, 20, 21	5, 9, 22, 23, 27, 31	17	30	16, 26, 28	17
Feb.	5, 6, 9, 22, 23, 27	4, 7, 19, 28	16, 17, 8, 15	11, 25	20	3	26
Mar.	1, 6, 19, 28, 30	2, 7, 16, 29	10	4, 12, 23		18, 26	9, 22
Apr.	2, 4, 15, 20	19, 21	1, 12, 14	9, 18, 28, 29	27	7, 30	22
May	16, 25, 26	9, 20, 21	15	6, 13, 31	4	7, 10, 14, 19, 22, 29	8, 23
June	2, 7, 12, 20, 30	5, 11, 14, 28	16, 27,	4, 10, 26	3	23	22
July	5, 9, 10, 12, 17	20, 26, 29	11, 13, 28, 31	22	8, 14, 18, 27		
Aug.	5, 6, 10, 18	22, 29, 31	4, 9, 19	7, 12, 17, 26	11, 23	2, 3, 24	25
Sep.	11, 19		1, 5, 14	17, 20, 21	6, 7	8, 10, 16	
Oct.	8, 13, 16	6, 15, 21, 23	9, 19, 20	3, 7, 14	2, 10	4, 24, 29	
Nov.	5, 13, 20, 26	1, 3, 7, 14, 19	8	9, 11, 16, 21		12	
ec.		11, 15	8, 28	12, 26	3, 9, 16	23	6

is not comprehensive. Does not include spells that cross over into multiple
ies.

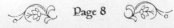

2011
Year of Spells

January is the first month of the Gregorian calendar, named for the Roman god Janus, god of doorways. Janus is often depicted with two faces, one looking forward and the other back, signifying the ending of one year and the beginning of another. January's Full Moon is called the Wolf Moon. Its astrological sign, Capricorn, the Goat (December 21–January 20), is a cardinal-earth sign ruled by Saturn. Though the ground is cold and bare, a sense of newness can be felt. Traditions around the world include personal resolutions to make a fresh start. This is a time to assess the past year, make future plans, and organize the home. Twelfth Night celebrations, which originated with the concluding Roman Saturnalia festivities, are held during January. In some cultures, a cake is baked with charms, such as a coin for prosperity or a ring for marriage, inside to predict the future for those who find them. In the Norse tradition, the Yule log is extinguished and the ashes saved to kindle next year's fire. This brought good fortune and ensured the transition of one year to the next. Making toasts is a popular way to ring in the New Year. Wassail has been a drink of good wishes since the 1400s. It's an ale-based drink with honey and spices, served in small bowls. Toast with the words *waes hael*, which is old English for "be well."

January 1
Saturday

New Year's Day – Kwanzaa ends

 4th ♐

Color of the day: Gray
Incense of the day: Patchouli

honoring the Three Fates

Called the Parcae (Roman), Moirae (Greek), or Norns (Germanic), the Fates are the controllers of destiny: one spins the thread of life, one measures it, and one cuts it. Today, therefore, this New Year's Day, is a day to open to the dance of free will and determinism. Allow yourself to find acceptance of what is and create intention around what will be. Call on the three Fates to work with you as you delve more deeply into your soul's purpose and put energy toward your heart's yearning:

O Fates! I call upon you to witness my work;

I trust in your wisdom.

As I walk my path, I release attachment to outcomes;

And I embrace the alignment of my inner and outer worlds.

Today, I make a commitment to myself and all that makes me

Who I have been, who I am, and who I will be.

Chandra Alexandre

Holiday lore: New Year's Day calls for safeguards, augurs, charms, and proclamations. All over the world on this day, people kiss strangers, shoot guns into the air, toll bells, and exchange gifts. Preferred gifts are herring, bread, and fuel for the fire.

January 2
Sunday

 4th ♐

Color of the day: Gold
Incense of the day: Frankincense

Nordic Blessings

Bring some luck and energy into your life with this very simple spell and celebrate the new beginnings that the new year brings. You need a stone with at least one flat

surface and a green marker or crayon. Cleanse the stone with whatever method you wish. Using the green marker, inscribe the rune Thurisaz (ᚦ) onto the stone's flat surface. Thurisaz can act as a gateway rune, which will help you choose a path for the new year. It would not hurt to ask Freya's blessing as well. Keep the stone somewhere safe, either carrying it on your person or placing it on your altar.

Laurel Reufner

January 3
Monday

 4th ♐
☽ → ♑ 2:39 am

Color of the day: Silver
Incense of the day: Clary sage

Bardic Spell for 12 Days of Yule
In Wales, January 3 was one of the Twelve Days of Christmas, and many wonderful traditions took place during this time. The Yule log was kept burning and its ashes kept as a charm for protection and fertility. Wassail was served (cakes and

apples cooked together and mixed with warm ale and spices). A procession known as the Mari Lwyd took place in Wales in which a decorated horse's skull led a procession door to door in a contest of poetic skill. Recite this traditional song of winter poetry and story to brighten the dark nights:

> Let us hear, wise ones, where you come from and what you request.
>
> The custom of wassailing has existed for a thousand years . . .
>
> Sing your best, as I shall too, and the winner shall drink ale!
>
> My talent is singing at night . . . I am an unbeatable rhymer!
>
> I'll sing for a year without fearing any evening during the holidays . . .

Sharynne MacLeod NicMhacha

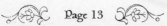

January 4
Tuesday

 4th ♑
New Moon 4:03 am

Color of the day: Red
Incense of the day: Geranium

The Courage to Begin

It's the first New Moon of the New Year—so much beginning energy that we can hardly stand it!—and it is Tuesday, blessed by the courage and sense of adventure of Mars. Make an oil today to use throughout the year whenever you need the courage to try something new or see something through. You'll need a dark glass bottle with a screw-on lid, like maybe an old vanilla extract bottle (fill with rock salt and water to get the vanilla smell out). Start with 2 tablespoons of olive oil and add 9 drops of oregano essential oil, 9 drops of bay essential oil, and 9 drops of cinnamon essential oil. Store the tightly capped bottle in a dark and cool place, and shake and charge whenever you use it to anoint yourself or something related to your endeavor, like your tennis shoes, school bag, or a special outfit (just don't stain the fabric!).

Castiel

January 5
Wednesday

 1st ♑
☽ → ♒ 11:08 am

Color of the day: Brown
Incense of the day: Marjoram

A Round Tuit Spell

Even with the best of intentions, sometimes we get caught up in our everyday lives and procrastinate activities we really feel are important. The "Round TUIT Spell" is to remind us to make the time to accomplish our goals. Here's what you need:

A round, wooden disk, any size
A sharp carving knife
A piece of dragon's blood (dark-red resin)

Lightly sand the disk, and then carve four symbols at the north, east, west, and south locations. The symbols can be anything you want to represent your desires. When you have completed the carving, rub the disk with the chunk of dragon's blood until the symbols are solidly colored. Hang the disk in a prominent place so that you see it every day and remind yourself of what you need to do to accomplish your goals.

Paniteowl

January 6
Thursday

1st ♒

Color of the day: Turquoise
Incense of the day: Clove

The Bull Games

According to Slavic tradition, today is Turisi, the holiday of the bull, Jar-tur. In ancient times, people celebrated this occasion by making and wearing masks of bulls, cows, and other figures. They made a great parade through the village, bellowing and prancing in imitation of the Great Bull. People of all ages played games of strength, stamina, and cleverness. These games, called *turisi*, gave the holiday its name. The bull represents the power of life and fertility. Observe this holiday today with rowdy outdoor games if possible (play indoor games if weather is harsh). A mask-making workshop full of colorful materials can help pass the long winter hours. Serve beef at your feast and honor the life force of the Great Bull.

Elizabeth Barrette

Holiday lore: Twelfth Night and the night following it are when wassailing used to take place. The word "wassail" comes from the Anglo-Saxon words *waes hael*, meaning "to be whole or healthy." People drank to each other's health from a large bowl filled with drink such as "lamb's wool," which was made of hot ale or cider, nutmeg, and sugar with roasted crab apples. In some parts of Britain, trees and bees are still wassailed to ensure a healthy crop. Having drunk to the tree's health, people fire shotguns into the branches. Different regions sing different wassail songs to the tree. Here's one from Worcestershire:

> *Here's to thee, old apple tree,*
> *Whence thou mayest bud,*
> *Whence thou mayest blow,*
> *Whence thou mayest bear*
> *apples enow.*

January 7
Friday

 1st ≈

☽ → ♓ 9:57 pm

Color of the day: White
Incense of the day: Violet

Filled with Faith

Today's the day the Russian Orthodox Church celebrates Christmas, as marked according to the old Julian calendar, thirteen days after Western Christmas. Having survived persecution and suppression during the communist era of Russia, it is a day of both solemn ritual and joyous celebration. Take your lead from the Russians, and do a spell reaffirming your faith and your right to practice it. Quietly affirm who you are, and what you believe. Then run your hands over your body from the top of your head to the tip of your toes, saying "Top to bottom, all of me is safe and free to be," affirming your right to live as you choose and practice your faith in your own way. Today, be filled with faith—express it through your words, actions, and intentions. In honor of Orthodox Christmas, give small gifts and blessings to the people you care for.

Dallas Jennifer Cobb

January 8
Saturday

 1st ♓

Color of the day: Blue
Incense of the day: Sage

Kaleidoscope Perspective Spell

When you get stuck while working on a creative project or when interpersonal relations become politically charged and entangled, changing your point of view or breaking the issue into smaller pieces is usually the best way to solve the problem. The next time this happens, get a kaleidoscope from any place that sells toys. Visualize something that represents your issue as you turn the kaleidoscope. Directing your emotions to the fragments you see, observe how the pattern splits and breaks, but remains beautiful. If you have a kaleidoscope that fragments images telescope-style, point it against something yellow, the color of creativity. Allow the fragmenting to also break apart your feeling into smaller bits—as you do this and after, new approaches will occur to you. As soon as you are done, write down the thoughts that came to you while looking through the kaleidoscope. They will guide you in your problem-solving.

Diana Rajchel

January 9
Sunday

 1st ♓

Color of the day: Yellow
Incense of the day: Eucalyptus

Leave Behind To Move Ahead

Janus is the two-faced god of the new year. One face looks ahead while the other looks to the past. The month of January takes its name from this Roman god—the god of gates and doorways, ending and beginnings. Today we have a waxing Moon and it's the first day of the week, so this is an opportune time to invoke Janus for putting the previous year behind us and welcoming the new opportunities. Light two white candles to symbolize new beginnings. Then repeat the charm:

> *Janus, two-faced god, keeper of the gates,*
>
> *I do now leave behind last year's mistakes.*
>
> *Help me to look forward and to begin anew,*
>
> *With prosperity, hope, and optimism true.*
>
> *By Sunday's magic this spell is spun,*
>
> *For the good of all, bringing harm to none.*

Ellen Dugan

January 10
Monday

 1st ♓

☽ → ♈ 10:24 am

Color of the day: Gray
Incense of the day: Lily

Ignite Your Intuition

After dark, in a quiet place, sit in front of a moonstone, a deep blue candle, and copal incense. Light the incense, close your eyes, and take some deep breaths. When your mind is relaxed, visualize a very still lake at night, reflecting the stars. When the visualization is strong, open your eyes and light the candle as you say:

> *I ignite my intuition.*

Warm the moonstone with the flame as you say:

> *I trust my intuition.*

Hold the moonstone to your third eye (just above the area between your eyebrows) and close your eyes, visualizing the lake once more. Only now, the lake is illuminated as if from the inside. You can see fish swimming, beautiful mermaids, and even the rocks all the way at the bottom. Keep the moonstone with you until the Full Moon, and make a point of noticing and trusting your hunches and inner guidance.

Tess Whitehurst

January 11
Tuesday

 1st ♈

Color of the day: White
Incense of the day: Bayberry

Carmentalía (Roman)

Today the Romans honored Carmenta, goddess of prophecy and childbirth. Since April was a traditional Roman marriage month, many women visited Carmenta's temple nine months later, in January. Carmenta was a midwife and sibyl—she sang her prophecies and often told the fortunes of babies. Only vegetarian sacrifices were allowed at her altar. In honor of Carmenta, here is a spell to promote prophetic dreams: Mix equal parts dried rose petals and mugwort, wrap in cloth, and tie with a white ribbon. Place the bundle in your pillowcase.

> Carmenta guide my dreams each night,
>
> Aid me with your gift of sight.
>
> Show me what I need to see,
>
> As I will, so mote it be.

Ember Grant

January 12
Wednesday

 1st ♈

2nd Quarter 6:31 am
☽ → ♉ 10:37 pm

Color of the day: Yellow
Incense of the day: Lavender

Put Your Problems on Ice

Winter brings many challenges, but also offers opportunities to work magic with the seasonal materials of snow and ice. Go outside on a day when plenty of snow covers the ground. Find a snowdrift or pack snow into a small pile. Use snow, icicles, fallen twigs, and any other natural materials lying around to sculpt an image of something that frustrates or upsets you. Then make yourself a generous supply of snowballs. Throw the snowballs at the figure, shouting out all the things you haven't been able to say in polite company. Continue until it's completely buried in the snow. Then go indoors and treat yourself to a cup of hot chocolate, leaving your worries outside in the cold.

Elizabeth Barrette

January 13
Thursday

2nd ♉

Color of the day: White

Incense of the day: Apricot

Altar Cloths

The slow pace of winter is a great time for projects, including crafting a new set of altar cloths. Visit your local fabric or craft store and scan the bolts of fabric. Stick with natural materials: cotton is an ideal choice, available in numerous colors and prints. You might design different cloths for the seasons, sabbats, esbats, or your own magical specialties. Before working with the fabric, preshrink by washing it in hot water and drying fully in a dryer. Cut the cloth into the shapes you wish: triangles for Goddess magics, squares for elemental work, circles for general purposes, etc., or design the coverings to fit your available spaces. Turn the raw edges over by ¼ inch and sew, or iron-bond the edges with fusible webbing. Save the scraps to use for amulet bags, tarot wraps, and other purposes. Enjoy decorating your magical spaces with your beautiful new altar cloths!

Susan Pesznecker

January 14
Friday

2nd ♉

Color of the day: Coral

Incense of the day: Thyme

Everyday Knot Magic

Do you find yourself having days when you feel absolutely elated, happy, and full of life's energy? Do you also find yourself having "down" days of stagnation, apathy, and lack of motivation? Sure, we all do. You can help carry on positive experiences by performing simple knot magic. Grab a piece of rope, cord, or twine, and tie five knots (an inch or more apart) when you're having an energetic "up" day. As you tie the knots, heavily focus your uplifted, positive energy into the rope or cord by seeing the energy flowing off your body. You can also breathe into the rope as you tie the knot, or even tie one strand of hair inside each knot. When finished, set the rope on your altar and untie the knots on one of your "down" days in order to release the trapped, positive energy.

Raven Digitalis

January 15
Saturday

 2nd ♉

☽ → ♊ 8:23 am

Color of the day: Gray
Incense of the day: Sandalwood

honoring the God

Today marks the second ancient festival of Carmentalia, this time elebrating the birth of boys in Rome. Think about the men in your life today. How do they support you? How do they heal you? How do they heal the world? Today, do something special for a man in your life. Offer it to the God in all His myriad forms. Go out to eat or to see a movie with him. If you are a man, do something special to honor your masculinity. How does the God flow through you? How does His playful dance touch your heart?

Beloved one,
God of laughter and love,
Lord of life and renewal,
Horned one of wild beauty,
Touch my heart this day.

May this offering draw
  me deeper into your
  mysteries,
Deeper into the world,
And deeper into myself.

Blessed be.

Abel R. Gomez

January 16
Sunday

 2nd ♊

Color of the day: Gold
Incense of the day: Juniper

Melt Your Problems Away

Negative energy tends to build up more at this time of year because our homes are closed up. If you have any bad habits or linger-ing problems, this spell will help get rid of them. In a small saucepan, combine a cup of water with a small amount of orange rind, a sprinkling of ground cloves, and a cinnamon stick. Bring to a gentle boil and sim-mer for a minute. Next, place an ice cube or some snow into the simmer-ing water. Watch as it melts, and at the same time visualize your habit or problem melting away. When done, take the water mixture outside and pour it onto the ground. Walk away and don't look back.

James Kambos

January 17
Monday

Martin Luther King, Jr. Day

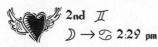 2nd ♊

☽ → ♋ 2:29 pm

Color of the day: Ivory
Incense of the day: Hyssop

"Dream" Spell for World Peace

We must concentrate not merely on the negative expulsion of war but the positive affirmation of peace.

—Martin Luther King, Jr.

Carve a peace symbol into a white candle. Fill a small dish with a little dirt from outside and place the candle on top. Relax and focus on the energy of peace. Hold your cupped hands near the candle and visualize very bright white light coming down from above, entering the crown of your head, going down to your heart, through your arms, out your hands, and into the candle. Light the candle, close your eyes, and see this white light of peace spread to the hearts of all people. See all humans everywhere filled with love and existing harmoniously with one another. Believe that this is our future. See if you can get your friends to do it too. The more people who do this spell, the better!

Tess Whitehurst

January 18
Tuesday

 2nd ♋

Color of the day: Black
Incense of the day: Cedar

Purification Spray

Banish germs and get rid of bacteria that cause illness with this practical, natural spray. Containing essential oils with natural disinfectant, antibacterial, antifungal, and antiviral agents, this spray cleanses the air, objects, and even hands, and leaves them smelling wonderful. The spiritual energy of lavender helps you to connect to spirit, resolve fear, and facilitate magical consciousness and focus. Combine:

30 drops tea tree oil
40 drops pure lavender essential oil
1 ounce food-grade alcohol
1 ounce of witch hazel
3 ounces triple distilled water

Mix all ingredients together in a spray bottle, and use regularly to spiritually and physically cleanse a space, an object (like a Pilates or yoga mat), or person. For other scents, substitute rosemary, lemongrass, orange, or eucalyptus for lavender.

Dallas Jennifer Cobb

January 19
Wednesday

2nd ♋

☽ Full Moon 4:21 pm

☽ → ♌ 5:16 pm

Color of the day: White
Incense of the day: Lilac

To Remember Your Dreams

Dream recall takes practice and repeated reinforcement. Along with regular bedtime habits, you can help the process along every evening with before-bed journaling to clear your head for dreamtime, smelling a sachet or muslin bag filled with rosemary and lavender, and reciting this appeal to the Greek god of dreams:

*Morpheus be merciful in my
night's dreamings,*

*Let me see in the morning
light what starlight brings.*

Take deep breaths, and picture yourself leaving a cave for a green field, accompanied by Morpheus or a spirit guide you know and trust. Follow the spirit into the depths of the cave. Allow this journey to take you into your dreams. When you wake up, write down any images, sounds, or sensations that come to mind. You may not remember your dreams the first few weeks, but with practice, recall will come easily and stay with you for longer throughout the day.

Diana Rajchel

January 20
Thursday

3rd ♌

☉ → ♒ 5:19 am

Color of the day: Green
Incense of the day: Nutmeg

Protect house and home

Just as the body houses the soul, the home houses the body. This spell focuses on protecting the house from negative energies, and is a good addition to any other protective exercises you may be enacting. Simply go to the main area of your home, take a match, and light a tealight candle that has the Raidho rune (ᚱ) carved on the top of the wax. The sulfur on the match head is known to drive away evil, and Raidho is an ancient letter and symbol, one of whose interpretations is "protection." Declare out loud:

I hereby banish and command all evils and malignancies in this place to FLEE!

At the base of any door that leads outside your house, as well as at the base of the candle, sprinkle an herbal mixture consisting of any parts of boneset, dill, fennel, juniper, mugwort, and mullein. Declare:

*Only protection, health, and
happiness are welcome here.
As I will, so mote it be!*

Finish by hanging additional charms

in the house (such as written rune, a sigil, a broomstick, or a wand of sage above a doorframe) and performing any additional protective magic you deem necessary.

Raven Digitalis

sacred intention to bring this magical tool into your life. To consecrate or rededicate a wand today, use the following blessing:

> Sacred tool supporting my spiritual journey, I bless and consecrate (rededicate) you as I open my heart to your inherent power. Aligning our life-force energies by this prayer, may we together magic make.

Chandra Alexandre

January 21
Friday

3rd ♂☾

☽ → ♍ 6:10 pm

Color of the day: Purple
Incense of the day: Alder

Consecrate a Magical Wand

Today is the beginning of the Celtic month of Luis, whose sacred wood is Rowan. A relative of the rose plant, rowan trees grow in harsh conditions and manifest beautiful red berries. Their wood is sacred to those seeking protection, the powers of divination, and other magical outcomes. Many practitioners consider rowan especially auspicious as a tool in spellwork and crafting. If you have a wand already, then today is the day to rededicate or consecrate it. If you do not possess a wand, then it is a good day to put out a

Holiday lore: Feast Day of Saint Agnes of Rome. Since the fourth century, the primitive church held Saint Agnes in high honor above all the other virgin martyrs of Rome. Church fathers and Christian poets sang her praises, and they extolled her virginity and heroism under torture. The feast day for Saint Agnes was assigned to January 21. Early records gave the same date for her feast, and the Catholic Church continues to keep her memory sacred.

January 22
Saturday

 3rd ♍

Color of the day: Brown
Incense of the day: Magnolia

Challenge the Status Quo

Sometimes things just need to change, and maybe you feel it's time to buck the status quo. Sketch a copy of the Hierophant card from your tarot deck, print the image of one off the Internet, or even draw your own. Gather the picture, a black candle and holder, and a broom (your magical broom is great, but the kitchen broom is just fine). Create your sacred space, and place the black candle on top of the picture. Repeat the following:

> Now remove the status quo
>
> Let the ideas flow and grow
>
> Remove what hinders and transform
>
> Sweep away the tired norm

As you chant, make the image under the candle synonymous with the situation you wish would change. When you feel the energy has reached its peak, tear the image into tiny pieces, cast it on the floor and sweep it away, cutting open your magic circle if necessary. Recycle or compost the paper for true transformation!

Castiel

January 23
Sunday

 3rd ♍
☽ → ♎ 6:59 pm

Color of the day: Orange
Incense of the day: Heliotrope

Frugality: Living Thrifty

The new year means new plans—often including a goal of frugality. To be frugal is to live sparingly and economically, with careful planning and little waste. In short, to be thrifty. In Horatio Alger's children's books, his heroes exemplified honesty, thriftiness, and hard work as a path to success. Since living frugally is easier said than done, try a little magic to help out. Work this spell during the waning Moon, when lunar energies draw inward. Use green ink (prosperity) to inscribe this charm into a pocket notebook, speaking it aloud as you work:

> Each dollar and coin I hereby vow,
> Will purpose have, 'ere it leaves this house.
> Its reason sure, its path so swift,
> This dollar's goal will charge my thrift!

Read the charm whenever you consider buying something, and keep a written account of everything you spend. With thrift comes prosperity!

Susan Pesznecker

January 24
Monday

 3rd ♎

Color of the day: Gray
Incense of the day: Neroli

The Power of Ice and Snow

In many shamanic traditions, one of the most powerful ways to work through difficulty is to honor the power of obstacles and learn to transmute these energies. When the world is locked in ice and snow, we tend to recoil, considering the wintry substances negative or devoid of life energy. Snow and ice contain powerful spirits who work to help the world sleep and rest in preparation for renewal in spring. Here is a spell to honor and harness the power of both ice and snow during the depths of wintertime:

> Great spirits of snow,
>   blanketing the earth
> Falling from the skies,
>   silently and in beauty,
> I honor your path, I honor
>   your wonder,
> I ask for the blessings of
>   nature's season of rest.
>
> Great spirits of ice,
>   magnifiers of winter sun,
> Crystalline powers creating
>   rainbows in the coldest
>   season,

> I honor your magic, I honor
>   your wisdom,
> I ask for the blessings of
>   winter's focus and inner
>   beauty.

Sharynne MacLeod NicMhacha

January 25
Tuesday

 3rd ♎
☽ → ♏ 9:15 pm

Color of the day: Scarlet
Incense of the day: Ginger

A Smoke Divination Spell

A winter evening is the perfect time to divine the future by using smoke. In a heatproof dish or your cauldron, combine equal parts thyme, sage, and wormwood. Ignite them and let them smolder. Let the smoke rise and spiral. You may wish to use a white feather to fan the smoke heavenward. Allow the smoke to curl about your fingers. Begin to let go of all cares or thoughts you may have. Don't think about any specific question. Let your eyes go in and out of focus. Watch for any signs or symbols. Some people see exact images, while others see

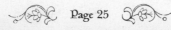

symbols. After about fifteen minutes, slowly return to your usual state of mind. Over the coming week see if any of your visions begin to manifest themselves.

James Kambos

outdoor ritual space works great, but if you don't have one, look for a wild place near your home. Visit this place as much as you can. Allow yourself to be open to all that nature can teach you. Listen. Weave magic in this place. Call to the gods and spirits of the land as your allies. Awaken to your connection to all things.

Abel R. Gomez

January 26
Wednesday

3rd ♏
4th Quarter 7:57 am

Color of the day: Topaz
Incense of the day: Marjoram

Create a Sit Spot

Magic is rooted in observation and interaction with the natural world. Sometimes our greatest lessons in magic come from just sitting in nature and opening our eyes to the vast intricacies of nature. Permaculture, an emerging system of ecological design, also observes the patterns of nature through the use of a sit spot. In this area, designers tune in to the patterns and wisdom of nature for deeper understanding of the land they wish to work with. Create your own sit spot today. An

January 27
Thursday

4th ♏

Color of the day: Purple
Incense of the day: Balsam

Banish Financial Worries

So the new calendar year is underway, and bills are coming in from holiday shopping. This is a great time to banish difficulties. You have a Jupiter day for prosperity, and a waning Moon phase to banish financial worries. Burn a green candle to encourage prosperity, and burn a black candle to remove any worry and stress over money. Repeat the following charm three times. When

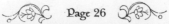

finished, allow the candles to burn in a safe place until they go out on their own.

> On this January night under a waning Moon,
>
> Lord and ladies of prosperity hear this Witch's tune.
>
> The green candle burns to promote prosperity,
>
> The black candle flames to remove any worries.
>
> The energies combine as one, through space and time,
>
> Bring to me triumph and wealth with this spell of mine.

Ellen Dugan

January 28
Friday

  4th ♏
) → ♐ 1:55 am

Color of the day: White
Incense of the day: Mint

Wind Chimes and Energy

Feng shui practitioners know how useful wind chimes can be within the home. Why not put this knowledge to use for yourself and dispel some household negativity at the same time? Is there a spot in your home where the energy seems to drag you down and make you tired, angry, or depressed? Pick a set of wind chimes appropriate in size and tone for that spot. Cleanse, bless, and consecrate them to protect your home using the method with which you are most comfortable. Finally, hang them in their chosen location and relax as the good energy flows in once more.

Laurel Reufner

January 29
Saturday

 4th ♐

Color of the day: Blue
Incense of the day: Rue

Freethinker's Spell

Today is commonly known as Freethinker's Day in honor of the birthday of Thomas Paine, author of *Common Sense*, which advocated American independence. Take time today to do a simple spell to affirm your individuality, your creative thinking, and all the ways that you are different. Be a freethinker. Sit quietly, in a safe space. Allow your breathing to deepen, lengthening each exhale, slowly drifting lower into an easy, relaxed state. Focus your awareness on the quirks and idiosyncrasies that make you uniquely you. Breath into each of these qualities, affirming it, and seeing it grow, swelling with your breath. Laugh a little at yourself, delighting in difference. Let your mind wander, and look at what you want to be free from. Allow yourself to envision freedom, independence, and ease. As you return to your daily life, take one small step toward independence, affirming your right to differ.

Dallas Jennifer Cobb

January 30
Sunday

 4th ♐

☽ → ♑ 9:04 am

Color of the day: Amber
Incense of the day: Almond

Transportation Spell

Need a new car? Here's a transportation spell that's been helpful to me! Supplies needed:

A round peridot cabochon
Plain carrier oil
A cup of spring water

Using a clockwise motion, rub the peridot with the carrier oil. Place the anointed cabochon in the cup of water. Set the cup outside at the New Moon. Picture the kind of vehicle you need and chant:

> Come to me, come to me,
> what I need is what I see.

When you're ready to go shopping, take the cabochon with you, placing it in your wallet so that the finances will be balanced with your need.

Paniteowl

January 31
Monday

 4th ♏

Color of the day: White
Incense of the day: Rosemary

A Spell to Encourage Employment

When you're job hunting, it never hurts to add some magical encouragement to your efforts. Use this spell to help increase your odds in obtaining an interview or after you've had an interview. You will need three candles. Arrange them in this manner: a yellow one in the center, an orange one on the left, and green one on the right. In front of the candles, write the job description or title on a piece of paper, or use the ad from the newspaper—any kind of paper symbol of the job you desire. On top of the paper, place a few sprigs of lavender (fresh or dried) and a piece of Devil's Shoestring (Viburnum). Visualize your goal as you light the candles. Focus on the reasons why you're the perfect candidate for the position. Allow the candles to burn out. Keep the herbs on your altar until you know the outcome of your effort.

Ember Grant

February is the second month of the Gregorian calendar. Its astrological sign is Aquarius, the Water-bearer (January 20–February 18), a fixed-air sign ruled by Uranus. The name February comes from the Latin term *februum*, which means "purification," referring to a Roman purification ritual called Februa that was held on the fifteenth. We also celebrate an important Celtic quarter-day, Imbolc, usually on February 1 or 2. The Wheel of the Year has turned toward the first stirrings of renewal, and Imbolc is a time to honor the spark of new life by paying homage to Brigid, the Celtic goddess of creativity (the spark of inspiration), the hearth and forge (spark of fire for the home), and childbirth and healing (spark of life). Honor her with candle flames and decorative lights. The church later named her Saint Brigid and Christians celebrate Candlemas on this day. This is a time to shake off the winter blues and look ahead. Groundhog Day has its origins in the Imbolc celebration, as this is a good time to practice divination. And don't forget the romance of St. Valentine's Day—a time to indulge in sweets and flowers while celebrating the warmth of love. The Finnish call this month *Helmikuu*, "the month of the pearl," to describe the beads of ice that form on tree branches when snow melts. The Full Moon of February is called the Snow Moon.

February 1
Tuesday

 4th ♑
)) → ♒ 6:21 pm

Color of the day: Red
Incense of the day: Basil

Pledge to Brigid

February 1 is the feast day of the Catholic Saint Brigid. According to Pagan lore, Saint Brigid was originally connected to the Celtic goddess Brigid, patroness of poetry, smithcraft, and healing. Brigid is a Maiden Goddess. She embodies the power of light to overcome the darkness and coldness of winter. Create a special ritual fire for Brigid today. Whether outdoors or safely in a cauldron, breathe in the energy of Brigid's flame and allow it to cleanse you of all that needs to be released. Offer a pledge to Brigid in return. As the light of life returns to the world, how can you be a force of healing, truth, and justice in the world? If you are unsure, take a few moments to breathe and meditate on what you can do. When ready, approach the flame and speak your intention. Let it flow from your heart and out to the world.

Abel R. Gomez

February 2
Wednesday

Imbolc – Groundhog Day

 4th ♒
New Moon 9:31 pm

Color of the day: White
Incense of the day: Honeysuckle

Out of the Belly

Today is especially magical because it combines the sabbat of Imbolc with the esbat of the New Moon. One meaning of Imbolc is "in the belly," the time when ewes grew heavy with lambs. The New Moon is also a time of inner life and ideas rising out of the subconscious. Use this rare confluence of energies to your advantage. Build your ritual around a black cauldron or bowl filled with soil. Use it as a focus for meditation on the meaning of this prefertile time. Contemplate what you want to bring into manifestation this growing season. Chant slowly:

In the belly
Life grows strong
It rises up
Toward the light
And then breathes out
One clear word.

Speak the word for what you seek to manifest. Light a candle and press it into the soil. Let the candles burn out after the ritual.

Elizabeth Barrette

Holiday lore: On Imbolc, a bundle of corn from the harvest is dressed in ribbons and becomes the Corn Bride. On February 2, the Corn Bride is placed on the hearth or hung on the door to bring prosperity, fertility, and protection to the home.

February 3
Thursday

Chinese New Year (rabbit)

 1st ≈

Color of the day: White
Incense of the day: Clove

Red Rabbit Fertility Spell

According to Chinese zodiacal lore, Rabbit people are admired, trusted, and are often financially lucky. Encouraging fertility this year is beneficial to the child born under this sign. You will need:

A small, white, furry toy rabbit
Finely ground dragon's blood
A small brush

Hold the rabbit in your receiving hand (the left hand for most of us). Dip the brush into the dragon's blood, and softly brush the rabbit as you croon a lullaby of your choice. When the rabbit is colored evenly by the dragon's blood, place it in the room designated for the baby, or a bassinet. If you don't have the room yet, you can put the rabbit on a shelf, placing an article of baby clothing under it. Eat healthy, exercise, and make love as often as possible.

Paniteowl

February 4
Friday

 1st ♒
☽ → ♓ 5:24 am

Color of the day: Rose
Incense of the day: Cypress

Keys to the Castle

As something you carry every day, your house keys can be powerful magical objects and talismans of protection. Cleanse, bless, and empower the keys to your home today. Sprinkle them with salt water and pass them through sage, lavender, or rosemary incense. You may want to buy or make a new key chain, perhaps with a pentacle, Moon, Goddess figure, or appropriate rune on it. Hold your keys to your heart and say:

> Guardians of my home,
> keeping thieves and harm at
> bay, link me to this space as
> I roam throughout the day.
> Give me insight into what
> passes in this place, alert me
> to trouble in this space, open
> that love may enter here, lock
> out trouble, lock out fear.

Practice using your keys as a pendulum to divine for possible problems at home while you're out, and use them as a talisman to send good ...es home when you're away.

Castiel

February 5
Saturday

 1st ♓

Color of the day: Brown
Incense of the day: Patchouli

Retrieve those Lost in Fantasy

Illusions and fantasy protect us, motivate us, and give us a way to create hope when it may not be available to us. Even so, fantasy is best consumed in moderation, lest it becomes a poison. If someone you love has become obsessed with something to the point of neglecting friends, family, and their daily lives, try this small intervention. In the brightest light you can find, stand with a picture of your loved one or his/her name written on a slip of paper, stored in a box. Open the box so that full light hits that name or face, and sprinkle coffee grounds and salt over the paper, while saying:

> Wake up, wake up! Come
> back to us!
> Stir now, hear us making
> a fuss!
> We need you in the here
> and now,
> Hear us calling — hear
> us now!

Diana Rajchel

February 6
Sunday

1st ♓
☽ → ♈ 5:45 pm

Color of the day: Gold
Incense of the day: Hyacinth

Winter Cheer

I've got just the ticket to beat the wintertime blues. This cheerful Sunday spell also has the energies of the waxing Moon to work with. All you need is a small yellow candle and a coordinating candleholder. Carve a simple Sun design on the side of the candle. Now, secure the candle back in its holder. Visualize happiness, cheer, and health coming straight to you. Finally, light the spell candle and repeat the spell verse three times.

> On this magical day of the bright golden Sun,
>
> Grant me happiness and health, as this charm is begun.
>
> Now make me more positive, enthusiastic and wise,
>
> As the waxing Moon illuminates this winter night's skies.
>
> By the power of the waxing Moon, and the rising Sun,
>
> As I will it, then so shall it be, and let it harm none.

Allow the candle to burn out on its own in a safe place.

Ellen Dugan

February 7
Monday

1st ♈

Color of the day: Silver
Incense of the day: Lily

honor Wolf-Month

In Scotland, the month of February was known by the Scottish Gaelic term *Faoilleach*, which meant "wolf-month." In Celtic tradition, it was taboo to speak the name of the wolf, and so it was known instead as a "wild dog" (*faol-chù*). In ancient times, the wolf was one of the animals associated with the horned or antlered god known as Cernunnos. It was also one of the animals honored by the ancient Picts. During this dark time of the year, honor the wolf and invoke its powers to survive *marbh-mhios*—"the dead month."

> I honor the power of the wild one
> The wild dog of the forests

*Brother of fox, cousin of
hound*

*I ask for your strength and
courage
Your cunning and your
wisdom
In this, the coldest time of
the year*

*Companion of the Horned
One
May I have your keen sight
And power to surviving the
wildness*

So may it be!

Sharynne MacLeod NicMhacha

February 8
Tuesday

1st ♈

Color of the day: Gray
Incense of the day: Cedar

The Passion Collage

Sometimes we need a little reminder of how passionate we feel about something—or a nudge to dig deep for the courage to go after our heart's desire. This little activity will produce a tangible reminder of whatever goal you are currently working toward. You will need some cardstock or light cardboard (such as a cereal box) cut to a 3½ x 2½ inch size, glue stick, magazines, or other source of images, and a piece of wide packing tape. You will also need a red candle. Spend some time searching through your images for those that resonate with your goal. Center yourself and focus on what you want to achieve. Now light the candle and, while it burns, begin creating a small collage on your card. After you're satisfied that it reflects your passion and that it encourages you toward that passion, cover it with a piece of wide packing tape to protect it. Carry it with you.

Laurel Reufner

Holiday lore: Today is the Buddhist Needle Memorial. On this day, as part of the principle of endless compassion espoused by the Buddhist faith for all sentient and nonsentient beings, all the sewing needles that have been retired during the year are honored. That is, needles are brought to the shrine and pushed into a slab of tofu that rests on the second tier of a three-tiered altar. Priests sing sutras to comfort the needles and heal their injured spirits.

February 9
Wednesday

 1st ♈

☽ → ♉ 6:22 am

Color of the day: Brown
Incense of the day: Bay laurel

Book and Bath Spell

Known as Read in the Bathtub Day, do a bathtub self-care spell today. Gather a good book, a warm cup of tea, and even a little sweet snack next to the tub. Get some oils or bubble bath, and make this a time of luxuriating. You deserve it. Choose a time when you won't be interrupted. Turn the phone off, leave a nice note on the outside of the door. Run a steamy bath, with bubbles or oil, and dip in. Take the time to indulge yourself, remembering that downtime is an important part of productivity—it renews and replenishes. Luxuriate in reading. Whether you indulge in mystery fiction, romance, or research, affirm your right to spend quiet time alone with a good book. While the cold winter winds howl outside, let the splendor of water and words restore you.

Dallas Jennifer Cobb

February 10
Thursday

1st ♉

Color of the day: Green
Incense of the day: Mulberry

Transformation

Thursday is Thor's day, the Norse thunder god—comparable gods from other cultures are Zeus and Jupiter. Since these are very powerful influences, today is a good day for magic of almost any kind. And with the Moon in a waxing phase, a spell for increase is appropriate. But, as always, be careful what you wish for! Begin by thinking about something in your life you'd like to change and focus on this clearly. Write your wish on a piece of paper. Fire is an element of transformation; for this spell, you will need a safe place to burn your wish. Do this outside if possible, or use a strong, heatproof container. Light the paper and watch it burn until it's done. Then pour water over it. As your paper burns, visualize your wish transforming into reality. Say these words:

*Fire, bring the change I
    need;
With this spell I plant the
    seed.*

Discard the ashes.

Ember Grant

February 11
Friday

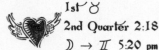

1st ♉
2nd Quarter 2:18 am
☽ → ♊ 5:20 pm

Color of the day: Purple
Incense of the day: Vanilla

"Be Irresistible" Spray Potion

This is a crafty little potion that will cloak you in a veil of irresistible charm. It's great for a job interview, party, date, or any other time you'd like to emphasize your charming qualities and attract positive attention. Fill a small mister half with rose water and half with witch hazel extract. Add 5 drops of hornbeam flower essence (available online and at many health food stores) and 6 drops of neroli essential oil. Hold the potion in both hands and mentally charge it with sparkling pink light as you repeat these magic words nine times (borrowed from the Kundalini Yoga tradition):

*Ra Ma Da Sa, Sa Say So
Hung*

To use, lightly mist your entire body and hair before you dress. You can also carry the mist along with you for a quick pick-me-up on your face, neck, shoulders, and/or hair. Always shake gently before using.

Tess Whitehurst

February 12
Saturday

 2nd ♊

Color of the day: Gray
Incense of the day: Ivy

Dedication Day

Have you played on the fringes of accepting a matron or personal deity into your life? If so, today is a good day to dedicate yourself to a special manifestation of the Divine resonant with your essence. Traditionally a time of purification, today is opportune to ask for a more direct relationship with a god or goddess. Create a simple ceremony to mark your dedication, and set an intention to work with your Chosen One for a cycle of the seasons. You may wish to have your rite witnessed by your coven or a spiritual partner, or you may keep it silent but strong at your heart. Either way, ensure that your intention aligns with your practice by making a specific honoring that you can repeat today and every day. Speak aloud:

> To thee, _____, I
> commit myself this year and
> a day. Work with me that I
> may become whole.

Chandra Alexandre

Holiday lore: Lincoln is called the Great Emancipator and is thought of as one of our greatest presidents. Know this, however: Lincoln was an almost unknown figure until the age of forty, when he first entered the Illinois state legislature. His later assassination threw the country into widespread mourning, inspiring Walt Whitman to write:

> Coffin that passes
>   through lanes and street,
>   through day and night
>   with the great cloud
>   darkening the land . . .
> I mourned, and yet shall
>   mourn with ever-
>   returning spring.

 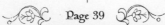

February 13
Sunday

2nd ♊

Color of the day: Yellow
Incense of the day: Almond

Shower Spell

Magic can happen anywhere, even during seemingly mundane activities. Many of us take showers every day. Add some focus and intention, and your daily shower can be a place of power and magical transformation. Begin by calling the gods and the elements of life to be present. Turn on the shower and begin to lather up. As you do so, visualize the suds of soap cleansing all thoughts or emotions that do not serve you in this moment. If you are unsure what those thoughts may be, will that what does not serve be cleansed from you. Visualize the suds washing away to reveal a glowing white light emanating from your body. Affirm:

> I am pure.
> I am present.
> I am fully in the flow of life.
> I am one with all things.
> So mote it be.

Thank the gods and elements for being present and go into the world as a child of earth and starry heaven.

Abel R. Gomez

February 14
Monday

Valentine's Day

2nd ♊

☽ → ♋ 12:48 am

Color of the day: Gray
Incense of the day: Narcissus

he Loves Me, he Loves Me Knot

This Valentine's Day, make a little special love magic with your sweetie (who must be a willing participant, of course!) by trying out some traditional knot magic. Get an 8 x 8-inch square of fabric (or larger) and hem the edges with red thread (or use a red kerchief). Tie two knots in the fabric and have your lover tie two knots. Then tie the whole thing in one big loose knot, and each hold one end. As you pull the knot tight, say:

> My love is knot, not untrue;
> with this I bind my love to
> you!

This will make it hard for anything to come between you. Keep the knot in a safe place and anoint it periodically with magical oils to keep it charged—cinnamon for spicy passion, rose for romance, and basil for fidelity. If for some reason you and your sweetie decide to part ways, just make sure to untie the knots!

Castiel

 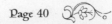

February 15
Tuesday

2nd ♋

Color of the day: White
Incense of the day: Ylang-ylang

Fortitude

Today we honor the birth of Galileo Galilei, born in Pisa, Italy, in 1564. Known for proving Copernicus' heliocentric theories of the Earth revolving around the Sun, Galileo was imprisoned and then shunned for what were regarded as dangerously heretical theories. Despite this, he clung with fortitude to his theories, becoming famous for his words, *euppur si muove*, "Nonetheless it [the Earth] does move." Are you looking for fortitude? Are you having trouble sticking to a plan or decision, or kicking a habit? Call upon the wisdom and strength of Galileo! Create a round talisman: a round stone, piece of cardboard, wood cookie, etc. Paint it yellow and inscribe with concentric circles and a central dot for the Sun. On the other side, draw or carve the rune Uruz (ᚢ) for belief and forbearance. Charge the talisman under Galileo's Sun and keep it with you at all times until your plans reach fruition.

Susan Pesznecker

February 16
Wednesday

2nd ♋

☽ → ♌ 4:14 am

Color of the day: Yellow
Incense of the day: Lilac

Buy Local Enchantment

In Japan, February 16 is Fumi-e, a day when people demonstrate their nonattachment to Western imports. Borrowing from the Japanese tradition, use the spirit of the day to celebrate the vitality of your local economy, practicing your nonattachment to imports. *Enchantment* comes from the French word *enchanter*, meaning to cast a spell over, to bewitch, to attract and delight. Traditionally, an enchantment was performed by the recitation of rhythmic or rhyming words that were chanted, whispered, or sung. The vibration of the words and music affects whoever hears them, producing an enchantment. Take time today to shop in small family-owned businesses, patronize local artisans, lunch from fresh local foods or make something from scratch. Chant or sing:

> *Buy it local, shop close to home,*
>
> *Buy from farmers that you know,*

Support your community,

Stand in unity,

Seek what locals make and grow.

Buying local works great magic affecting many.

Dallas Jennifer Cobb

On this night of the waxing Moon, I call for prosperity,

Jupiter's influence will send abundance swiftly to me.

Four tumbled stones around a green candle so fair,

Will bring me money, success, and riches to share.

By the power of the crystals true,

May I be blessed in all that I do.

Ellen Dugan

Ｆebruary 17
Thursday

 2nd ♌

Color of the day: Purple
Incense of the day: Myrrh

Prosperity and Charity

It's a Jupiter day and we have a waxing Moon—an ideal time to work spells to promote prosperity! Light a green candle and surround it with the following tumbled stones; malachite, aventurine, bloodstone, and tiger's eye. Then repeat this prosperity spell that works with candle and crystal magic. When the prosperity you are casting for manifests in your life, be sure to give a small portion of it to charity to symbolize your gratitude.

February 18
Friday

2nd ♌

 Full Moon 3:36 am

☽ → ♍ 4:39 am

☉ → ♓ 7:25 pm

Color of the day: Pink
Incense of the day: Orchid

Enchant Your Tools

Every Witch or magician works with some magical tools. It's a good idea to recharge these tools on a regular basis. Some practitioners may only enchant particular tools on particular days. Generally, this has to do with the material that forms the tool, or with the tool's magical usage (e.g., whether its magic is projective, receptive, commanding, containing, etc.). Times for enchanting generally vary as a result of astrological factors, certainly including the day's precise lunar and solar alignments. Whether or not you choose precise days, times, or hours to more deeply enchant your tools, a "quickie recharge" can be performed on any Full Moon. Simply grab your tools and set them on a silver platter or in a silver cooking bowl or baking pan. Place all of this on the ground outside, directly under moonlight. Sprinkle water and sea salt on the tools (consecrate these as you normally would), and situate a tealight candle and a stick of all-natural

incense on either side of the tray. Summon the elements and visualize the tools surrounded in glowing white moonlight. You may also direct energy from the Moon into the tools. Leave these overnight and repeat on any Full Moon you desire!

Raven Digitalis

February 19
Saturday

3rd ♍

Color of the day: Indigo
Incense of the day: Pine

Sensitivity Spell

The sign of the Fish is traditionally imaginative, sensitive, compassionate, selfless, and unworldly. Sometimes, our own sensitivity can overwhelm us emotionally. Along with an active imagination, we can scare ourselves silly! A plain crystal can be used to help you be aware of a situation, without being drawn into someone else's drama. Find a crystal that resonates with you. Either carry it with you or wear it as a pendant. When you feel yourself getting too caught up in another person's issue

 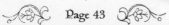

hold the crystal in your "sending" hand (for most of us, this is the right hand), and focus on the situation while mentally stepping back and being more of an observer than a participant. This will aid you in helping others without damaging your own psyche. Cleanse your crystal often by setting it in the moonlight at least once a month.

Paniteowl

environment? The following divination spell can add to your insights. Choose four pennies. Put them with the target object, or a photo or other representation of it, for at least a full day. Cup the pennies in your hands and drop them onto a flat surface. Count the heads:

4 heads = highly useful, no significant problems.
3 heads = significantly useful, only minor problems.
2 heads = so-so; somewhat useful, but fraught with challenges.
1 head = probably more trouble than it's worth.
0 heads = not very useful, causing significant problems.

Elizabeth Barrette

February 20
Sunday

 3rd ♏

☽ → ♎ 4:01 am

Color of the day: Amber
Incense of the day: Eucalyptus

Divination for Early Adopters

Technology offers many benefits, but often comes with a cost, sometimes hidden. Before deciding whether to adopt a new device, service, or program, consider its pros and cons: What will it do for you? What will it take from you? How will using it affect other people and the

February 21
Monday

Presidents' Day (observed)

 3rd ♎

Color of the day: White
Incense of the day: Neroli

Call the Winds of Winter

In the Scottish Gaelic folk calendar, the third week of February was known as an *Feadag*, "The Whistle," because of the cold, whistling winds heard at this time of year. It came between the period of time known as an *Faoilleach* (the Wolf Month) and an *Cailleach* (the Hag). In some areas, it was followed by short periods known as an *Gobag* (the Sharp-Billed One), an *Sguabag* (the Sweeper), and an *Gearan* (the Complaint). These names referred to particular types of wind and weather which were keenly observed by the Highlanders. The spirits of weather and season were ritually acknowledged, and many ancient sayings about them have been passed down to this day. This is a traditional charm that speaks to the weather at this time of year:

> *Season in which the flaying wolf-month arrives*
>
> *Cold hailstones, a storm made of bullets*
>
> *The Whistle, the Sweeper, the gloom of the Complaint*

And the shriveling sharp-bristled Hag!

Sharynne MacLeod NicMhacha

February 22
Tuesday

 3rd ♎
☽ → ♏ 4:29 am

Color of the day: Maroon
Incense of the day: Bayberry

Part the Clouds in Your Head

Some days, a cup of coffee or yerba mate and a loud noise just won't get rid of a strong brain fog. This could come from lack of sunlight, hunger, problems you need to see a doctor about, or just having a lot on your mind. One way to get yourself focused in a pinch is to hum the theme of the bossa nova classic "Girl from Ipanema" to yourself while tapping your forefinger and turning your head slowly from left to right, and then sitting perfectly still while engaging your core stomach muscles for a count of five. If this almost works but not quite, stand up and jog in place for a full minute and then try the process again. Repeat as needed until your head is clear enough to grab some coffee/make that phone call/balance your checkbook. This also works when you have a song stuck in your head.

Diana Rajchel

Holiday lore: We all know the lore about our first president—cherry tree, silver dollar, wooden teeth—but the truth behind this most legendary of American figures is sometimes more entertaining than the folklore. For instance, did you know that once when young George went for a dip in the Rappahannock River, two Fredericksburg women stole his clothes? This story was recorded in the Spotsylvania County records. Picture then the young man scampering home flustered and naked, and the icon on the dollar bill becomes just a bit more real.

February 23
Wednesday

 3rd ♏

Color of the day: Topaz
Incense of the day: Lavender

For Continued Health and Wellness

Our bodies, minds, and spirits require balance. When one part of our system is out of whack, it's our responsibility to realign ourselves. Imbalance leads to more imbalance, so it's essential to come back to a place of holistic wellness. A fun and practical way to keep this balanced energy flowing is to make a spellbag. Spellbags, medicine bags, sachets, mojo hands, and so on, are easy magical workings that can produce wonderful results. Simply get any sort of small drawstring bag and fill it with gingko, life everlasting, and sunflower. Add a piece of hematite or a fossil for additional strength. Gaze at the bag and put yourself in a meditative frame of mind. Loudly chant the word "SANITAS" (which is Latin for "health") into the bag ten times. Energy will continue to flow and radiate from the sachet, and recharging the sachet regularly keeps its own energy in tip-top shape. A spellbag such as this can not only help keep your own physical health and wellness functioning, but can aid you in self-healing work. Keep the bag close for any personal healings,

and put it somewhere in the house so that it's frequently in your presence.

Raven Digitalis

responsibilities, names, and deeds that you assign to Him. Deepen into awareness too of the challenges to Him wrought by patriarchy, and the ways in which you wish to be in relationship to His energy and presence. How do you wish Him to return this year, and what you will do to support His unpathologized flourishing?

Chandra Alexandre

February 24
Thursday

3rd ♏

☽ → ♐ 7:46 am

4th Quarter 6:26 pm

Color of the day: Crimson
Incense of the day: Carnation

Return of the Sacred Male

In ancient Rome, today was known as the Regifugium or Fugalia. It signified the offering of sacrifices by the Rex Sacrorum, or religious king, in the place where political matters—those in which he could not participate—were conducted. Some also say it was the day when the Goddess crowned the New Year King after the old one was sacrificed or displaced. Today then is a day to honor the Sacred Male in his role as consort and consciousness in the mundane world. Take time to meditate on the presence of the sacred masculine within you, on the roles,

February 25
Friday

 4th ♐

Color of the day: Rose
Incense of the day: Thyme

A Bath Spell for Love

To have love in our lives, we must first be receptive to it. During this waning Moon phase, you can begin with a cleansing spell that opens your heart. Begin with a piece of rose quartz, a piece of amber, or a clear quartz crystal. If your stones are set in a piece of jewelry, wear it. If not, simply take the stone with you into the bath (or shower). Imagine the nurturing water washing over

you and your stone. Chant these
words:

> I deserve love, to give
> and receive.
> I deserve love, in this
> I believe.

After your bath, keep the stone with
you for a week. You can carry it,
sleep with it in your pillowcase or
under your mattress, or wear the
piece of jewelry.

Ember Grant

February 26
Saturday

 4th ♐
♫ → ♑ 2:32 pm

Color of the day: Black
Incense of the day: Sage

Get Ready for Spring

S now may still cover the ground
and the wind still has the bite
of winter in it, but Mother Earth is
stirring with new life. Crocuses are
beginning to push through the fro-
zen ground and the birds are finding
their nesting sites. Now is the time
to attune yourself to the life force
which is beginning to pulse through
all of nature. Upon your altar, place
a pot of spring flowering bulbs such
as crocus or daffodils. And on either
side place one green and one yellow
candle. Sit on the floor before your
altar. Light the green candle and say:

> I welcome the Green Man.

Next light the yellow candle and say:

> I welcome Father Sun.

Feel the life force increasing around
you; breathe deeply. Send the power
you feel through the palms of your
hands back into Mother Earth.
Spring is almost here.

James Kambos

February 27
Sunday

 4th ♑

Color of the day: Orange
Incense of the day: Marigold

Weight–Loss Water Empowerment

This magical weight-loss strategy works on the vibrational level to create positive shifts in your mind, body, and emotions. And today is a great day to begin! Obtain a 32-ounce (or so) water bottle that you really love. With a permanent marker, write "lightness" on the outside of the bottle. Then write "joy." Fill the bottle with water and add 2 drops of crabapple flower essence (available online and at many health food stores). Hold it in both hands and visualize very bright white light filling the water as you say:

> Goddess, please establish lightness, beauty, and perfect health in every cell of my being.

Throughout the day, drink the entire bottle of water and then repeat. Each day, drink two empowered bottles of water until you reach your perfect weight. Over time, you'll notice your habits naturally starting to transform into healthier ones. Allow this to happen.

Tess Whitehurst

February 28
Monday

 4th ♑

Color of the day: Ivory
Incense of the day: Clary sage

Shielding Trigger

If you're empathic, it's very easy to feel drained and exhausted after being in a crowd. However, with a little advance preparation, you can protect yourself and your energy levels. You need to put yourself into a meditative state for this to work. (I use the method described in Laurie Cabot's *Power of the Witch*.) Now, begin building your shields, letting your intuition guide you in choosing a form. Mine is a vortex of energy that absorbs stray emotional energy not only from others, but also from me, so I don't project my emotional state on anyone else either. Really focus on the shield, making it as strong as you can. Finally, fix a gesture in your mind as an automatic trigger for pulling those shields up. It could be tugging on your earlobe, crossing your fingers in a special way—anything small and not too obvious. Bring yourself out of the meditative state and it is done. Next time you're in a draining environment, just use your trigger and invoke your shields. Keep in mind that this will get better with practice.

Laurel Reufner

March is the third month of the Gregorian calendar, and it was the first month of the Roman calendar. Its astrological sign is Pisces, the Fish (February 18–March 20), a mutable-water sign ruled by Neptune. Named in honor of Mars, the Roman god of war, March can be a tumultuous month with blustery winds, storms, and snow, yet it carries on its breath the promise of spring. It feels as though the seasons are waging a battle for control. In some places, cold temperatures still reign, but inevitably the days are growing longer. This is the month of the Vernal Equinox; day and night are equal in length. March is a good time for reflection (wells and springs can be good places to visit) and seeking balance when weather can be unstable. A feeling of renewal can be sensed in nature as birds begin nesting and the brave crocus peeks out through the snow. Spring bulbs such as tulips and daffodils begin to emerge in our gardens and brighten the landscape. This is a good month for blessing seeds and preparing for the gardening season. The Full Moon of March is often called the Worm Moon or Sap Moon.

March 1
Tuesday

 4th ♑

☽ → ♒ 12:14 am

Color of the day: Scarlet
Incense of the day: Cinnamon

Magic at Your Fingertips

Yoga is a practical way to increase physical flexibility and spiritual awareness. Mudras are hand gestures or poses that influence personal energy flows—in essence, a concise and discreet form of yoga that you can perform anywhere. Here is a set of mudras to do when you are stuck in line or a waiting room:

Guyan Mudra: Touch the tip of your thumb (symbolizing ego) to the tip of your index finger (representing Jupiter). This stimulates knowledge and ability, while encouraging receptivity and calm.

Shuni Mudra: Touch the tip of your thumb to the tip of your middle finger (representing Saturn). This promotes patience.

Ravi Mudra: Touch the tip of your thumb to the tip of your ring finger (symbolizing Uranus). This invigorates health, energy, and intuition.

Buddhi Mudra: Touch the tip of your thumb to the tip of your little finger (symbolizing Mercury). This enables clear and intuitive communication.

Elizabeth Barrette

Holiday lore: On March 1, Roman matrons held a festival known as Matronalia in honor of Juno Lucina, an aspect of the goddess Juno associated with light and childbirth. Some records indicated that her name was derived from a grove on the Esquiline Hill where a temple was dedicated to her in 375 BCE. Whenever a baby entered the world in Roman times, it was believed that the infant was "brought to light." Women who worshipped Juno Lucina untied knots and unbraided their hair to release any entanglements that might block safe delivery.

March 2
Wednesday

 4th ♒

Color of the day: Brown
Incense of the day: Bay laurel

Binding Spell

B inding spells prevent others from
doing harm against us. As with
any sort of magic aimed at another,
consult your guides and divinatory
oracle before casting. You will need
a poppet to represent the person, a
black candle, a large piece of paper, a
black cord, and equal parts of thyme,
dragon's blood, garlic, basil, and bay
leaf. In your ritual space, stuff the
poppet with the herbs. (Alternatively,
you could also use a photograph
to represent the person.) Place the
image on the paper and drip a circle
of wax around it for protection. Begin
wrapping the cord around the image
or poppet as you say:

> Your words (actions) are
> harsh,
> Your words (actions) are
> dense,
> I bind you now in my
> defense.
>
> Your words (actions) bring
> harm
> That you cannot see.
> I bind your harmful words
> (actions) from thee.

> There is no other choice.
> There is no other hope.
> I bind you (name) with this
> rope.
> So mote it be.

Keep the image or poppet in a dark
place until the harm has ended. Bury
in the earth to release the energy.

Abel R. Gomez

March 3
Thursday

 4th ♒
☽ → ♓ 11:47 am

Color of the day: Purple
Incense of the day: Myrrh

Peace Corps Day

T he first week in March, commemorates the founding of
the Peace Corps in March 1961 by
President John F. Kennedy. What we
know as the "peace sign" is a combination of the semaphore signals for
the letters N and D, i.e., "nuclear
disarmament," a remnant of the Cold
War. You can create your own peace
symbol for empowering your own
peace works. Select an alphabet or

symbol set: you might consider the Futhark runes, Theban font, semaphore, or even the regular alphabet. Combine the letters P-E-A-C-E in different ways to create a pleasing sigil. Or, work with letters from the words *pais* or *pax*, French and Latin for "peace." Capture your sigil by inscribing it on a wooden surface, etching it into a disk of oven-firing clay, or painting it onto ceramic plate. Use white for tranquility, and enjoy a peaceful focus for your altar.

Susan Pesznecker

March 4
Friday

 4ħ ♓
𝔑ew 𝔐oon 3:46 pm

Color of the day: Pink
Incense of the day: Yarrow

Conjure Up Romance

A New Moon symbolizes beginnings and fresh starts. During this New Moon phase you could work to bring new romance into your life (or bring more romance into an existing relationship). Today we have the planetary associations of Venus in play, so why not work with this and conjure up some romance, just for fun? Burn a pink candle for Venus and to represent the romance that you wish to bring into your life. Add a fresh white rosebud to add a touch of flower fascination to the spell. For a little extra pizzazz, you could scatter fresh rose petals across your work surface or use a rose-scented, pink candle. Use your imagination and see how you could personalize today's spell.

> On this night sacred to
> Venus and under a New
> Moon,
>
> Goddess of love, please hear
> my call and then grant me a
> boon.
>
> The pink of the spell candle
> is an affectionate hue,
>
> The white rose symbolizes
> virtue and promises true.
>
> Combine these elements and
> bring romance to light,
>
> With harm to no one this
> New Moon spell springs to
> life.

Ellen Dugan

March 5
Saturday

 1st ♓

Color of the day: Blue
Incense of the day: Rue

honor Isis

Did you know that the Romans honored the Egyptian goddess Isis? She was magical, beautiful, and nurturing. Around March 5, an annual festival was held to honor her as the patroness of sailors. Offerings of spices and other valuables were made to her by setting them afloat on a special ship with a white sail. A parade of worshippers carrying torches and candles would leave flower petals, perfume, and milk in the streets. Create your own centerpiece or altar to honor Isis today. Start with a bowl or dish of water; add a few drops of perfume, essential oils, or milk. Float candles or flowers on the water. (Be careful of the flowers near flame.) You can float candles on the water and put flowers around the dish, or vice versa. Meditate on the characteristics that caused many to call Isis the "Queen of Heaven" and draw this energy into your life.

Ember Grant

March 6
Sunday

 1st ♓

☽ → ♈ 12:14 am

Color of the day: Amber
Incense of the day: Marigold

A Spell to Cause Sleep

Are you an insomniac? Many people suffer from insomnia for a number of reasons. To help cause sleep, you can either make a sachet or stitch your own "dreamtime pillow." For the latter, simply get some cotton and cut a piece of fabric (preferably black, white, or indigo) to size. Stitch up the sides, leaving the end open. Stuff the pillow both with cotton and with a combination of any of these herbs: agrimony, lavender, mugwort, bay leaf, hops, and poppy. Under the light of the Moon, dedicate the bag (in your own manner) to the gods and spirits of sleep and dreaming. Declare the bag as a tool that invokes slumber in the user. Be sure to state your intention clearly, saying that a "full night's rest" is latent in each use of the pillow. (You wouldn't want this spell to put you asleep too long!) When you lay your head down to sleep, make sure the conditions are pleasing (soft music, a guided meditation, darkness—whatever you like!) and draw the soft energy from the pillow into your body.

Raven Digitalis

March 7
Monday

 1st ♈

Color of the day: Ivory
Incense of the day: Hyssop

Peace Powder

Conflict is inevitable and can lead to positive change, but we always hope it will be resolved peacefully. To help ensure the conflicts in your life resolve without aggression, make a peace powder that you can sprinkle when things get tense. Gather up some of the following dried herbs: rose petals, chamomile, lavender, jasmine blossoms, thyme, sage, lemon balm, or catnip. Crumble everything as small as you can with your fingers, and then grind even finer with a mortar and pestle, spice grinder, or small food processor. Put the powder in a white cloth bag or small bottle and charge with this chant, which you can repeat when you use it:

> Calm the tension, calm the
>   fight,
> Everything will turn out
>   right.
> Open our hearts and clear
>   our minds,
> The best solution we will find.

If you substitute essential oils for some of the dried herbs, this powder can also be a tension-easing incense.

Castiel

Holiday lore: Although the month of June is named for Juno, principal goddess of the Roman pantheon, major festivals dedicated to her are scattered throughout the year. For instance, today marks Junoalia, a festival in honor of Juno celebrated in solemnity by matrons. Two images of Juno made of cypress were borne in a procession of twenty-seven girls dressed in long robes, singing a hymn to the goddess composed by the poet Livius. Along the way, the procession would dance in the great field of Rome before proceeding ahead to the temple of Juno.

March 8
Tuesday

Mardi Gras (Fat Tuesday)

 1st ♈

☽ → ♉ 12:52 pm

Color of the day: White
Incense of the day: Ylang-ylang

The King Takes the Cake

Among the most interesting Mardi Gras traditions is the King Cake, a ring-shaped loaf of sweet bread or cake. Its three colors of sugar represent desired qualities: purple (sovereignty), green (prosperity), and gold (purity). Charms made of metal or another oven-safe substance (often with trailing strings, so you can find them without biting into them) are baked into the cake for divination to tell what the coming year holds for you. These include a coin for wealth and a heart for love. The best is the baby, or king, which indicates great good fortune—and the person responsible for baking the next King Cake!

Elizabeth Barrette

Holiday lore: While most holidays across the world celebrate the lives and achievement of men, March 8 is one day wholly dedicated to the achievement and work of women. Originally inspired by a pair of mid-nineteenth-century ladies' garment workers' strikes, today the holiday is little known in its country of origin; though this day's legacy is clear in March's designation by the U.S. Congress as Women's History Month. Throughout the month, women's groups in many American towns hold celebrations and events, concerts, exhibitions, and rituals that recall heroic and gifted women of every stripe.

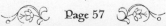

March 9
Wednesday

Ash Wednesday

 1st ♉

Color of the day: Topaz
Incense of the day: Honeysuckle

Go Vegan (or Vegetarian) Ritual

I find that veganism (or vegetarianism) lends itself to the magical lifestyle because it's a diet that honors our health, our animal allies, and the entire planet. It also lifts our vibrations and connects us more deeply with our guidance and our power. If you've been thinking of making the switch, today—the first day of Lent—would be an appropriate time, as giving up the eating of animal products can be a powerful act of spiritual devotion. Light a white candle and take a sea salt bath. While you're in the tub, say:

> I now release all lower
> vibrations associated with
> consuming animal products,
> and prepare myself for this
> happy new phase.

After bathing, say something like:

> In an act of love and
> devotion toward the God, the
> Goddess, all animals, and all
> of life, I now fully surrender
> the consumption of all animal
> products. And so it is.

Tess Whitehurst

March 10
Thursday

 1st ♉

Color of the day: Turquoise
Incense of the day: Balsam

Businesslike Basil

Basil has long been considered a profitability plant, good at attracting money and increasing business. Boost your own business profits by blessing a basil plant with attracting more customers. Keep the plant on your desk, work counter, or somewhere near the front door. Every so often, around the Full Moon, let the plant spend a day in the sunlight to recharge. If you have a green thumb, you can even grow your plant from seed, charging it a little every day with attracting more money your direction.

Laurel Reufner

March 11
Friday

1st ♉
☽ → ♊ 12:31 am

Color of the day: White
Incense of the day: Orchid

Celebrating Births

Springtime is the time for birth, with Earth's renewal all around us. This magical ritual makes a lovely accompaniment to Wiccanings, christenings, or other infant welcoming ceremonies throughout the year. Hold the new baby in your nondominant arm. Whisper, so only the infant can hear you, "Not above you, not below you, but within you." As you whisper, use your other hand to gesture above and below the baby, matching the words you speak. Finish by touching the baby's forehead and heart, or all seven chakras, if you prefer. If you can't be physically present, make or purchase a baby blanket (blue is ideal for health and protection). Cradle it as if it was the new baby, and perform the above ceremony with the blanket-effigy. You might print a rune of protection, such as Algiz (ᛉ)or Thurisaz (ᚦ), into one corner. Send the blanket to the new family, where it will serve as a power piece for the new child.

Susan Pesznecker

March 12
Saturday

1st ♊
2nd Quarter 6:45 pm

Color of the day: Black
Incense of the day: Magnolia

Know if You're Ready for Love

Everyone suffers a broken heart even if what hurts you happens in an unusual way. If it's still a rather short time since your last romance ended and someone on the horizon looks rather tasty, give yourself a moment's pause and grab your tarot deck. Rather than fishing for romantic possibility and ignoring all warnings about negative outcomes (we all do it!), ask this question: "Have I learned what I need to learn from my last love?" Throw down the cards—if the Tower or the Hanged Man appears in any configuration, you need to wait and simply admire the new friend from afar. However, if the Fool or Death right-side up appears, go ahead and drop a hint that you're interested—you're ready for the next phase of your life. When you're ready again, the Sun and Cups cards below the number five will appear.

Diana Rajchel

March 13
Sunday

Daylight Saving Time begins 2 am

 2nd ♊

) → ♋ 10:29 am

Color of the day: Gold
Incense of the day: Heliotrope

Awakening to the Sun

Today, make sure you get out of bed on the right side—literally. Now aligned with the energies of the rising Sun as experienced in your body, plant your first footfalls on the ground with intention. Before doing anything else, take a moment to breathe: right nostril for the Sun and left nostril for the Moon, alternating in and out each side. With three deep breaths, balance these energies within you. Offer them as a container for the cycling of the elements through your physical and subtle bodies. Now imagine the rays of Sun and Moon held perfectly in union at your third-eye center, and allow this awareness to be present throughout your day, coming back to it again and again in moments of stress or uneasiness. Today, as in every day, you have the resources inside of yourself to find peace with the whole of creation.

Chandra Alexandre

March 14
Monday

 2nd ♋

Color of the day: Silver
Incense of the day: Rosemary

Eating the Apple of Knowledge

The forbidden fruit is the fruit of wisdom. When Eve took a bite in the Garden of Eden, after being tempted by the serpent, her (and Adam's) delusions—illusions of the nature of reality—came crashing down. Naïveté was lost. Whether or not you resonate with Judeo-Christian mythology, you may wish to perform this spell in order to see what is "hidden" in your own sphere of consciousness. Are you ready to invoke true wisdom, even if it may be unpleasant? Situate yourself in a magical circle. The ideal environment is within nature, under trees, in a quiet and sacred space. With an apple in hand, put yourself in a meditative state and concentrate on issues in your life where you may not be seeing clearly. You may wish to think about other people's perceptions in various issues (such as disagreements), or re-examine your own changes in perception over time. When you've concentrated on the issue or issues, declare:

> As Eve once took of this forbidden fruit, I now invoke the wisdom of the Isle of Avalon

and the Garden of Eden into
my consciousness. Yahweh!
Reveal truth to this seeker!
So mote it be!

Raven Digitalis

March 15
Tuesday

2nd ♋
☽ → ♌ 3:33 pm

Color of the day: Gray
Incense of the day: Geranium

Prayer to Enhance Growth in Life

In Celtic tradition, March was the
traditional time for planting and
sowing seeds. In Scotland the seed
was sprinkled with clear, cold water
for three days prior to planting, the
person doing the ritual walking in a
deosil direction. Then the seed was
ritually consecrated and used in an
ancient ritual to enhance the power
of the sacred planting:

*I will go out to sow the seeds
In the name of those who
    gave it growth
I will stand before the wind
And throw a handful in
    the air.*

*Seed day, auspicious day
The dew will come down to
    welcome
Every seed that lay asleep
Since the coming of the cold.*

*Every seed will take root in
    the earth
As the rulers of the elements
    desire
The grain will come forth
    with the dew
It will inhale life from the
    gentle wind.*

Sharynne MacLeod NicMhacha

 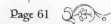

March 16
Wednesday

 2nd ♌

Color of the day: Yellow
Incense of the day: Marjoram

The Go to hell Spell

Today the Finnish celebrate Saint Urho, who when faced with a plague of locusts devouring Finland's wine-grape crop, simply told them, "Grasshopper, grasshopper, go to hell" and they left. Now, you probably don't have much of a grasshopper problem in March, in most of North America, but perhaps there is something else that is eating away at you. Be like Saint Urho and banish it to hell. Name your problem, writing it down on a piece of paper. Over a ceramic bowl, or the toilet, carefully light the paper on fire. As it burns say:

Problem, problem, go to hell.

It is most effective if you substitute the exact words of your problem, as in:

Self-doubt, self-doubt, go to hell.

As the paper burns, envision your problem in the flames of the metaphorical hell. See Hades gleefully take it in. Be free of devouring locusts.

Dallas Jennifer Cobb

Holiday lore: Why is March 15 so notorious? On this date in 226 BCE, an earthquake brought the Colossus of Rhodes—one of the Seven Wonders of the Ancient World—to its knees. But a more famous event likely accounts for the notoriety of the "Ides of March." Julius Caesar's rule, somewhere along the way, became tyrannical. In February of 44 BCE, Caesar had himself named Dictator Perpetuus—Dictator for Life. Brutus assassinated him on March 15. Caesar's murder was foretold by soothsayers and even by his wife, Calpurnia, who had a nightmare in which Caesar was being butchered like an animal. Caesar chose to ignore these portents and the rest, of course, is history.

March 17
Thursday
St. Patrick's Day

 2nd ♌

☽ → ♍ 4:53 pm

Color of the day: Crimson
Incense of the day: Nutmeg

Luck Spell

Tapping into the "Luck of the Irish" can be both a blessing and a curse! However, the energy of this day is certainly beneficial to any luck charm you would like to make. You will need:

A small clay pipe (easily found during this season)
Copal incense (enough to fill the pipe)
A green ribbon, or a live shamrock plant
An emerald

Fill the pipe with the incense. Wrap the stem of the pipe with the green ribbon, or place it in the middle of the shamrock plant. Light the incense and hold the emerald in the smoke of the incense, chant . . .

> Luck of the Irish come to me,
> as I will so mote it be. Love
> and laughter, each times
> three, as I do, so mote it be.

Wear or carry the emerald with you all through the year.

Paniteowl

Holiday lore: Much folklore surrounds Saint Patrick's Day. Though originally a Catholic holy day, Saint Patrick's Day has evolved into more of a secular holiday today. One traditional icon of the day is the shamrock. This stems from an Irish tale that tells how Patrick used the three-leated shamrock to explain the Trinity of Christian dogma. His followers adopted the custom of wearing a shamrock on his feast day, though why we wear green on this day is less clear. Saint Patrick's Day came to America in 1737, the date of the first public celebration of the holiday in Boston.

March 18
Friday

2nd ♏

Color of the day: Rose

Incense of the day: Mint

A Garden Blessing

In many regions, the soil can now be worked in the garden. It's not too early to plant cool-weather vegetables—lettuce, onions, and spinach are good choices. While you're in the garden, this would be a good time to perform this simple blessing. Begin by crumbling some soil in your fingers and inhale its earthy scent. With deep reverence, begin hoeing and loosening the soil. Let your hoe serve as your wand. Direct your energy down the handle of the hoe and into Mother Earth. Silently thank her for allowing you to plant and eventually harvest her bounty. Take a moment to connect with the natural world surrounding you at this time of year—the sound of birdsong, the budding trees, and early-blooming spring flowers. The Earth is alive, and you are part of this magic.

James Kambos

March 19
Saturday

2nd ♏

Full Moon 2:10 pm

☽ → ♎ 4:03 pm

Color of the day: Gray

Incense of the day: Sage

Healing Bath Spell

Tap into the transformative power of the Full Moon tonight by taking a healing bath. As you draw a bath, gather equal amounts of dried calendula, nettle, comfrey, oatmeal (uncooked), and three pinches of salt and place the contents in an old sock. When the bathtub is filled, place the sock in the water. Hold your hands above the water and charge it with intention by saying something like:

> I charge and consecrate this healing water. As I bathe, so shall I become healthy and whole.

As you immerse yourself in the water, allow yourself to feel the warm water on your skin. Take the warm, herb-filled sock and squeeze it above your skin, letting the herbal brew soak into your pores, opening you to deeper healing. Continue this for as long as is pleasurable and then simply soak in the healing waters. You're bathing in a huge potion, after all. When ready, step out of the tub,

visualizing any disease remaining in the bathwater. As the water flows down the drain, so shall you become healthy and whole.

Abel R. Gomez

March 20
Sunday

Purim

Ostara – Spring Equinox –
International Astrology Day

3rd ♎

☉ → ♈ 7:21 pm

Color of the day: Amber
Incense of the day: Hyacinth

Spring into Sun and Fun

Ostara is the Germanic Maiden Goddess of the spring. She lends her name to this festival. Her symbols are the hare, spring flowers, and, of course, eggs. This year the Spring Equinox sabbat falls on a Sunday, which is associated with the Sun, new beginnings, and success. Pick up some fresh flowers for your home. Dye some hard-boiled eggs for the sabbat with your friends and family today. Go ahead and make

Ostara baskets for your kids. Include Ostara's hare (the chocolate bunny), hide those eggs, and have some fun! Also, don't forget to go outside and celebrate the beginning of spring. Look around you, what signs of the approaching spring do you see? Are daffodils and crocuses blooming? What about the buds on the trees— see how they are swelling? Celebrate the turning of the wheel of the year by spending some time in nature!

Ostara, gentle Goddess of the spring,

Sweet Maiden, new beginnings you do bring.

Your symbols of the hare, eggs, and springtime flowers,

I'll include into my own magical powers.

By this sabbat's magic, the spell is spun,

For the good of all, bringing joy and fun.

Ellen Dugan

March 21
Monday

3rd ♎︎
☽ → ♏︎ 3:17 pm

Color of the day: Gray
Incense of the day: Lily

To Release Justice to the Gods

Something in life happened that just wasn't fair, and you're feeling stuck and distrustful. Whatever happened, you're left with a loss of faith in the universe. This just means that you're human, and that justice in this situation is not for humans to handle. If you still need to see the situation addressed, go to a crossroads after midnight and leave a little cloth bag with an offering of High John the Conqueror root, a bit of cypress oil, and some graveyard dirt. Take a piece of chalk and draw a circle around the bag, laying a feather on top and saying:

> Ma'at, I petition you—pass
> your judgment on _____.
> If justice is done, then I am
> done. But if his heart weighs
> more than a feather, lay
> down your sentence.

Write the person's name around the outside of the circle and walk away without looking back.

Diana Rajchel

March 22
Tuesday

3rd ♏︎

Color of the day: Red
Incense of the day: Ginger

Hilaria

Near the time of the Vernal Equinox, the ancient Romans honored the goddess Cybele with a festival—they borrowed this tradition from the Greeks. Cybele is an Earth Mother, a goddess of nature—especially caverns and mountains. This spring festival celebrated the death and rebirth of Cybele's son, Attis. A felled pine tree representing his body was decorated with sashes of linen and violets—which are said to have grown from his spilled blood. This festival actually lasted for several days. Symbols of rebirth are found in most cultures around this time of year. Create a rebirth altar by decorating with pine and violets, or burn candles in shades of purple and green. Place a few drops of pine essential oil in an aromatherapy burner and meditate on images of rebirth by taking a few moments of silence to reflect on the cycles of life.

Ember Grant

Holiday lore: Cybele was the Great Mother of the gods in Ida, and she was taken to Rome from Phrygia in 204 BCE. She was also considered the Great Mother of all Asia Minor. Her festivals were known as *ludi*, or "games," and were solemnized with various mysterious rites. Along with Hecate and Demeter of Eleusis, Cybele was one of the leading deities of Rome when mystery cults were at their prime. Hila'aria, or "Hilaria," originally seemed to have been a name given to any day or season of rejoicing that was either private or public. Such days were devoted to general rejoicing and people were not allowed to show signs of grief or sorrow. The Hilaria actually falls on March 25 and is the last day of a festival of Cybele that commences today. However, the Hilaria was not mentioned in the Roman calendar or in Ovid's *Fasti*.

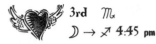 3rd ♏

☽ → ♐ 4:45 pm

Color of the day: White
Incense of the day: Lilac

Wisdom and Love, Love, Love

The coming together of the birthday of Minerva, goddess of wisdom, and the rites of the Great Goddess mark the perfect time for love. Today, spend time thinking about the components of love that are most important to you (not who possesses them) and especially engage the challenges with love you have had in the past. Ask yourself what you have learned. With this knowledge pressed into wisdom through time, you have the ability now to create a love spell that shines brightly enough to attract a worthy partner. Before a mirror, breathe cleansing and releasing breaths. Surrender to higher wisdom and release attachment. Become willing to be truly met. From this place, look into the mirror, gazing past your face and into your soul. Speak your truth about love and your desire to be met. When you have finished, use rose oil to seal the spell at your heart.

Chandra Alexandre

March 24
Thursday

3rd ♐

Color of the day: Green
Incense of the day: Clove

Sowing New Seeds

In Scottish folk tradition, March 24 was the beginning of a ritual period known as Seed-Time. This was the busiest time of spring, as planting had to be underway by this time. Having ground that was moist at this time was considered a good-weather omen. There was much ritual associated with plowing and sowing seed, and the community elders preserved ancient advice and lore associated with planting seeds. Recite this folk charm for sowing seeds while symbolically planting seeds or grains for new beginnings in your life:

> Let the first Tuesday in
>   March pass by
> And the second Tuesday, if
>   need be,
> But if the weather is good
>   or bad,
> I sow my seeds in True
>   March
> Though I cannot send a
>   pebble
> Against the strong north
>   wind.
> At this time, Seed-Time
> Is the right time to sow!

Sharynne MacLeod NicMhacha

March 25
Friday

3rd ♐

☽ → ♑ 9:57 pm

Color of the day: Purple
Incense of the day: Cypress

Festival of Joy

Today is Hilaria, the Roman Festival of Joy. Corresponding with the ancient date of the Spring Equinox, this was the day Romans celebrated the resurrection of Attis, a Phrygian god beloved of the Great Mother Goddess Cybele. Romans could dress up like anyone, even the Emperor himself, and wild parties were the norm. Decorate your altar or house today with fresh pine or violets, both sacred to Attis. You can use this prayer at your altar today:

> Attis, beloved of Cybele,
>
> Your return brings with you
>   the renewal of joy.
>
> Fill my life with bounty
>
> That I may delight in it and
>   so honor you. Blessed be!

Now, since it's a Friday, go out and get a little wild! Dress to the nines and go out with friends, or do something else you really, really enjoy doing. Try to incorporate music somehow, especially something with lots of drums and cymbal crashing!

Castiel

 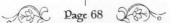

March 26
Saturday

 3rd ♑
4th Quarter 8:07 am

Color of the day: Indigo
Incense of the day: Sandalwood

Spring Cleaning

Spring has sprung! Many of us have an urge to clean and reorganize at this time of year, and it's an urge with biological and magical roots. Spring cleaning is a great time to treat yourself to a new besom—a broom. The besom is strongly associated with witchcraft and Wicca, with Witches long thought to ride their brooms across the skies. In reality, the besom is the symbol of a hearth or kitchen Witch, who works with magic and herbs at the fireplace in her home's center. A besom may be made or acquired. For best results, choose a handmade broom of natural materials. Name your besom as you would an animal familiar, then consecrate it in a dedicated ceremony. Hold the broom over your heart and make a wish: legend says the wish will come true if you keep your besom close for the next seven days, then place it in a safe, permanent location in your home.

Susan Pesznecker

March 27
Sunday

 4th ♑

Color of the day: Yellow
Incense of the day: Juniper

Tansy Spell

Although tansy can be toxic when used either internally or topically, the nature of the plant itself can be used to protect your home from parasites and illness. I'd suggest you first read about the plant before focusing on how you wish to use it. When you are ready, either buy a plant from a reputable nursery, or take a cutting from an established plant that was grown by someone you trust. Choose a spot near your front door, and prepare the soil for your plant. Dig the hole during the Dark Moon, and leave it alone for three days. On the fourth day, plant the tansy, and water the area thoroughly. As you plant, say this chant:

> Tansy fair, so green and
>   bright,
> Keep my doorstep in your
>   sight.
> Guard and ward from pests
>   and ills,
> And enhance my healing
>   skills.

Paniteowl

March 28
Monday

 4th ♑

☽ → ♒ 7:00 am

Color of the day: Lavender
Incense of the day: Narcissus

Personal Cleansing for Inner Peace

All you need for this ritual is sea salt, a bundle of dried white sage, and a white quartz pendant. Begin by performing forty minutes of fairly rigorous cardio exercise. Throughout your workout, silently repeat the phrase:

> *It is safe to still my thoughts
> and relax my mind.*

If your mind wanders, just gently return to the phrase. Then, relax deeply as you take a forty-minute sea salt bath that's as hot as you can comfortably stand. (Be sure to drink plenty of water during the workout and the bath.) Get out, dry off, light the sage bundle so that it's smoking like incense, and move the bundle around your body to purify your energy with the smoke. Extinguish the sage. Hold the quartz in your right hand and say:

> *My energy is clean and clear
> and I am peaceful through
> and through.*

Hang the pendant around your neck.

Tess Whitehurst

March 29
Tuesday

 4th ♒

Color of the day: White
Incense of the day: Cinnamon

Self-Defense Spray

We live in an increasingly violent world. While most of us hope for the best, it's a good idea to prepare for the worst. It's easy to buy canisters of self-defense sprays, but it's also possible to make your own. And while doing so, you can concentrate on banishing any harm or violence that may come near you. Place 2 tablespoons ground red pepper into a small bowl or glass. Pour in about a cup of rubbing alcohol and slowly mix the two together using a spoon. Make sure they are completely combined. Allow the pepper to thoroughly infuse itself throughout the alcohol for a couple of hours. Strain through a coffee filter to get out the remaining solid bits. Add 1½ tablespoons baby oil and stir well. Pour the final product into a small spray bottle that you can easily carry with you. (Make sure this is legal to use wherever you're living.)

Laurel Reufner

March 30
Wednesday

4th ≈

☽ → ♓ 6:38 pm

Color of the day: Brown
Incense of the day: Lavender

Good for You—and Everyone

On this day, ancient Romans worshipped Salus, the goddess of public welfare and personal health. Her temple in the Quirinal dates from 302 BCE. Her symbols include bowls and serpents. Salus taught the Romans that a healthy citizen makes for a healthy society, and vice versa. To honor Salus, do one thing for the public good and one thing for your own health. For the public good, you might volunteer at a charity or pick up litter in a park. For your own health, you might go hiking, jogging, or swimming; or treat yourself to a home-cooked organic meal in Italian style. Write out your accomplishments on slips of paper and place them in a bowl for Salus to admire. If you have snake figurines, add them to your altar as well.

Elizabeth Barrette

March 31
Thursday

4th ♓

Color of the day: White
Incense of the day: Apricot

Borrowed Days

Roman superstition called the last three days of March "borrowed" days, a term that might have its roots in the change over to the Gregorian calendar. "Borrowed days" were rumored to be dangerous, filled with bad weather, bad spirits, and treacherous taboos. Do a detaching spell to pull back parts of you that stretch like psychic tentacles out into the universe. In a private space, envision the tendrils of your energy that stretch out to people and places: physical, mental, emotional, and psychic energy. Like an octopus with many arms, remove your tentacles from bad spirits, draining people, hopeless situations, and treachery. Draw them in, coiling golden light in your core. Use your energy for self-protection, a golden cloak enveloping you. Heed the taboo "neither a borrower nor a lender be," and today return things (tangible and intangible) to their right place in your universe.

Dallas Jennifer Cobb

April is the fourth month of the Gregorian calendar and the first month of the astrological calendar. Its astrological sign is Aries, the Ram (March 20–April 20), a cardinal-fire sign ruled by Mars. The Roman war god Mars equates with the Greek Ares, or Aries, the first sign of the zodiac. The Latin word *aperire* means "to open" and is thought to be one possible origin of the name. April brings the blooming time, a dazzling display of fragrant flowers and budding trees. Spring makes her presence fully known in April. Redbud, dogwood, crab apple, forsythia, lilac, and many other plants create a splendid color palette in neighborhoods, parks, and forests. Trees are bursting with fresh, tender green leaves—yet unexpected cool weather can threaten new growth. We are reminded of this by April Fools' Day on the first—a day to honor the Trickster. As Anglo-Saxons found April sacred to Eostre or Ostara, the goddess of spring, they referred to it as Oster-monath or Eostur-monath. This is the origin of the modern Easter. April is a month of beauty and new life—symbolized by popular fertility symbols such as eggs and rabbits. And don't forget Earth Day on April 22. Do something special in honor of Mother Earth—plant a tree or find ways to go green and make every day Earth Day. April's Full Moon is called the Pink Moon.

April 1
Friday

April Fools' Day

4th ♓

Color of the day: Coral
Incense of the day: Mint

Take a Risk Spell

On April Fools' Day we celebrate the Trickster or the Fool. Behind all the jokes and pranks people partake in today, take time to think of what the Fool symbolizes. As depicted in the tarot, the Fool doesn't watch where he's going. He is a carefree traveler and doesn't think about what the future holds. Let today be the day you take a risk; do something that's out of the ordinary for you. Upon arising, ground and center. Think about what you want to accomplish today. Say Words of Power, such as:

> Divine Power today I will
> (state your goal here), and I'll
> achieve this in the most per-
> fect way. With harm to none
> and for the good of all.

Go about your day, and follow your instincts so that you may achieve your goal. Learn to listen to your "inner bell" and have fun.

James Kambos

April 2
Saturday

4th ♓

☽ → ♈ 7:16 am

Color of the day: Gray
Incense of the day: Pine

Vitality Spell

Feeling apathetic about life? Melancholy? Uninspired? Draw upon the power of the Sun today for vitality and renewal. Put on some sunblock and find a place outside where you can spend some time in sunlight. Remove as many garments as you feel comfortable and allow the rays of the Sun to kiss your skin. Call to the Sun, visualizing the sunlight around you burning away all that does not serve. Breathe deeply and allow the Sun to fill you with strength, passion, and vitality. As you breathe say something like:

> Fire, Sun, Eternal Star
>
> Power of life and renewal
>
> Burn in me!
>
> Purify me of all distraction.
>
> And fill me with your Light
>
> That I might be passionate
>
> That I might be radiant
>
> That I might be fully alive.
>
> So mote it be.

When you feel full of solar light, allow it to sink into your skin, healing the deepest parts of yourself. Offer a prayer of gratitude for this exchange. The light of life lives within you.

Abel R. Gomez

a cleansing shower or bath in the dark. Step into the water. Know that darkness is not dangerous, but a part of the natural cycle. As the water washes over you, let go of what you want to release. Be cleansed, and let your worries wash down the drain. When you feel cleansed, step out of the water, towel off, and open the bathroom door. As you step out into the light, envision your new beginning. Affirm in detail what you want to start anew, and know that as the Moon swells and grows, so will the energy of what you have initiated. Dress, and take one small step toward your new beginning.

Dallas Jennifer Cobb

April 3
Sunday

 4th ♈︎

New Moon 10:32 am

Color of the day: Gold
Incense of the day: Eucalyptus

New Beginnings

Do you wish you could start over, erase mistakes, and begin anew? Maybe you have a bad habit you want to let go of, replacing it with something healthier or happier. Well, today's your lucky day. As the Moon begins a new cycle, so can you. With today's New Moon, you can pick yourself up, wash yourself off, and start all over again. Turn off the bathroom light, leaving just enough light to see by. Think about what you want to be rid of. Take

 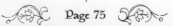

April 4
Monday

 1st ♈

☽ → ♉ 7:46 pm

Color of the day: Silver
Incense of the day: Clary sage

Spring Flower Purification Ritual

Springtime is the perfect time to perform cleansing and purification rituals for the body, mind, and spirit. Here is a gentle ritual for springtime cleansing: Take a metal or glass vessel of pure, clear water and set a crystal in the center of it. Let this water sit in direct moonlight for three nights. On the morning of the third day, gather as many types of spring blossoms as you can find—white for cleansing, pink for healing, yellow for rejuvenation, and purple for connection with spirit. Set these flowers in and on top of the vessel of water and purify your thoughts. Meditate on what you would like to release, and what you would like to see blossom in your life. Recite the following words over the vessel before pouring into a ritual bath:

> With the power of these
> sacred blossoms
>
> I cleanse myself of all that
> does not serve
>
> With the blessings of the
> spirits in these holy flowers

> So am I renewed and
> empowered.

Sharynne MacLeod NicMhacha

April 5
Tuesday

 1st ♉

Color of the day: Red
Incense of the day: Bayberry

Personal Power Potion

Glue a small (approx. 4-inch) square of red flannel onto a similarly sized piece of cardboard and let dry. Then, fill a tiny bottle three-quarters full of patchouli essential oil. Add 6 drops of ylang-ylang essential oil, close the lid, and shake. Hold the bottle in both hands and direct positive energy into it through your hands as you repeat this phrase (borrowed from Kundalini Yoga) nine times:

> Ong So Hung

Place the bottle in the middle of the flannel square and surround it with a small circle of tiger's eye crystals. The next day, it will be ready to use. When you want to boost your con-

fidence and personal power, lightly anoint your belly, heart, and throat, saying "Ong So Hung" at each point. Return the bottle to the flannel when not in use, and cleanse the crystals with sunlight every couple of weeks to keep their energy fresh.

Tess Whitehurst

April 6
Wednesday

 1st ♉

Color of the day: Brown
Incense of the day: Lilac

Finding the Lost

If you're like me, the warmer weather finds my schedule filling quickly, and my forgetfulness increases threefold. I depend on my pendulum to help me when these things happen, so I'll share my technique for finding the lost, whatever or whoever that may be. I draw a diagram of my home, my car, or the area in which I live. I position my pendulum over one of the diagrams and specifically ask the pendulum about the lost item. Looking for a "Yes or No" answer, I ask the pendulum if the lost item is in my home. If the answer is "No," I will then use another diagram. If the answer is "Yes," I'll narrow the focus of the pendulum, one room at a time. When I get a positive response to a specific room, I'll then ask if it is in the north, south, east, or west. At that point, I can begin a search in a specific area, and find the object. Remember to "recharge" your pendulum before each use by asking it to "Tell me Yes," and then "Tell me No." The movement, in response to your request, will tell you what to expect when actually making your "Lost" request.

Panitcowl

April 7
Thursday

 1st ♉

)) → ♊ 7:22 am

Color of the day: White

Incense of the day: Nutmeg

Warming the Spirits

Historically, this was an occasion when Slavic people honored their ancestors; today is sacred to Karna, the goddess of crying and wailing. She watches over the ancient ones who have gone before. For this holiday, gather up the dry branches, leaves, and other yard waste left after the winter. Build a bonfire and make the traditional declaration:

Walking here near this fire,
the spirits have warmth.

Set a bowl of fresh water on the altar to refresh the spirits as they pass by. If you watch closely, you may see the surface of the water ripple in their presence. Any person who has lost someone during the previous season may cry and wail to Karna. After the ritual, pour the water over the firepit, and scatter the ashes over the garden or fields. The dead of winter has been cleared away, making way for the new life of spring.

Elizabeth Barrette

April 8
Friday

 1st ♊

Color of the day: Rose

Incense of the day: Thyme

Increase the Love Vibes

There is no stronger vibration than the energy of love. Indeed, Love is the Law, and is the true key to the wisdom of the self, reality, and the cosmos. As a simple working to increase the vibration of love, simply keep a small dish of caraway seeds on your altar, and set a stone of rose quartz in the middle. Whenever you feel the need to increase love (for yourself or others), grab a pinch of the seeds and lie down, placing the rose quartz over your heart chakra. Chew the caraway seeds while repeating the following in your mind:

Love is evolution, Love is
knowing. Love is pure, and
Love is growing.

Continue to perform this exercise regularly. It's particularly beneficial to perform this every Friday, which the planet Venus rules. Venus is, of course, a planet of divine love. To take this a step further, perform this little love-invoking ritual seven Fridays in a row. Seven is a number of Venus. You may wish to jot a reminder on your calendar!

Raven Digitalis

April 9
Saturday

 1st ♊

☽ → ♋ 5:02 pm

Color of the day: Indigo
Incense of the day: Ivy

Super-Charged Spring Cleaning

If you want to get your house spic-and-span this spring magically as well as physically, make yourself an air/energy freshener. You will need a clean empty spray bottle, some cheap gin or vodka, lemon juice, water, and some essential oils. Try combinations of lemon, lavender, cedar, rosemary, orange, peppermint, pine, and thyme, based on scent preference and the atmosphere you want to create—lavender to relax, peppermint to stimulate, rosemary to clear out negative vibes, etc. Fill the bottle with ⅓ lemon juice, ⅓ alcohol, and ⅓ water, and add 3 to 9 drops of your chosen essential oils, depending on their strength. Put the top on the bottle, hold between your hands, and shake as you say:

> Clear and cleanse
> I clean this space
> Light and peace
> Claim this place

When charged, spritz generously in the air, on curtains and furniture, and even on pet bedding. Use whenever you need a little freshening up.

Castiel

April 10
Sunday

 1st ♋

Color of the day: Orange
Incense of the day: Frankincense

For Walking a Labyrinth

Labyrinths differ from mazes in that the path is actually planned for you, but the twists and turns make it hard to see whether you are coming or going. Should you get to walk a labyrinth, try speaking this prayer as you go:

> Each step before me has been walked before
>
> Each turn I turn on has been turned before
>
> What goes behind me has gone before
>
> And before you now I go.

Repeat this prayer while picturing your own concept of the divine; when you reach the center of the labyrinth, pause and listen to the sounds and sensations around you, and then while walking back out of the path repeat the prayer again. At the entrance of the labyrinth, pause and listen again while dwelling on your own idea of how divine energy manifests. Look around you for what seems different from when you walked into the labyrinth.

Diana Rajchel

April 11
Monday

1st ♋
2nd Quarter 8:05 am
☽ → ♌ 11:37 pm

Color of the day: Gray
Incense of the day: Lily

Pax

Be it world peace or inner peace, this little spell should help. Take a small, blue birthday candle and place three bay laurel leaves around it to form a simple ring (you may substitute rose petals). Ground and center yourself and focus on a sense of peace and calmness. Once you feel truly centered and at peace, light the candle. Meditate on the flame for a few moments and then leave it to burn out. Shred and scatter the leaves (or petals) in the wind at a favored spot. A simple holder for the birthday candle can be made using some clay or a small container of dirt. If you'd like to spread this spell's influence out over several days, use a larger candle and allow it to burn a certain amount of time each day, such as a half-hour or an hour. Try to perform the spell's ritual at the same time each day.

Laurel Reufner

April 12
Tuesday

2nd ♌
Color of the day: Maroon
Incense of the day: Geranium

Luck Charm

Today is sacred to Jupiter, the supreme Roman god of luck, victory, and thunder. Draw upon Jupiter's power today to draw luck into your life. For this spell you will need four bay leaves, a photocopy of the Wheel of Fortune tarot card, and a deep blue cord. In your ritual space, wrap the bay leaves in the tarot card. Use your breath to charge the ingredients with your intention. Begin visualizing yourself lucky, achieving all goals, successful in all endeavors as you chant:

By the powers of Fate

Open the gate

The path shall be clear

My success will draws near

Luck flow my way

Grow by night, grow by day

As the energy has almost reached its peak, tie the leaves and tarot card closed with the cord with four knots. Keep it close to your person to attract luck.

Abel R. Gomez

Historical note: On April 12, 1961, Yuri Gagarin piloted the first manned spaceship to leave the pull of our planet's gravity. This achievement is given much less attention than it deserves. Part of that is politics, since Gagarin was a cosmonaut for the Soviet Union. Part of it, too, is time; today, space pilots live and work for months aboard space stations, so a simple space flight seems routine. Still, Yuri Gagarin's 108-minute flight in space represented a triumph of science and engineering, and it also broke a psychological barrier. It was literally a flight into the unknown. "Am I happy to be setting off on a cosmic flight?" said Yuri Gagarin in an interview before the launch. "Of course. In all ages and epochs people have experienced the greatest happiness in embarking upon new voyages of discovery . . . I say 'until we meet again' to you, dear friends, as we always say to each other when setting off on a long journey."

April 13
Wednesday

 2nd ♌

Color of the day: White
Incense of the day: Bay laurel

Shake Up Change Shrewdly

This day belongs to the Greco-Roman, winged-footed god Hermes/Mercury. With Wednesday being aligned with the planet Mercury, and the Moon waxing, today is a perfect for casting spells for shrewdness and transformation. If you feel like things will never change and you are ready to shake things up in your life, then Mercury and Hermes are the ones to call on. But remember, these are trickster gods. So this spell closes with a tag line, making certain that the transformative magic will unfold in the best possible way. Burn an orange candle and repeat the spell.

> Wednesdays are for
> Mercury/Hermes, the
> messenger of the gods,
>
> A clever and canny soul, on
> winged feet he does swiftly
> trod.
>
> By the waxing Moon, please
> send positive change to me,
>
> With no trouble or harm,
> As I will, so mote it be.

Ellen Dugan

April 14
Thursday

2nd ♌

☽ → ♍ 2:40 am

Color of the day: Green
Incense of the day: Carnation

A Candle Spell for Expansion

The spring season is a good time to begin something new, and Thursdays are good days for magic involving expansion. Think of an area of your life where you would like to grow. This could be financially, spiritually, intellectually, or perhaps advancement in your career field. But beware: make sure you don't ask for more than you can handle. The magical influence of this day can be unpredictable. Use a purple or dark blue candle if possible. If not, use white and use a colored altar cloth or candleholder. Charge your candle by carving your goal into the wax. Sprinkle a pinch of nutmeg in the bottom of your candleholder and put the candle on top of it. Outside your candleholder, place a stone of amethyst or turquoise. Visualize your goal and light the candle. Allow the candle to burn out completely today, or over the next few days.

Ember Grant

April 15
Friday

2nd ♍

Color of the day: White
Incense of the day: Yarrow

Take a Walk

Walking is great exercise for all of us. Here's a small ritual to bless you and your walking shoes. Write this charm on a piece of paper, reading aloud as you write:

> Strong my heart,
> And fleet my feet,
> Soon to start,
> My blood to beat.
>
> Send me power
> That I may last
> For minutes and hours
> Along this path.

Dissolve a bit of salt in some water and light an orange candle (for health and vigor). Sprinkle salt water over your shoes, saying:

> By earth and water
> I empower these shoes.

Pass the shoes above the candle, saying:

> By fire and air
> I empower these shoes.

Roll up the paper charm and burn it with the candle, visualizing the power of your words being concentrated by the flame. When cool, dab a spot of ash inside each shoe and

over your heart. Visualize the glowing aura of empowerment!

Susan Pesznecker

As the breezes blow, the wind chime will gather energy from the moving air. When you need inspiration or clear thought, touch the chimes and draw the air energy into yourself.

Elizabeth Barrette

April 16
Saturday

 2nd ♏

☽ → ♎ 2:59 am

Color of the day: Blue
Incense of the day: Patchouli

A Breath of Air

Spring is the season of air. The element of air represents clarity, inspiration, the mind, and new beginnings. Now is an auspicious time to work magic for these purposes and to blow away the old, sleepy energy of winter. For this spell, you need a wind chime made of metal, glass, or stone. It should have a good clear sound. Ideally, use one with images of butterflies, birds, or other air creatures. Hang it outside and say:

> Spring time
> Wind chime
> Hanging in the air
> Blow through
> Sky blue
> Bringing power fair

April 17
Sunday

Palm Sunday

 2nd ♎

Full Moon 10:44 pm

Color of the day: Yellow
Incense of the day: Almond

Scottish Full Moon Charm

In Scotland it was believed that the essence or power of living things increased during the waxing Moon and was at its highest potency at the Full Moon. For that reason, people would not cull plants during the waning Moon (when their essence was decreasing), but did this during the waxing or Full Moon. There were many traces of Moon worship in the Western Islands of Scotland in the early part of the last century. When old people walked outside at night to see "what the night was doing," they observed the Moon, the stars, and the constellations, and often repeated prayers and charms. Here is a traditional Scottish prayer to the Moon:

Hail to you,
Jewel of the Night!

Beautiful one of the Heavens,
Jewel of the Night!

Mother of the Stars,
Jewel of the Night!

Foster child of the Sun,
Jewel of the Night!

Majesty of the Stars,
Jewel of the Night!

Sharynne MacLeod NicMhacha

April 18
Monday

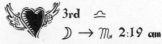 3rd ♎

☽ → ♏ 2:19 am

Color of the day: Lavender
Incense of the day: Rosemary

Release Jealousy

Jealousy lies heavy on your heart, wastes energy, and restricts your natural flow of blessings and joy. This journaling ritual will help you release jealousy and be free. Write the heading: "Jealousies." Then make a list of every person and/or situation that arouses the negative feeling of jealousy in you. Now light a white candle and relax. Look at the first item on your list. Close your eyes and visualize this person and/or situation. Remind yourself that this is an infinite universe: what one person has can never diminish you in any way. Realize that the more you release jealousy and celebrate the good fortunes of others, the more open you'll be to receiving your own blessings. As much as you can, wish this person well and surround the situation with love. Continue with each item. Afterward, (safely) burn the list and flush the ashes down the toilet.

Tess Whitehurst

April 19
Tuesday

Passover begins

 3rd ♏

Color of the day: White
Incense of the day: Cinnamon

Eggstra Protection

It's a good idea to regularly refresh the wards around your home, and there's no reason they can't be seasonal and decorative! Blow out an eggshell. Gather some craft or beading wire, white glue, large and small beads, red paint, dried rosemary, and bay leaf. Cut a piece of wire three inches longer than your egg, and secure a large bead on one end. Thread the wire through the egg until it rests on the bead, and secure the two together with glue. When dry, paint the egg red while holding it by the wire, and let dry. Fill the egg with rosemary, bay leaf, and your intentions for a safe, happy home. String a large bead onto the wire at the top, securing with glue. Put small beads on the remaining wire then twist it into a loop so you can hang your egg in a window or over a door.

Castiel

April 20
Wednesday

 3rd ♏

☽ → ♐ 2:50 am
☉ → ♉ 6:17 am

Color of the day: Yellow
Incense of the day: Marjoram

Day of Self-Nurturing and Gratitude

We enter the earth sign of Taurus today, and with this transition invoke the power of the Horned Moon Goddess by her many names: Hathor, Selene, Luna, Diana, Io, Isis, and Hera. Goddess of home, hearth, magic, intuition, and the subtle realms, call on Her to inspire you to act for your own well-being. It is too easy to forget to nourish our own wellspring, so today, you have the Goddess' permission to engage in moments of laughter, self-love, devil's food cake, and wild abandon. Spontaneity is your guide, with accompaniments of comfort, care, love, affection, and sweetness. Remember to feed not only your body, but also your mind, soul, and spirit. In the evening, put out an offering of water and before going to bed, voice your gratitude, releasing the water and your prayers back to Earth.

Chandra Alexandre

April 21
Thursday

3rd ♐

Color of the day: Purple
Incense of the day: Balsam

Dismiss Negative Self-Views

If there's one thing lacking in the lives of humble Witches and magicians, it's self-confidence. Negative self-views (a common occurrence for those who do not overcompensate with egotism) can manifest at the worst times, blocking us from our true paths. To help banish these negative thoughts, wait until you're in a bitter, apathetic, and otherwise negative state of mind. When you sense a "beating yourself up" attitude, grab a piece of all-natural paper and a pencil. Sketch, draw, and write down these negative self-views. It doesn't matter how you express these things; it's more important to get them out on paper, even if it's in a crazy, random, abstract form. When ready, place a few pinches of banishing herbs on the paper (such as nettles, nightshade, flax, mandrake, and so on), and place a medium-sized rock in the middle. Crumple the paper around the rock and herbs, securing it in a tight ball. Walk to a bridge (that spans flowing water) at midnight and cast the spell over the edge. Declare the following:

Watery abyss, womb of life; take this pain, take this strife. I banish these thoughts, I banish these things; so that they may not return again! So mote it be.

Raven Digitalis

April 22
Friday
Good Friday
Earth Day

3rd ♐
☽ → ♑ 6:24 am

Color of the day: Pink
Incense of the day: Vanilla

Our Good Earth

Today is Good Friday, when Jesus Christ is reputed to have been crucified. It's also Earth Day, a time to celebrate environmental victories, and commit to ecologically sound practices for the future. Started in 1970 as a grassroots movement of national learning for the sake of the environment, Earth Day has morphed into an international event of activism and awareness. The con-

vergence of these holidays makes it a great time to do a Good Earth spell. Ground and connect yourself to the energy of the Earth. Pull the strong, long-lived energy into you with each breath, exhaling love, gratitude, and care. Continue this exchange until the energy rises up your spine and into your scalp. Filled with the loving, abiding, Good Earth energy, make a solemn vow to protect the planet. Make it finite, such as:

> I will make my yard a carbon sinkhole, a sanctuary for butterflies, a testament to my love for the Earth.

Now, go live it.

Dallas Jennifer Cobb

April 23
Saturday

 3rd ♑

Color of the day: Brown
Incense of the day: Pine

The Magic of Spring Flowers

In April the world turns green and spring flowers splash color across the landscape. Daffodils, hyacinths, pansies, and tulips brighten flowerbeds. There was a time when people "spoke" with flowers. When bouquets were given they carried special messages because the flowers were rich with symbolism. Here are some of the special meanings of popular spring flowers. Daffodils were given to express love and increase fertility. Hyacinths were used to represent love and protection; when the scent is inhaled it also helps to ease grief. Pansies were used to draw love, and if you are trying to perform a love divination ritual, keep a bouquet of pansies nearby. For protection, add some tulips to a bouquet. And during love spells, place a few tulips on your altar. Learning about the language of flowers will increase your magical power.

James Kambos

April 24
Sunday

Easter
Orthodox Easter

 3rd ♈

☽ → ♒ 1:59 pm

4th Quarter 10:47 pm

Color of the day: Gold
Incense of the day: Heliotrope

Easter Egg Spell

A spell is a wish that takes form by your direction and intent. The tradition of coloring Easter eggs can be part of your spellwork! Using a simple egg-dyeing kit, you can inscribe your wishes for anyone by writing on a hard-boiled egg with a wax pencil before dipping it in the dye. Names have power, so be sure to spell the person's name correctly. Then add a word, or phrase, that describes what you would like for them, such as "Health, Wealth, Happiness," or more specific things like passing a test or buying a car. Be sure to dip the egg at least three times in the dye bath. The darker the color, the more intense is the wish/spell. My wish is that YOU receive an Easter egg wishing happiness for you. Eating the egg made especially for you means that you accept the good wishes!

Paniteowl

April 25
Monday

 4th ♒

Color of the day: Silver
Incense of the day: Neroli

A Wellness Brew

Infusing herbs and plants with water, like making tea, is a kind of "Witch's brew." Today, focus on your well-being and finding balance in your life by creating a magical brew using any tea bags that contain chamomile or jasmine flowers. Begin by simply brewing yourself a cup of hot or iced tea. While your tea is steeping, hold your hands over the cup (be careful of the hot steam) and say the following words:

May this brew bring harmony

And balance to my life.

May this brew bring wellness, too,

In times of stress and strife.

When you're ready to drink your tea, imagine the water infused with the magic of the plants and flowers, their energy filling you with a calm, balanced state of mind. Drink and be well. Repeat the spell as often as you like; make this visualization part of your daily cup of tea.

Ember Grant

April 26
Tuesday

Passover ends

 4th ≈

Color of the day: Gray
Incense of the day: Ginger

The Magic of Gratitude

Start a gratitude journal. Select a small notebook, or, if you're more technologically inclined, open a new computer file. If choosing a notebook, green is an excellent color for invoking abundance and calm. Set a time each day to write in your journal. For best results, choose a time when you're calm and well rested. Working in the morning enables a concrete view, helping you consider those things you're grateful for and how they might lead to positive actions in the day to come. Writing in the evening is more magical and reflective, encouraging a writer to reflect on personal benefits already reaped. When writing in your gratitude journal, ask yourself what you're thankful for. Who or what do you appreciate? Who are you indebted to? Who deserves your thanks? Your recognition? Make your notes, and then consider a way to thank or honor those you're grateful for. Pay forward the magic of gratitude!

Susan Pesznecker

April 27
Wednesday

 4th ≈
☽ → ♓ 12:57 am

Color of the day: White
Incense of the day: Honeysuckle

Administrative Professional's Day

Hooray for the administrative professional! They are the backbone of the office—nothing would ever be accomplished without them! Since Wednesday is ruled by Mercury, this puts the emphasis on communication, and, believe it or not, computers. This spell to protect your computer at work is subtle enough that you could perform it at the office, and no one will even notice. Take a couple of tumbled agate stones and place them near your computer monitor. (Agates are aligned with Mercury and aid in communication.) Set your dominant hand upon the crystals and then repeat the charm either silently or out loud.

> Agate stones aid me in
> communication and clarity,
>
> Mercury protect my computer
> with all possible speed.
>
> Now circle me with your
> energies, around and about,
>
> Bring efficiency in and keep
> negativity out.

Ellen Dugan

April 28
Thursday

 4th ♓

Color of the day: Crimson
Incense of the day: Mulberry

Festival of Flora

Honoring our bodies and sexuality in a time and culture that so generally denies corporeal pleasure is a must for all spiritual practitioners dedicated to an embodied path. Today, resonant with the Roman Floralia, connect to the sensual through all means at your disposal: buy flowers, taste dark chocolate, caress your beloved, listen to sweet music, and take in the world's inherent beauty. Be willing to alight your senses on waves of bliss and catapult your limiting notions and taboos into the embrace of the Goddess of Love, where they can be transformed into potent elixirs of adoration, enjoyment, and devotion. Experiment today with honoring the fullness of who you are in this body, noting with wonder its physical perfection and ability to give and receive delight. Exchange simple offerings of words, affections, and trifles with both your circle of loved ones and your special someone.

Chandra Alexandre

April 29
Friday

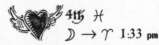 4th ♓
☽ → ♈ 1:33 pm

Color of the day: Purple
Incense of the day: Violet

Scented-Candle Friendship Spell

While this spell won't repair serious damage in a relationship between two friends, it can help ease over those occasional rough spots we all go through. For a simple version of this spell, you'll need a scented candle with an aroma makes you feel calm, relaxed, and at ease. Hold the candle in your hands and inhale deeply. On a piece of paper, write down what is causing tension between the two of you. Now light the candle, watching it burn, while focusing on all the positives in your relationship. Finally, light the paper in the candle's flame and allow it to burn to ashes in a heatproof bowl. Feel free to burn the candle often, remembering your friendships as you light it. You can also give matching candles to your closest friends as an offering of how much they mean to you.

Laurel Reufner

April 30
Saturday

  4th ♈

Color of the day: Black
Incense of the day: Magnolia

Encouraging Plants to Grow

Even if you follow all the garden manuals like a new parent following Doctor Spock and feed your leafy greens the caviar of fertilizer, sometimes they just don't blossom. Before you commit any plants to the Great Compost Heap in the Sky, try placing a clear quartz crystal, amethyst, or rose quartz stone near the plant on a sunny day. Place a hand on the stone, and see your love for the plant as a living thing sinking into the soil for the plant to absorb and rising up through stem, leaf, blossom, and fruit. Whisper to the plant:

> Come and breathe and grow
> and live,
>
> What you take I gladly
> give—
>
> Green thing, give love back
> to me,
>
> Breathing breath of harmony.

Spend a little time each day simply giving your attention to the plant; the more you connect to it, the more it will thrive.

Diana Rajchel

May's astrological sign is Taurus, the Bull (April 20–May 21), a fixed-earth sign ruled by Venus. Named for Maia, a Roman goddess of growth, May is a month of abundance and fertility. The Full Moon of May is appropriately called the Flower Moon, as the land rests fully in spring's fragrant embrace. Lush gardens are in bloom, roses are beginning to appear, and most grass and trees are a vibrant green. The breezes of May carry the scent of honeysuckle and black locust; this is a good time for tree magic and garden blessings. On the first day of May—May Day or Beltane—fertility festivals celebrate the union that creates life. Traditions include dancing around the Maypole and igniting sacred bonfires. Other new beginnings such as commencement celebrations also occur, and Mother's Day honors all who nurture. In ancient times throughout Europe, performers—dancers, musicians, and masked characters known as mummers—would create a procession through the streets, exchanging flowers and tree branches for gifts of food and money. This ritual brought the promise of a successful growing season. Gather flowers between sunset and sunrise on Beltane to make magical wreaths, garlands, and bouquets. Create a May Bough by decorating a small tree branch with colored ribbons to display as a centerpiece in your home.

May 1
Sunday

Beltane

 4th ♈

Color of the day: Yellow
Incense of the day: Juniper

high Spring
(Northern hemisphere)

No matter where we might be in the world, today marks a time when the veil between the seen and unseen realms is thinnest, for we are at a crossquarter turning to our greatest seasonal intensity, whether light or dark. The dance of the worlds here is sublime, for we are riding the edge of order and chaos—that fertile ground where the tensions of living, dying, being born, and accepting rebirth are all happening. With us, the spirit realm delights and our every breath engages the eroticism of the unknown. Here, set an intention, and today, celebrate! Create merriment, commune with the old ones, the ancestors, and the future generations. Honor your teachers and open to the abandon of the Fool. Allow your senses to feast on the magic sparkling all around; end your day with a time of self-reflection on the Great Mystery and your part in it.

Chandra Alexandre

May 2
Monday

 4th ♈
☽ → ♉ 1:58 am

Color of the day: Lavender
Incense of the day: Lily

Thunderstorm in a Bottle

Thunderstorms cleanse the Earth, combining the powers of earth, air, fire, and water, and can cleanse you, too. Capture that power by catching rainwater in a bottle. Watch the entire storm from a window. Visualize the bottle expanding to embrace the storm. Allow the rain to create a trance-like rhythm. As you chant, imagine the rain falling on you, and notice thunder in the distance vibrating your body.

> Thunder beat, my heart
>   drums
> Lightning strike, my skin
>   thrums
> Rain of rivers, lakes, and
>   ocean
> Through me, to me, from the
>   sky

Grab your bottle right after the rain stops. Cap the bottle and store it in your refrigerator or a cool, dry place. Add a little of the rainwater you captured to your shampoo or to your bath water when you need extra cleansing or an energy boost.

Diana Rajchel

May 3
Tuesday

 4th ♉
New Moon 2:51 am

Color of the day: Black
Incense of the day: Cinnamon

New Moon Growth Spell

The New Moon in May is an auspicious time to wish for growth and prosperity. May is considered the real beginning of the growing season; spells cast during a May New Moon take on special power. Begin by gathering some green grasses, weeds, or flower stems. Bind them with garden twine and shape them to resemble a human figure. Tuck a few leaves, pieces of bark, or flowers into the figure, which may represent your wish. Lay the grass figure on your altar and surround it with symbols of the four elements. Light a green candle for fire, sprinkle some peat moss or soil for earth. Burn some incense to represent air, and a bowl of spring water. Think of your wish and pass your power hand over the figure, then form the shape of a pentagram above the figure. At noon, the solar hour, carry your figure to a stream or river and release it. See your spell growing and being carried to fulfillment by the flowing water. At the Full Moon, scry into a bowl or cauldron filled with water to check the status of your spell.

James Kambos

May 4
Wednesday

 1st ♉
☽ → ♊ 1:09 pm

Color of the day: White
Incense of the day: Bay laurel

Safe Travel Charm

Harnessing the powers of the planet Mercury, create a charm today to protect yourself or a loved one while traveling. You will need a stone aligned with Mercury such as jasper or orange calcite, a photocopy of the Magician tarot card, a white candle, a piece of blue cloth, string, and equal parts of the following: dill, chamomile, oats, lavender, fennel, sandalwood, almonds, and sage. Bless and charge all of the items within your sacred circle. Drip a bit of wax onto a candleholder, carve the symbol of Mercury in it, and allow it to harden. Place all the ingredients on the cloth. Tie and say something like:

As I travel far away
Keep all danger and harm
*   at bay*
That I may return safe
*   and sound*
By sea and sun, sky and
*   ground.*

Carry the charm with you as you travel.

Abel R. Gomez

May 5
Thursday
Cinco de Mayo

 1st ♊

Color of the day: Turquoise
Incense of the day: Jasmine

National Day of Prayer (U. S.)

Today, in the United States, it is the National Day of Prayer. It is also Cinco de Mayo, a day in Mexico when folks celebrate a major triumph over the French in 1862. Offer up a prayer today for courage and triumph in the face of world, or personal, adversity. On a plain, unlined piece of paper, write or draw your prayer. Allow the winds to carry your prayer out into the world by affixing it to a tree branch in the fashion of *Shinto omikuji*, or fortune scrolls, or Eastern European prayer scrolls, as well as *ema*, wooden plaques left at Shinto shrines with wishes written on them.

Laurel Reufner

Holiday lore: Don't confuse Cinco de Mayo with Mexican Independence Day on September 16. Cinco de Mayo marks the victory of the brave Mexican army over the French at the Battle of Puebla. Although the Mexican army was eventually defeated, the *Batalla de Puebla* became a symbol of Mexican unity and patriotism. With this victory, the people of Mexico demonstrated to the world that Mexico and all of Latin America were willing to defend themselves against any foreign or imperialist intervention.

May 6
Friday

 1st ♊

☽ → ♋ 10:32 pm

Color of the day: Rose
Incense of the day: Cypress

Gather the Beauty of Violets

One of the most wonderful plants in the Scottish folk tradition is the móthan or bog violet. Violets grow abundantly at this time of year and were used in charms and spells for love, happiness, and protection. When used for love spells, the wise woman gathered nine roots of the plant while leaning on her left knee and then formed them into a ring. This was placed in the mouth of a young girl who would pass the ring into the mouth of the young man she desired, ensuring his everlasting devotion. Here is a charm for gathering violets for magical protection and wisdom:

> I will gather the sacred violet,
> Plant of the nine roots,
> To overcome all oppression
>   and negativity.

> I will pluck the gracious
>   violet,
> Most precious plant in the
>   field,
> So that the holiness of the
>   seven sacred eldors,

Their eloquence, their
    wisdom, and their counsel
Will be mine.

Sharynne MacLeod NicMhacha

May 7
Saturday

1st ♋

Color of the day: Indigo
Incense of the day: Magnolia

Go Green

With the Moon waxing and Beltane magic still rippling through the air (and earth!) it's a great time to plant. Gardens take many forms—even a few pots on a windowsill counts—but all can be sacred spaces to commune with the Mother Goddess, the Green Man, the Fey, or yourself. If you have a garden, spend some time today tending, and maybe putting in a new addition. If you don't have a garden, put a potted basil or sage in your sunniest window, or claim a corner of the yard if you're feeling really ambitious. The following blessing can be used regardless: fill a bowl or pitcher of water and stand in or next to your garden. Charge the water by chanting:

> Life of water, life of air, life of fire, life of earth, life begets life, grow in life.

Then water your garden, focusing on your connection with the green beings there.

Castiel

May 8
Sunday
Mother's Day

 1st ♋

Color of the day: Gold
Incense of the day: Marigold

Love Your Mother Earth

Happy Mother's Day! Today is an ideal day for reconnecting to the Great Goddess, the mother of us all. For starters, you can help secure this connection by spending a bit of time with your mother or grandmother, acknowledging the holiday. If you are either not close to your mom or grandma, or if they are not in your life for some reason, you can,

of course, perform this Great Mother working regardless. Whatever your own situation, today is the day to connect to this force. Today, I suggest you perform a ritual of surrender, gratitude, and connection—all centered around Mother Earth. Go to a secluded place outdoors, carrying three fresh organic apples, and feel the energy of the Earth. Lie on the ground, feel the soil and grass, commune with the trees and the spirits. Allow yourself to cry. Weep deep tears, thinking about the destruction of the Earth and her creatures. Think of all the painful, Earth-related images you've seen, and stories you've heard. Bring to mind clear-cutting, factory farming, and other issues that are killing our Mother. Let your tears spill on the soil. Once you've gathered yourself, express the depth of your gratitude. Tell the Mother why you love her. Reflect on all the positive Earth aspects that come to mind, and give thanks. Offer the three apples by leaving them behind. To conclude, head to the bathtub and take a bath with the herb parsley, to further attune and bind you to the Great Mother of us all.

Raven Digitalis

May 9
Monday

1st ♋
☽ → ♌ 5:35 am

Color of the day: Gray
Incense of the day: Narcissus

Lemuria

This is one of three days the ancient Romans practiced a ritual of exorcism to dispel the lemures, ghosts of the restless dead. If anyone had these spirits lurking in their homes, they would lure them out by leaving a trail of black beans, throwing them over their shoulder without looking back. This should be done at midnight. Some say the homeowner should be barefoot while doing this; others say he should spit black beans from his mouth, and some say the person should walk backward. Mondays are good days for practicing magic of hearth and home, so perform a cleansing ritual for protection and to clear away negative energy. Place nine black beans on the floor in your home, leading out a doorway. As you position each bean, say:

Beans of nine, this home is mine.

Sweep the beans out with a broom, and then wash your hands.

Ember Grant

May 10
Tuesday
Census Day (Canada)

1st ♌
2nd Quarter 4:33 pm

Color of the day: White
Incense of the day: Basil

Enchanted Garden Blessings

May is here and the bewitching season of spring is in full swing. To celebrate, why not bless your enchanted gardens with this garden Witch's charm? Go outside and walk around in your garden. Find your favorite spot and hold your hands out above the young plants, flowers, and herbs. Then visualize your loving energy streaming from your hands and down into the plant life.

A Garden Witch's magic begins with the earth,

Bless these herbs and plants with power, health, growth, and mirth.

Happy plants do create enchantment all year long,

May the gods bless my garden as they hear this song.

By all the powers of the Earth, the Moon, and Sun,

As I will so shall it be, and let it harm none.

This charm also works well as an all-purpose blessing when you add new plants into your Witch's garden.

Ellen Dugan

May 11
Wednesday

 2nd ♌
☽ → ♍ 9:59 am

Color of the day: Yellow
Incense of the day: Lavender

Binding a Book

We've all had the experience of loaning a book to a friend but then forgetting who we loaned it to. To help your book find its way back home, carry out this simple binding spell. Measure the book from top to bottom. Add four inches to this measurement, and then double the total. Cut a red cord or ribbon (for empowerment) to this length. (Example: If your book is ten inches tall, you'd calculate 10 + 4 = 14; 14 x 2 = 28.) When you're ready to loan the book, hold the cord in your hand and say these words aloud:

However far this book may travel,

Never will this strand unravel.

O'er land, through air, or stirring sea,

Return this volume back to me.

Cut the cord in half, knotting each of the four ends with overhand ("stopper") knots. Insert one half-cord into the book; keep the other in a safe place until the book is returned.

Susan Pesznecker

May 12
Thursday

 2nd ♍

Color of the day: Green
Incense of the day: Carnation

Limerick Enchantment

Words are sacred tools used for incantations, spells, and enchantments. To celebrate the birthday of the eighteenth-century champion of the limerick, Edward

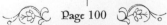

Lear, write your own five-line rhyming poem using an A, A, B, B, A pattern of rhyme. Use your words to engage and entertain, educate and involve. Use your words to make magic, altering consciousness at will. Like the traditional mummers who shaped group energy, and magical practitioners who craft spells and incantations, use your words to make change. Craft a limerick that will remind you time and again what you want to remember.

> There once was a Pagan
>   daughter,
> Who loved earth, air, fire,
>   and water,
> She followed the seasons,
> That taught her good reason,
> And gave thanks for all they
>   brought her.

> When my life needs
>   correction,
> I use meditation and
>   reflection,
> I look to the Wheel,
> Because seasons are real,
> And nature teaches direction.

Dallas Jennifer Cobb

May 13
Friday

 2nd ♏
☽ → ♎ 11:56 am

Color of the day: Purple
Incense of the day: Rose

Airy Fairy Love Altar

This ritual calls upon the fairies to draw a whirlwind romance into your life. Find a picture or statue of two or more winged fairies. Spread a sparkly, pastel-colored cloth over a small table, shelf, or box. Position the image(s) as the centerpiece, and add a white or light-colored votive candle, a stick of vanilla incense, and a lepidolite crystal (which has been cleansed with sunlight). Light the candle and incense and hold the crystal to your heart. Say:

> Fairies of joy and delirious
> bliss,

> Send me the one with the
> magical kiss.

Close your eyes and feel the dizzy, whimsical feeling of falling in love. Place the crystal back on the altar. Let the incense burn all the way down and extinguish the candle. Leave the altar until the next New Moon, and then put the crystal at the base of a tree as a gift to the fairies.

Tess Whitehurst

May 14
Saturday

2nd ♎

Color of the day: Gray
Incense of the day: Pine

Cleanse Your House

The showers of April bring the flowers of May, so it is appropriate to use a floral arrangement in your plans for spring cleaning! Gather a bunch of spring-blooming flowers and place them in vases. When you've cleaned a room, place a vase in a prominent place asking the flowers to bless and brighten your home by simply chanting:

> Flowers of May to brighten
> the day.

As you chant or hum these words to a favorite tune, the actual cleaning will seem less of a chore if you visualize each room as being clean and cheerful with the flowers in place.

Paniteowl

May 15
Sunday

2nd ♎
☽ → ♏ 12:31 pm

Color of the day: Yellow
Incense of the day: Almond

Mercury's Business

Today is Mercuralia, a Roman celebration meaning "Festival of Mercury." The god Mercury oversees merchants, commerce, and travel. Traditionally, Roman merchants would sprinkle themselves, their merchandise, and their ships with water taken from Mercury's sacred well in Porta Capena. Honor Mercury today by taking care of your business. Place ten silver coins in a bowl of water and ask Mercury to bless the water. Use this in your bath or shower. Also wash your car, your desk, your work tools, and anything else you associate with your career. As you do these things, chant:

> Swift planet
> Swift wealth
> Strong planet
> Strong health
> Mercury
> See me
> Mercury
> Bless me

At the end of the day, pour the water in front of your threshold (NOT down a drain!) and thank Mercury for his blessings. Donate the coins to charity.

Elizabeth Barrette

seeing your body whole and healthy. Leave the votive for a couple of hours to begin drying, and then carry it on your person until the next evening. Bury it somewhere safely in the ground and walk away.

Laurel Reufner

May 16
Monday

 2nd ♏

Color of the day: White
Incense of the day: Rosemary

Votive healing

Folks in the ancient world would make votive offerings to the gods asking for healing. The votives represented the body part with which the petitioner was concerned. Make your own votive by mixing ½ cup salt with 1 cup flour. Slowly add in ½ cup water and continue mixing. On a lightly floured surface, knead the dough well. If it seems too dry, add small amounts of water until it is pliable. If it is too wet, mix in equal proportions of salt and flour. When the dough is ready and you've cleaned up the mess, ground and center yourself. Begin shaping a small ball of dough to resemble the body part you are requesting healing. Really focus on

May 17
Tuesday

 2nd ♏

Full Moon 7:09 am
☽ → ♐ 1:22 pm

Color of the day: Red
Incense of the day: Cedar

Abundant Light

Tonight we celebrate the Full Moon—this is a time of abundant magic and a good time to honor all Moon goddesses. The energy of the Full Moon can bring us peace, comfort, love, and joy. Prepare a centerpiece for your altar or table. Use a clear glass bowl or dish and place a small mirror in the bottom, round, if possible. Add water, and place three white floating candles in the dish. An alternative is to use a glass plate, with or without a mirror, and arrange three white votive candles or tealights on it. Surround your entire center-piece with white flowers and stones associated with the Moon, such as quartz crystal and moonstone. Gaze into the mirror and meditate on the reflected candlelight. Remember that the Moon does not shed light of her own, but reflects the light of the Sun. This means we can see the life-giving light of our world, even in times of darkness. Repeat this chant:

> As the Moon controls the tides,
>
> So its rhythm rules our lives.
>
> Through cycles changing, wax and wane,
>
> In different phases, yet the same.

Ember Grant

May 18
Wednesday

 3rd ♐

Color of the day: Topaz
Incense of the day: Lilac

A Prayer to the Sun

Many magicians and Witches fancy aligning themselves to the cosmic energies upon waking. To carry on this tradition, get some incense-burning charcoal—not the stuff used in BBQ pits—and a tray with sand to place it on. Go outside when you wake up for the day (or when the Sun is high) and ignite the charcoal. Place either chamomile or frankincense on the ember, and offer it to the Sun. Waft its smoke to the mighty Star of Stars, and think about the reasons why you are grateful for its cosmic light. Once you've made your offering, set the charcoal down or extinguish it (to ensure it doesn't start a fire!), and hold your hands to the Sun. Form a triangle with your hands by touching your thumbs together and touching your pointer fingers together. Hold this triangle up to the Sun, framing it. Take in six deep breaths, envisioning the sunlight funneling through the frame and into your body. Once finished, bathe under the Sun for as long as you'd like. Repeat this every morning for as long as you please!

Raven Digitalis

 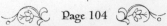

May 19
Thursday

3rd ♐

☽ → ♑ 4:16 pm

Color of the day: White
Incense of the day: Clove

The Kallynteria–Day of Sweeping

Perhaps the origin of spring cleaning, this ancient festival marked the time of annual temple purification, changing of the flame, and readornment of the Goddess after a ritual bath in the sea. Priestesses used brooms to sweep out the marble and tile rooms, making ready for the return of Pallas Athena. Offerings of figs were considered especially proper because they were the first cultivated fruit, symbolic of a new beginning in the Goddess' care—a kind of fresh start for everyone. With this in mind, today is a day to clean your house, take a ritual bath and reassemble your altar. Cleanse your ritual tools, dust out the remnants of old magical work, and make a fresh start with your spiritual practice. Commit, for example, to doing one thing every day that brings you into communion with deity. Finally, anoint your images and implements, blessing them for the year ahead.

Chandra Alexandre

May 20
Friday

3rd ♑

Color of the day: Coral
Incense of the day: Violet

Protection While Walking

Even in quiet towns, sometimes things go a bit awry, making a normal activity like walking more perilous than you might expect. To cushion yourself from both accidents and mishaps of design, choose a ring to wear whenever you go out for a walk. A metal ring of any design is ideal. Hold it closely in your hand when the Sun is highest in the sky, and petition the Sun's energy:

Light my path and guard my
step, so that I am ever safely
kept. Where I walk the Sun
may shine, even in the dark-
est night.

Say this several times as you charge the ring, and repeat the rhyme whenever you put the ring on. The ring will form a protective shield around you whenever you wear it; use this along with a good sense of caution and attention to your surroundings. Magic does not impart invincibility!

Diana Rajchel

May 21
Saturday

3rd ♑

☉ → ♊ 5:21 am
☽ → ♒ 10:32 pm

Color of the day: Blue
Incense of the day: Patchouli

Armed Forces Day

Today we honor the brave men and women of our armed forces. Light a red candle, a white candle, and a blue candle for the armed forces today and remember the sacrifices that they and their families have made for us all. May their missions both at here and abroad be successful and may they all return home safely to their loved ones. Since it is Saturday, this is a perfect time to work protection magic. Light the three candles and repeat this charm thrice:

> Marine, airman, sailor,
>   and soldier,
> May you be safe while on
>   land, in the air, and
>   at sea,
> Walk with integrity, courage,
>   and honor,
> Returning safe and whole to
>   your families.
> By Saturday's magic this
>   spell is spun,
> For the good of all, bringing
>   harm to none.

Ellen Dugan

May 22
Sunday

3rd ♒

Color of the day: Amber
Incense of the day: Frankincense

Clear Clutter for Clarity and Creativity

Light a yellow candle and a stick of cedar incense. Hold your hands in prayer pose, close your eyes, and focus your attention at your third eye (above the center of your brows). Relax and set your intention by envisioning/feeling perfect clarity and creativity in your life. Now, clear clutter from your home. Box up or discard clothes you don't wear or that don't make you feel good, papers you don't need, gifts you never liked, and everything else that's just taking up space. Drink lots of water while you do this, and take as much time as you need (even taking extra days if necessary). When you're finished, take a shower. Then light a bundle of dried white sage. Move the smoke around your body and home. Finally, stand in a central location with your hands in prayer pose and say the following nine times:

> Clear, creative, joyful, free.

Tess Whitehurst

May 23
Monday

3rd ≈≈

Color of the day: Ivory
Incense of the day: Hyssop

World Turtle Day

Today is World Turtle Day, a day set aside to raise awareness for the preservation of these wise, ancient creatures. Turtles and tortoises have been around much longer than humans, and some can live for more than a hundred years. Many cultures incorporate turtles into their stories about the creation of the world, and thus they are a symbol of Mother Earth for many people. Tortoises teach us about being grounded and patient—that children's story is an old one, but always pertinent!—and turtles, who live on the boundary between water and land, teach us about creation, transformation, and transition. Do something today to honor these special creatures—light a candle, draw a picture, or donate to a charity that protects them. Try working with the Turtle Totem. Place images of turtles on your altar and ask the totem to come to you in meditation. Remember that living things are connected to Mother Earth.

Castiel

May 24
Tuesday

3rd ≈≈
☽ → ♓ 8:24 am
4th Quarter 2:52 pm

Color of the day: Black
Incense of the day: Geranium

Memory and Mindfulness

Mnemosyne is a goddess of memory and mother to the nine Muses. The ancient Greeks believed that fine and stage arts were gifts from the gods. Artists would invoke the apt Muse for inspiration. Mnemosyne's name comes from the Greek root, "mindful," and and is the basis of "mnemonic," a pattern-based memory device, e.g., ROY G. BIV is the color spectrum: Red, Orange, Yellow, Green, Blue, Indigo, Violet. Invoke Mnemosyne when seeking mindfulness or stronger memory. Work at dusk, a threshold time when mental acuity is high. Brew peppermint or blueberry tea; burn rosemary incense or smudge; use moonstones, emeralds, fluorite, hematite, or turquoise; work with blue or indigo colors. Create a mnemonic device, if you wish. Then call upon Mnemosyne:

Dear Mnemosyne,
Heed my request,
To boost my memory,
Is my behest!

Susan Pesznecker

May 25
Wednesday

 4th ♓

Color of the day: Brown
Incense of the day: Marjoram

Thyme for health and Magic

Thyme should be looking lush in the herb garden now, and is excellent in spring health and magic rituals. First, use a bit of thyme in your bath to cleanse away any negativity that has built up from the past. To do this, simply sprinkle a few thyme leaves, or place a sprig of thyme in the bath water. You may add it to your favorite bubble bath to clear away negativity. Burn some thyme on your altar in May to cleanse your magical space. Thyme burned with incense will increase psychic power. For a restful night, place a sprig of thyme beneath your pillow. To cleanse your body, include thyme in a soup recipe such as green split pea for some soothing tasty comfort food.

James Kambos

May 26
Thursday

 4th ♓
☽ → ♈ 8:36 pm

Color of the day: Purple
Incense of the day: Nutmeg

A Spell to Sleep Well

Spin a spell today to quiet your body and soothe your senses. Call to the Egyptian goddess Nuit, the embodiment of the starry heaven. All you'll need is a blue candle and lavender oil. At your ritual space, or under the night sky, charge the candle with your intention of restful sleep and dress the candle with the oil. (Rub oil on your temples for added relaxation). Take a deep breath and lift your gaze at the beauty of the sea of stars. Raise your arms in honor and call to Nuit:

> Beauteous Nuit
> Eternal One of starry heaven
> Hold me in your warm
>   embrace
> As I journey through the veil
>   of dreams
> Grant me a deep and
>   peaceful sleep
> That I may dream of the
>   worlds unseen.
> Blessed be.

Snuff out the candle and allow your breath to guide you into a deep and restful sleep. Sweet dreams!

Abel R. Gomez

May 27
Friday

 4th ♈

Color of the day: White
Incense of the day: Orchid

Water Elemental Spell

After a long, cold winter, there is nothing like that first swim in a lake or the ocean. The end of May signals the beginning of summer days, yet the waters are still cold enough to present a challenge to the hearty! Plan a waterside picnic, and focus on reconnecting with water on a personal level. Write a few lines on paper describing ways in which you'd like to change or enhance your life. Think carefully, and set out some short-term goals, and then some long-term goals. Burn your notes and take the ashes to the water. Stand in the water and release the ashes saying:

> I cast my promises for the
> future into your care. May
> your example be my guide.
> The placid flow, the raging
> torrent, sculpts the earth in
> its movement. May the flow
> of the waters within me sus-
> tain my dreams.

Paniteowl

May 28
Saturday

 4th ♈

Color of the day: Black
Incense of the day: Ivy

Make Your Mind Blossom

Your mind is what controls your magic. The stronger and more versatile you can make your mind, the better your magic will get. This exercise hones your skills of visualization, concentration, and mental endurance. Close your eyes and imagine a glass vase. See its shape and feel its cool weight in your hand. Now visualize a rose in your other hand. See its color, smell its sweet fragrance, and feel its stem in your fingertips. Place the rose in the vase. While still maintaining your visualization of the rose in the vase, imagine a daisy in the same detail. Add it to the vase. Continue creating flowers in your mind and adding them to the bouquet in your vase, always holding the earlier flowers as well. Stop when you start to feel tired (or get a headache), or when you lose track of some of the flowers.

Elizabeth Barrette

May 29
Sunday

4th ♈

☽ → ♉ 9:02 am

Color of the day: Gold
Incense of the day: Eucalyptus

Create a Magical Threshold

The main entrance to your home is a very magical place. Household spirits are thought to dwell there and your threshold also serves as a protective buffer between your living space and the outside world. Now that the weather is warm, it's a good time to create some positive magical energy around your front door. Begin by giving the space a good physical cleaning. Get rid of any cobwebs and dirt. Sprinkle a bit of salt outside your front door, and sweep it away from your home to clear away any bad vibrations. Place a few plants on your porch or by your door. Ferns, potted or hanging, are protective and are loved by the fairy folk. Red geraniums are protective and energizing, while pink geraniums draw love. A rose quartz placed near the door brings peace. To let your house spirits know they're welcome, hide an old key you no longer need near your front door. Then grab a good book and a comfy chair and enjoy your magical threshold.

James Kambos

Holiday lore: Opinions are divided concerning the origins of the holiday of Memorial Day in the United States. This is a day set aside for honoring the graves of American war dead. While most historians credit the origins of the custom to Southern women, there is also a rumor, historically speaking, of an anonymous German who fought in the American Civil War (no one is sure on which side). At the end of the war, this soldier was allegedly overheard commenting that in the Old World people scattered flowers on the graves of dead soldiers. In May 1868, a Union army general suggested to Commander John A. Logan that a day be set aside each year to decorate Union graves. Logan agreed, and he set aside May 30 for this ritual. His proclamation acknowledged those "who died in defense of their country" and "whose bodies now lie in almost every city, village, or hamlet churchyard in the land." This patriotic holiday was later amended to include all the dead from all the wars, and its date was shifted to a convenient Monday late in May.

May 30
Monday
Memorial Day (observed)

 4th ♉

Color of the day: Lavender
Incense of the day: Narcissus

Ritual to honor the Ancestors

Memorial Day is an excellent time to remember those who have gone before, whether they fell defending land or loved ones, or from other causes. We are here because of our ancestors and it is important to honor their spirits. Ancestors can be powerful allies once they have fully passed over and received their healing. Here is a ritual for remembering the ancestors: On the ground, make a circle of small stones, which represent the ancestors, known and unknown. Around this, make another circle of salt, indicating you wish to work with healed ancestors who are ready to help. In the center, make a small mound of grain, nuts, or dried fruit that would have been part of your ancestors' natural diet. Invite them to feast on this ritual meal and recite these words to remember them:

> Old Ones, Great Ones, Wise Ones, and Elders
>
> I call upon you to guide me, once your healing is over

> I remember your wisdom, I remember your ways
>
> Help me and bless me each night and each day.

Sharynne MacLeod NicMhacha

May 31
Tuesday

 4th ♉
☽ → ♊ 7:56 pm

Color of the day: Scarlet
Incense of the day: Ginger

Many Mothers Celebration

In Catholic countries, May 31 is Flores de Mayo (Flowers of May) day. After a month of celebrations in honor of the Virgin Mary, the final night is a grand party featuring torchlight parades, games, banquets, and open houses. Children bat at piñatas filled with candy and toys, and adults celebrate with food and music. Enact your own little celebration in honor of May, mothering, and creativity. Plan a block party or community gathering, and be sure to invite people with children. Potluck is best, welcoming the creative energy of everyone to the table. Make a piñata shaped like the Earth, our mother. Fill it with treats: sweets and toys for the kids, flowers for all the mothers. Celebrate the mothering energy of creativity, food, friends, and families. Then let the children bat the piñata, grab candy, and take flowers to the mothers.

Dallas Jennifer Cobb

June is the sixth month of the year. Its astrological sign is Gemini, the Twins (May 21–June 21), a mutable-air sign ruled by Mercury. The month is named for Juno, the principal goddess of the Roman pantheon, and wife of Jupiter. She is the patroness of marriage and the well-being of women. This is one reason June is the most popular month for weddings. June brings the magic of midsummer—the Summer Solstice, longest day of the year. Summer is ripe now with bird song and the pleasant buzz of evening insects. The gentleness of spring has given way to the powerful heat of summer—the Full Moon of June is called the Strong Sun Moon. Various cultures pay homage to Sun gods this time of year. In some places summer is just getting started and the hottest months are yet to come, yet after the solstice we don't even notice the days beginning to get slightly shorter. This is the time for enjoying the splendor of summer: playful picnics and hikes through the woods, long nights beneath the stars, and tending gardens and flowerbeds. Roadsides are a riot of color, and herbs such as St. John's wort, vervain, and yarrow can be used in herbal amulets. This is the time of year to honor the faeries—leave offerings of ale, milk, fruit, or bread before cutting flowers or herbs and they may help your garden grow.

June 1
Wednesday

 4th ♊
New Moon 5:03 pm

Color of the day: Topaz
Incense of the day: Lavender

Shadow Spell

Today there will be a solar eclipse, so a shadow spell is quite appropriate to use for any number of things we may want to address. Stand in the sun and face your shadow. Move slowly toward your shadow, then back away from it. Move to your left, and then to your right, you can even hum a tune and dance a box step. Watch your shadow as you move. Now talk to your shadow, expressing your thoughts on what you want to achieve. Simply say:

> I am you, and you are me.
> Follow my lead so that we
> may be, all we can, so mote
> it be!

Paniteowl

June 2
Thursday

 1st ♊

Color of the day: Green
Incense of the day: Mulberry

Cool Your Temper

Fire rules over anger. Its essential oils are sharp ones like cinnamon and dragon's blood. Its color is red. Its stones include garnet, ruby, and red jasper. For this anger-management spell you need a solid red votive candle, cinnamon oil, and a chip of red stone. First, dress the candle with essential oil, stroking from base to wick. Put the candle on a fireproof plate and light it. Meditate or talk about what angers you—yell if you want to—until a pool of wax forms at the base of the candle. Press a chip of red stone into the soft wax and fold wax to cover it completely. Blow out the candle. As the wax cools, so does your anger. Carry the blob of wax with its embedded stone as a charm to remind you that no matter how hot your temper gets, you can always cool it.

Elizabeth Barrette

June 3
Friday

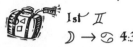

1st ♊

☽ → ♋ 4:36 am

Color of the day: Pink
Incense of the day: Thyme

A Car-Protection Spell

Vacation time is beginning, and now is a good time to magically protect your vehicles before heading out on the road. This simple protection oil may help. Select three protective herbs such as basil, fennel, and thyme. Place a sprig of each, or crumble equal parts of each herb, in a small jar and combine with a quarter cup of olive oil. Seal the jar with a lid and allow the mixture to steep for three days. Now you're ready to anoint your vehicle. To do this, place a small amount of the oil on your finger or a cotton swab, and trace the sign of a cross on hidden areas of your vehicle. Do this on all four sides, and visualize all the occupants of your vehicle surrounded with protective energy. At the same time, silently bless the other cars you'll encounter on the road.

James Kambos

June 4
Saturday

1st ♋

Color of the day: Black
Incense of the day: Rue

To Wish Love to a Friend

Some of us are just born yentas. Ultimately, however, only the person seeking love can find the right partner. It's best not to go hunting for specific people yourself. Even so, if a dear friend seems lonely, you can ask nature to help—and then stay out of it! Light a pink or white candle with your friend's name carved onto it. Hold it up to the sky—as if the Moon can see—and say this:

> Dear friend, walk alone no more,
>
> Aphrodite, show him/her what his/her heart is for—
>
> Lead him/her to a lover or friend,
>
> Let him/her find happiness at his/her path's end.

Blow out the candle and store it in your freezer. After your friend meets someone, gift him/her the candle—re-melted into a new candle if possible. You do NOT need to tell your friend about the spell, and after doing this, leave it be!

Diana Rajchel

June 5
Sunday

1st ♋

☽ → ♌ 11:03 am

Color of the day: Amber
Incense of the day: Heliotrope

Animal Repelling Spell

This spring a skunk moved in under my porch, creating a large hole dug under my deck and leaving frequent fragrant reminders. I don't harm animals, so I needed to clearly communicate to the skunk my desire for it to go elsewhere. I got rid of the skunk with the following spell. Purchase a pound of black peppercorns—animals with a developed sense of smell hate these. Make sure the animal is not in the space, then scatter the peppercorns on the pathway to it, in the entrance of it, and as far into the hole or space, as you can. Incant:

> This house is mine, I live here,
>
> So you must go, far or near,
>
> Find your own more suitable space,
>
> But not here, this is my place.

You usually only need the one application of peppercorns, but repeat if necessary.

Dallas Jennifer Cobb

June 6
Monday

1st ♌

Color of the day: Lavender
Incense of the day: Rosemary

Dream Pillow

Monday is ruled by the Moon, and dream spells draw on the magical influence of the Moon. During this waxing Moon phase, create a dream pillow to help you remember your dreams and draw wisdom from them. Stitch together a small piece of fabric, or use a drawstring bag. Fill it with plain white rice and add any three of the following ingredients: a few drops of lavender oil, a small quartz crystal or a small tumbled moonstone, sandalwood powder, jasmine, gardenia, lavender, or chamomile flowers. As you seal the pillow, chant the following:

> Moon when dark and Moon when bright,
> Guard my dreaming every night—
> Lend me wisdom, let them guide,
> Learn the meanings that they hide.

Keep the dream pillow in your pillowcase or tuck it beneath your mattress. Use it for as long as you like, refreshing it with new ingredients from time to time.

Ember Grant

June 7
Tuesday

1st ♌
☽ → ♍ 3:33 pm

Color of the day: Scarlet
Incense of the day: Cedar

Invigoration Invocation

When we wake up, our mind is stuck somewhere between the dreaming and waking life. Naturally, many of us pray daily to the goddess Caffeina, asking her to fill us with wakefulness and the energy of the day! Why not make your morning cup of coffee (or caffeinated tea) a ritual? When you add the coffee grounds to the filter, or when you put the tea bag in the cup, say:

> Sacred caffeine—invigoration! Fill my day with motivation. Imbue this elixir, merge with my being, that I may be inspired, that I may sing! This day is mine, through space and through time. Fill me now, So mote it be!

As the coffee or tea steeps, envision it surrounded with a bright blue light. Chant any extra energies you wish to imbue your day with by speaking them directly into the elixir—the water will carry this energy into you. Repeat this "instant magic" spell as often as you like.

Raven Digitalis

June 8
Wednesday

Shavuot

1st ♍
2nd Quarter 10:11 pm

Color of the day: White
Incense of the day: Honeysuckle

Spontaneous Ceremony

Through improv we can access our authentic, instinctual self. Improv in magic and ritual allows us to delve into the wisdom of our bodies. It teaches us to trust our intuitive sense. Spin a spell on a whim today without any scripts or prewritten material. Cast a circle and call to the gods and the elements of life through song, movement, silence, or however your heart inspires you. Take a breath. What is it you need at this moment? Begin to move and embody your desire. What does it look like? What does it taste like? Continue to move and allow the energy to build and take the form of your desire. When the energy is at its peak, send it out into the universe to manifest your intention. Offer any excess energy to the gods and to your own god-self. The Divine Mystery lives within you.

Abel R. Gomez

June 9
Thursday

 2nd ♏

☽ → ♎ 6:31 pm

Color of the day: Turquoise
Incense of the day: Myrrh

Ritual of the Ashes

This is a kind of sympathetic magic—magic in which a physical substance is used to create a magical link between people, places, or ideas. The ritual of the ashes is a wonderful tradition that will empower your candle magic, altar craft, ritual fires, and even your family hearth. Start by selecting a glass or ceramic jar with a tight lid. You may wish to select a special vessel for this purpose. Begin by placing some ash from a hearth fire, smudging, or candle magic into the jar. Thereafter, every time you work with fire, start the process by adding a pinch of ash from the ritual jar. Once done, add a bit of the cooled ashes back to the jar. Keep a list of which ashes are added, the date, and the circumstances. As your jar of ashes accumulates, they become a powerful sympathetic link binding intention, time, and place.

Susan Pesznecker

June 10
Friday

 2nd ♎

Color of the day: White
Incense of the day: Alder

The Irresistible Charm

Wear this necklace and you'll possess dazzling beauty and irresistible charm. String a lepidolite or rhodochrosite bead or pendant (that has been cleansed in running water) onto a silver or hemp cord. Light jasmine incense and a lavender candle. Hold the pendant in the smoke from the incense and say:

> Goddess Venus and Spirit
> of Dove,
> Let this stone glow with the
> power of love.

Then warm the stone with the candle flame as you say:

> While I wear this magical
> prize,
> Let all my charms be
> emphasized.

Continue to hold the pendant above the flame as you envision and/or feel what it will be like to be irresistibly charming and dazzlingly beautiful to all you meet. When the visualization feels complete, surround the necklace with fresh mint leaves, wrap them together in white flannel, and store it in a special place until the Full Moon.

Tess Whitehurst

June 11
Saturday

2nd ♎

☽ → ♏ 8:33 pm

Color of the day: Blue
Incense of the day: Sandalwood

Child Protection

As our children get older and they spend more and more time away from us, it gets harder and harder to keep them safe from the troubles and dangers of the world. This simple protection spell uses a cell phone charm. Ground and center before lighting a small blue or white candle. Hold the chosen charm in your receptive hand and focus your will upon it, filling it with white protective light. Visualize that light swirling out from the charm to surround your child with a protective barrier between them and the dangers of their world. Place the charm near the candle and allow it to burn down completely. Fasten the charm to your child's cell phone. It is done. Make sure to program an ICE (In Case of Emergency) number into their directory.

Laurel Reufner

June 12
Sunday

2nd ♏

Color of the day: Gold
Incense of the day: Hyacinth

Feeding the Divine Creation

Feast Day of Mut in the Egyptian calendar and grain festival sacred to Ashtoreth in the Hebrew year, today is a day to leave offerings of food for those in need, reflecting your commitment to engaged spirituality. To nurture yourself, take a break from the errands, demands, and other time-constrained activities of your daily life. Make time to prepare your own food, no matter how simple. Avoid takeout, fast food, or premade options and let the creation of a meal be your ritual. Today, you may wish to speak a special prayer acknowledging the abundance you do have. Give thanks for the elements, spirits, and souls who contribute to all that nourishes you. Let your meditation be on the ways in which your body takes food and converts it to the energy you use in daily life. Reflect on what you're able to accomplish by the grace of this divine process.

Chandra Alexandre

June 13
Monday

 2nd ♏

☽ → ♐ 10:38 pm

Color of the day: White
Incense of the day: Hyssop

Your Magical Camouflage

Today we have a Moon's day and a waxing Moon phase, which creates a double dose of power on any lunar magics that you perform. The Moon can help you blend in and have your actions go unnoticed. Whether you are keeping your head down at work from a tyrannical boss or if you just want your nosy neighbors to stop spying on you when you are out working magic in your yard at night, try this spell tonight to increase your magical camouflage. Go outside and look up at the face of the Moon. Call upon the Moon goddess Selene by repeating the charm.

> Greek Goddess of the Moon,
> Selene, hear my cry,
>
> Shine your blessings down on
> me from up on high.
>
> Protect my privacy from those
> who wish me harm,
>
> This magic takes effect as I
> finish this charm.

Ellen Dugan

June 14
Tuesday

Flag Day

2nd ♐

Color of the day: Black
Incense of the day: Geranium

Banish Threatening Energy

If you ever feel threatened by another person, it's a good idea to work with that energy rather than taking the typical response of either backing off in fear or countering with aggression. Instead, venture to protect yourself. Take a small piece of ginger root and chew it. Taste the unique gingery flavor and meditate on the issues you're having with the other person. Bring to mind their words, their intentions, and the energy they've projected to your person. After visualization is complete, and after you've chewed up the root, step outside and face the direction of the person. If, for example, the person lives on the other side of town from you—or the other side of the country—just face that direction. If they live with you, face the house. When ready, close your eyes and spit the ginger in that direction. Declare:

> Conflict eased, threat ceased.
> In this mind, there's only
> peace. So mote it be.

Raven Digitalis

June 15
Wednesday

 2nd ♐
Full Moon 4:14 pm

Color of the day: Brown
Incense of the day: Lilac

Full Moon Mysteries

A Full Moon accompanied by a lunar eclipse intensifies Moon magic and gives us a chance to delve deeper into the Mysteries. The Moon is a symbol for illusions and secrets; it reminds us we may not see everything clearly. This is especially true during a lunar eclipse. On this night when the Moon rides high and becomes shrouded by darkness, think of the mysteries in your own life you'd like solved. Perhaps this divination will help answer some of your questions. For this you'll need the Moon card from the tarot, a pendulum, black paper, and a craft pen with silver ink. Place the Moon card on a table or altar and meditate on it. Is there something hidden in the shadows you've been wondering about? Think of three questions you'd like answered. Write each question clearly on the black paper with silver ink. Begin moving your pendulum over each question. Repeat the question silently in your mind. The pendulum will begin to move, giving you a "yes" or "no" answer. If it moves in a circle, the answer hasn't

Holiday lore: It was on June 14, 1777, that Congress standardized the flag of the United States with 13 stripes in alternating red and white and 13 white stars on a blue background. Forty-one years later, in 1818, Congress voted to keep the number of stripes at 13 representing the 13 original colonies, but to add a new star for each new state. A star's addition becomes official on the Fourth of July following the state's admission. The current flag of 13 stripes and 50 stars has been in use since July 4, 1960, following Hawaii's 1959 statehood.

been formed yet in the unseen realm. When done, save your questions and review them at the next Full Moon. Has anything been revealed to you since your last session?

James Kambos

I bind financial woe from me

Away as the Moon does wane

I make room for prosperity

To come when it's full again.

Keep the bag with your wallet or checkbook to ward it from monetary loss, and bury the bag at the dark Moon. As the Moon begins to wax, feel free to work for and expect monetary increase!

Castiel

June 16
Thursday

 3rd ♐
☽ → ♑ 1:59 am

Color of the day: Purple
Incense of the day: Nutmeg

Exile Money Woes

Thursday is a good day to work for prosperity, but when the Moon is waning, what's a Witch to do? It's always possible to approach a magical need from the perspective of banishing instead of calling, so try this spell for exiling money problems. Sew or obtain a purple charm bag. Write your money woes down in black ink, and place in the bag with a small handful of cloves—whole are less messy, but ground is fine. Bind the bag shut with black ribbon or thread as you say:

June 17
Friday

 3rd ♑

Color of the day: Coral
Incense of the day: Mint

Making a Window Altar

Do you have a favorite window? One that you spend a lot of time looking through? You can honor your special window with its own altar. Start by cleaning the sill and cleansing it with salt or a sage smudge. Polish the window, too. Cut a strip of decorative scrapbooking

paper equal to the depth of the windowsill, plus ½ inch. Line the windowsill with the paper, folding the extra ½ inch over the sill edge. (Our grandmothers used to line windows and shelves with paper: they knew what they were doing!) Arrange selected items on the windowsill. You might choose stones, statuary, a shot glass filled with water, candles, tools, or whatever pleases you. A string of small LED lights adds a nice effect when tucked among the items. When you stand before your window altar, pause mindfully, offer thanks, or just enjoy a moment of serenity.

Susan Pesznecker

June 18
Saturday

3rd ♑

☽ → ♒ 7:47 am

Color of the day: Gray
Incense of the day: Sage

Charm for Gathering Yarrow

Yarrow was a widely used herb in the Scottish folk tradition. It had many medicinal uses and numerous magical applications. As yarrow began to bloom, it was ritually gathered and kept for future use. Recite this ancient charm from Scotland to honor the yarrow plant and use its power for strength, compassion, courage, eloquence, and guidance:

*I will gather the fair herb
  yarrow,
So that my speech will be as
  the beams of the Sun,
And my lips like the juice of
  the strawberry.*

*I will gather the fair plant
  yarrow,
So that my hand will be
  brave,
And my foot will be swift.*

*May I be an island in the sea,
A hill upon the shore,
A rock upon the land.*

*May I be a star in the
  waning of the Moon,
And a staff to the weak.
With the power of yarrow,
  none can harm me.*

Sharynne MacLeod NicMhacha

June 19
Sunday

Father's Day

3rd ≈

Color of the day: Yellow
Incense of the day: Marigold

honor All Father Figures

Today is the day set aside in America to honor all fathers. Unfortunately, there are people who have had to grow up without having a strong male role model. If you are fortunate enough to have someone like this in your life—your real father or a father figure—you are blessed. Honor that person today. Use this ritual to honor the spirit of the Father, draw someone like that into your life if you wish, or send energy to those people who need a father in their lives. On your altar or table, place a yellow candle of any size. Surround it with pictures and anything that reminds you of a positive male role model in your life, find an image that conveys this feeling in general, or simply write the word "father" on a piece of paper and place it under the candle. Burn the candle throughout the day.

Ember Grant

June 20
Monday

3rd ≈

☽ → ♓ 4:45 pm

Color of the day: Lavender
Incense of the day: Clary sage

The Alchemy of Oxygen

Magic is the act of changing consciousness at will. A daily walk can cleanse your head and heart, release your worries, and change your life. Take thirty minutes each day, sacred space away from outside demands. Walk easily for five minutes, allowing muscles to warm. Bless your body. Pick up the pace for intervals. Walk fast for two minutes, then easy for two minutes. Do this twice. Feel your heart beating faster, delivering more oxygen to your body and brain. Bless your heart. Walk easy for five minutes. Feel gratitude and peace as worries slip away in the wash of endorphins. Do four one-minute intervals, fast then easy, fast then easy. Feel your heart pump hard. Give thanks for cardiovascular health. Finish with an easy eight-minute cool down, letting your pace and heart rate slow down. These thirty minutes will prevent depression, heart disease, and diabetes, and magically make you feel great.

Dallas Jennifer Cobb

June 21
Tuesday

Litha –
Summer Solstice

3rd ♓

☉ → ♋ 1:16 pm

Color of the day: Gray
Incense of the day: Basil

Understand Your Dreams

What better night to peer into dreams than Midsummer? Understanding dreams takes practice, free association, and divination. If you find a dream particularly disturbing and you can't quite determine where it came from after looking through journals, try this technique: list the major symbols/characters from your dream. For each item, pull a tarot card or rune. The meaning of the card or rune will give additional insight into your subconscious. If the dream is in any way prophetic, the High Priestess or the Hierophant will appear. If the meaning from the divination is still not clear to you, take the card or rune and place it under your pillow when you go to bed the next night, and hold the image of the rune or card in your mind for as long as you can before drifting off to sleep. Your next dream will reveal further details about the meaning of the troubling dream.

Diana Rajchel

June 22
Wednesday

3rd ♓

Color of the day: Topaz
Incense of the day: Bay laurel

Earth Altar

Summer is a great time to go outside and do magic, especially if you cannot do so in the winter months. A great way to do some magic in nature is to create an earth altar that can bless all who see it. Meditate on a magical intention that you would like to share with others and head to a nearby park or hiking trail. Gather rocks, sticks, plants, and other natural materials available to create your altar. How can these tools represent your desire? Assemble your altar at the side of a trail where it is easily visible so that others can see it and receive the magic you have conjured.

> By the powers of Earth and Sky,
>
> By the might of the Mysterious Ones,
>
> I bless and charge this altar.
>
> May all who see it be blessed.
>
> May all who see it know they are loved.
>
> So mote it be.

Abel R. Gomez

 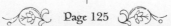

June 23
Thursday

 3rd ♓
☽ → ♈ 4:24 am
4th Quarter 7:48 am

Color of the day: White
Incense of the day: Balsam

Mindfully Decluttering

Sometimes our clutter gets in the way of greater prosperity. True generosity allows our lives to be richer in more ways than those involving money. This simple activity helps you to mindfully declutter. Put on some good music and some old clothes. Pick a spot in need of a good sorting out. Wade in, sorting things into piles of what can be donated to charity and what can be pitched in the trash or recycling. If possible, put things away as you come to them. When you're finished with your chosen spot, take care of the piles of sorting. Immediately put trash where it goes. If you made a pile of things to put away, then go put them away. Finally, set your donations in a spot where you'll remember to take them to a secondhand shop. If possible, go and take them now. Do so joyfully, knowing that you've opened up your life to more possibilities and that the energy can flow a little more freely in your home.

Laurel Reufner

June 24
Friday

 4th ♈
Color of the day: Rose
Incense of the day: Vanilla

Three's the Charm

Some things are harder to change directly and easier to change indirectly. For these, consider the Druidic tradition of "triads" or "threes." These are sayings that compare things, such as:

> Three holy terrors: the baying hound, the cat who hunts, and a mother protecting her child.

To work indirect magic, first craft a triad that includes the thing you want to affect and two other things easier to influence directly. For example:

> Three things wilt in good time: a weed in the gardener's hand, greens in the cooking pot, and the habit that does only ill.

Whenever you work on one of the easy things, recite your triad, so the energy will spill over to the third thing. In this example, you might weed your garden, cook supper with spinach, and then work on breaking your bad habit—thus enjoying the momentum built up.

Elizabeth Barrette

 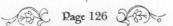

June 25
Saturday

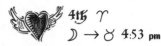 4th ♈

☽ → ♉ 4:53 pm

Color of the day: Brown
Incense of the day: Rue

honey Spell

Since June has become a traditional wedding month, and the
honeymoon has grown to such sig-
nificance, a honey spell seems appropriate as this month draws to a close.
No, this is not a love spell, but more
of a "be kind to yourself" spell!
My grandmother used to dose us
with honey to help us get through
the allergies of the season. Eating
local honey helps build your immune
system to your own environment.
Choose any recipe that calls for
honey, or concoct one of your own.
Make enough to share with family
and friends. As you prepare the recipe, think about the busy bees and all
the work that went into making the
honey. As you share the food, think
about your intent to help people get
comfortable in the environment.
There are no words needed for this
spell, your hands and thoughts as
you prepare the food will cast the
spell of wellness.

Paniteowl

June 26
Sunday

 4th ♉

Color of the day: Orange
Incense of the day: Almond

Grieving Loss and Letting Go
(Day of Saint Pelagius of Oviedo)

Have you lost someone or something meaningful to you? Have
you abandoned yourself thought-
lessly, forgetting your true nature to
please others? Today, grieve the loss
and empty yourself of the pain you
hold. To help let go, draw a bath and
sprinkle in lavender and comfrey.
Take a moment to set the space with
white candles. Copal is conducive to
your healing process, so burn this
if you wish. Alternatively, light sandalwood to soothe your soul. Soak
now, relaxing your muscles and your
heart center, focusing on the release
of all forms of tension: physical, psy-
chic/emotional and causal. Breathe
in compassion and forgiveness as you
work through each loss, and breathe
out any unnecessary holding. Use
sound to help let go. When you are
done, exit the bath and return a small
portion of the bath water to soil
beyond your home. Drain the bath
only after you have done this.

Chandra Alexandre

June 27
Monday

 4th ♉
Color of the day: Gray
Incense of the day: Clary sage

Clear the Way for Wealth

To manifest abundance, we must first clear away energetic congestion and create the space for wealth to enter. This ritual is a bit time consuming, but it's worth it. Make sure you drink water throughout.

• Clear as much clutter as you can from your home.

• Add eight drops of cedar oil to your cleaning solution(s) and thoroughly clean your house.

• Go through your wallet and/or purse, discarding receipts, gum wrappers, and other extraneous items.

• Shower or bathe

• Light eight sticks of frankincense incense and hold them together in a bundle. While holding a dish under the incense to catch ash and embers, walk around the perimeter of each room in your home while repeating:

> I now clear the way for
> wealth to enter.

Once you've finished, burn the incense around your wallet and/or purse, and then your body, while still repeating the magic words.

Tess Whitehurst

June 28
Tuesday

 4th ♉
☽ → ♊ 3:56 am

Color of the day: White
Incense of the day: Ylang-ylang

Banishing Talisman

Today we are in a waning Moon phase and we have the planetary associations of the god of war, Mars. So what do you say we banish fear and any obstacles in our path? You will need a small piece of red jasper and light a red candle for Mars. Hold the tumbled stone in your projective hand and focus your concentration on removing any and all obstacles to your happiness and success. Now repeat the charm:

> Mars, I call upon you to
> bless me with courage and
> confidence,
>
> Help me overcome the obstacles in my life, with strength
> and style.
>
> May the energies of the waning Moon safely remove all
> obstacles from my life,
>
> While this red agate stone
> becomes a talisman to remind
> me of your magic.
>
> For the good of all, so mote
> it be.

Pocket the stone and keep it with you for courage and fortitude.

Ellen Dugan

June 29
Wednesday

 4th ♊

Color of the day: Yellow
Incense of the day: Marjoram

Charm to Gather St. John's Wort

In Scotland, Saint John's wort or *Alla-Bhuidhe* ("noble yellow plant") was one of the most prized of all sacred herbs. It was used to protect against sorcery, evil eye, and death, and also to bring the bearer peace, abundance, prosperity, and growth. It was kept secretly in the bodice of a woman's dress or in the vest of a man's outfit, always under the left arm. The plant was only considered to have power when it was accidentally found. If you come across the plant, recite this spell to harness its power:

> Sacred yellow plant
> Found without seeking or
>   searching
> Beside me forever!

> For luck of people and
>   prosperity
> For luck of desires and
>   wishes
> For luck in battle, and
>   victory

> For herds and crops
> Plenty in fields and
>   household
> On land, on sea, and on
>   ocean

> I will gather this sacred plant
> So that mine may be its
>   power
> Over all I see.

Sharynne MacLeod NicMhacha

June 30
Thursday

 4th ♊

☽ → ♋ 12:13 pm

Color of the day: Green
Incense of the day: Apricot

Balancing Act

Now that it's summer, the routine has relaxed. There are things like weekend parties and vacations—in short, the balance we work so hard to achieve can get thrown off. Use an element spell to restore your equilibrium. Gather a white candle, a white charm bag, a small oak twig, a small shell, a small feather, and a small piece of moss agate. Light the white candle and carefully char the oak twig in it to represent fire. Place it south of the candle. Place the moss agate north, the feather east, and the shell west. Put your hands on either side of the arrangement and focus on the candle flame. Call on each element in your own words and feel its energy work with your own. Do this as often and as long as you need to. When the candle is out, place the element tokens in the charm bag and carry them with you.

Castiel

July is the seventh month of the year. Its astrological sign is Cancer, the Crab (June 21–July 22), a cardinal-water sign ruled by the Moon. Named for Julius Caesar, July brings a time of ripening and fulfillment. The ancient Celts were attuned to the cycles of Sun and Moon, and now, during the height of summer, is a perfect time to study the night sky and take camping trips to enjoy star-gazing away from city lights—take advantage of connecting with the natural world. Outdoor activities are in full swing now and Independence Day, July 4, is the major holiday this month—a time when many people enjoy barbeques and vacations. Since July's astrological sign is associated with water, this is a good time to practice water magic or visit lakes, rivers, and oceans. Enjoy the splendid flowers of these warm, sunny days: purple liatris (blazing stars), coneflowers, orange day-lilies, and the glow of blue chickory along roadsides. This time of year is referred to as the "dog days of summer." Sirius, the "dog star," rises and sets in conjunction with the Sun. The heat of July can be oppressive, so relax in the shade or enjoy the sultry nights by taking a magical, moonlight swim. The Full Moon of July is sometimes called the Blessing Moon.

July 1
Friday

 4th ♋
New Moon 4:54 am

Color of the day: White
Incense of the day: Rose

The Personal Retreat

Throughout history, women and men have withdrawn (retreated) from the world around them in order to contemplate problems, focus energy, or engage in spiritual growth. You, too, can invoke the power of the cloistered retreat, and the settling energy of the New (Dark) Moon provides a perfect opportunity. Your retreat can be anywhere from hours to days long. Arrange a time and place off your usual radar screen, giving you the quiet needed to reflect and evaluate. Timing your retreat with the Dark Moon will "sync" your efforts with her gathering energies. Identify a purpose for your getaway: you may want time to study, meditate, or practice a magical skill. Or, perhaps you're completing a period of initiation or transition and would like time to reflect. Go alone, and begin your retreat with an agenda, but leave time for spontaneity. Eat lightly to keep your mind unbound. Leave the computer and cell phone behind. While on retreat, embrace the silence. Listen to it. Welcome it. Allow yourself to hear and respond to your own inner voice, the well from which personal growth and insight spring. Be ready for the moments of revelation that gift you with new knowledge and directions.

Susan Pesznecker

Holiday lore: Today is the first day of the season for climbing Mt. Fuji in Yamabiraki, Japan. Mt. Fuji is the highest peak in Japan and is revered in Japanese culture. Considered the foremother or grandmother of Japan, Fuji is an ancient fire goddess of the indigenous Ainu people. In modern times, the Ainu mostly resided on the northern island of Hokkaido. The name *Fuji* was derived from an Ainu word that means "fire" or "deity of fire." Each year since the Meiji era, a summer festival has been held to proclaim the beginning of the climbing season and to pray for the safety of local inhabitants and visitors or pilgrims to the sacred mountain. The two-month climbing season begins today and ends on August 30.

July 2
Saturday

1st ♋

☽ → ♌ 5:43 pm

Color of the day: Indigo
Incense of the day: Ivy

To Conceive a Child

Today is the day to speak your prayers to birth and fertility goddesses such as Astarte, Parvati, Artemis, Tonantzin, Yemaya, Demeter, and Isis. First, find a stone. Holding it in your left hand for a girl and right hand for a boy, breathe your intention onto it and wrap colored string, preferably red, three and a half times around. Secure it with a knot. Within three days, tie the stone to a willow tree, birch tree, or hazelnut bush. Give gratitudes to the tree by leaving a small offering of seeds, fruit, water, or wine. Come back in three months. If the stone is still there and you have not yet conceived, then bury it nearby while again making your wishes known. If the stone is not there, then within the next three months you will receive word that your child is coming.

Chandra Alexandre

July 3
Sunday

1st ♌

Color of the day: Orange
Incense of the day: Frankincense

A Water Scrying Ritual

July is an appropriate time to perform water magic of all kinds. The Sun is in the water sign Cancer, vacationers head to the shore, and thunderstorms rumble in the afternoon. The ancient art of water scrying will enable you to tap into this water energy. This ritual should be performed outdoors on a moonless night. For this scrying session, use a birdbath with clean water, your cauldron, or a pond. In silence, approach the water and concentrate on your question. With your finger, stir the water three times in a clockwise direction. As the ripples move, begin to scry. Become lost in the water as you gaze. Whisper:

Water flow, let me see what I
need to know.

As the images fade, return to your normal state of mind and thank the water element.

James Kambos

July 4
Monday

Independence Day

 1st ♌

☽ → ♍ 9:15 pm

Color of the day: Ivory
Incense of the day: Lily

Weaving the Web

Independence Day is a long-standing American tradition. It marks the birth of our nation. However, July 4 has been celebrated as a holiday of civics as far back as ancient Greece and Rome. This was the Roman festival of the goddess Concordia, whose ceremonies also honored the Roman goddess Pax and the Greek goddess Eirene, both in charge of peace. This was a general holiday of peace, freedom, and community bonds. Observe this holiday by weaving a web with covenmates or friends. Toss a ball of yarn from one person to another, holding onto the corners of the web as it forms, until everyone has passed the yarn to each other person. Chant:

> Thoughts of war and
>
> Conflict cease
>
> Weaving freedom
>
> Weaving peace
>
> Through our friendship
>
> Find release
>
> Weaving freedom
>
> Weaving peace

You can anchor the web to tree branches, grass, etc., to hold its shape after you step away.

Elizabeth Barrette

Holiday notes: On July 4, 1776, the Second Continental Congress adopted the Declaration of Independence. Philadelphians were first to mark the anniversary of American independence with a celebration, but Independence Day became commonplace only after the War of 1812. By the 1870s, the Fourth of July was the most important secular holiday in the United States, celebrated even in far-flung communities on the western frontier of the country.

July 5
Tuesday

 1st ♏

Color of the day: Scarlet
Incense of the day: Basil

Vibrant health Tonic

Just before sunrise, go outside, face east, and place nine leaves of fresh basil in a glass bowl. Add a pinch of calendula blossoms and a clean white quartz. Pour spring water over the ingredients, almost filling the bowl. Now, place your hands on either side of the bowl and close your eyes. Relax, breathe, and focus as you inwardly repeat the words:

> Perfect love, perfect strength,
> perfect health.

Open your eyes when you sense that the sun has risen. Using a dropper from a small bottle, put 9 drops of the water from the bowl into the bottle. Fill the remainder of the bottle half with spring water and half with brandy. Pour the remaining contents of the bowl around the base of a tree as an offering. Close the bottle, shake gently, and put 3 drops under your tongue. Take daily until you've reached your desired health level.

Tess Whitehurst

July 6
Wednesday

 1st ♏

☽ → ♎ 11:54 pm

Color of the day: White
Incense of the day: Lavender

Inspire Arts and Crafts

High summer is upon us and with the waxing Moon phase, this is an opportune time to work for increasing your creativity. Since it is Wednesday, you could work with the goddess Athena, the patron of handmade crafts and the arts. Ask Athena and for her blessing and inspiration as you go to finish up your arts and crafts projects. Light a purple candle for Athena, and then repeat the charm three times.

> Goddess of handicrafts, bless
> me with inspiration
> today,
> Guide my heart and my
> hands as I work
> diligently away.
> Athena bless me under a
> waxing Moon so bright
> Help me bring all my
> creativity to light.
> By Wednesday's magic this
> spell is spun,
> For the good of all bringing
> harm to none.

Ellen Dugan

July 7
Thursday

 1st ♎

Color of the day: Purple
Incense of the day: Clove

honor the Power of the Sun

Many modern Pagan rituals focus on the veneration of the Moon, but we must also remember the other inhabitants of the celestial realms who guide and bless us every day. In Celtic tradition, words for both the Sun and Moon were feminine in gender, and both were honored in rituals and prayers. In the last century, old people in the islands of Scotland would uncover their heads when they first saw the Sun in the morning and intone a hymn. Here is a traditional Gaelic prayer to the Sun:

> Hail to you, Sun of the
> seasons
> As you course through the
> skies above
> Your steps are strong on the
> wings of the heavens
> You are the glorious mother
> of the stars
>
> You lie down in the mighty
> ocean
> Without harm and without
> fear
> You rise up on the gentle
> crest of the wave

> Like a queenly maiden in
> bloom
> Glory to you, O Wondrous
> Sun!

Sharynne MacLeod NicMhacha

July 8
Friday

 1st ♎
2nd Quarter 2:29 am

Color of the day: Coral
Incense of the day: Vanilla

Psychic Vision with Mint Tea

One of the mint family's unique properties is increasing psychic vision. Because all of us can use a little clarity in our life, let's brew some tea just for that purpose. As you're going about your daily routine, pick a good time to brew a cuppa. Using either a bag of peppermint tea or a loose blend, pour the boiled water over the leaves. As it steeps, inhale the vapors through your nose, sensing and smelling the purifying properties. Look at the tea and say:

> Lightness dark and darkness
> bright, come to me through

*day and night! Empower this
brew, enchant it right; bring
me psychic vision, give me
psychic sight! So mote it be!*

Repeat this chant a number of times,
focusing on your goal. Envision the
tea surrounded by an indigo-colored
light, and drink the cup in silence,
visualizing its essence entering your
body and filling your mind with psychic prowess.

Raven Digitalis

you stir, talk about the tree and how
it needs help. If possible, add a leaf or
branch from the tree to "introduce"
it to the herbs, allowing them to
"sense" what needs healing. Let the
mixture cool, and then bottle it (use
a funnel if you have it) and take it to
the tree. Pour your potion over the
tree's injuries, and then sit with your
back to the base of the tree while
saying:

Root to sap to wood to bark,

*Rustling leaves eating light,
giving dark–*

*In the shade of the
whispering tree,*

I give healing unto thee.

Diana Rajchel

July 9
Saturday

2nd ♎

☽ → ♏ 2:31 am

Color of the day: Brown
Incense of the day: Sage

heal a Tree

Trees suffer disease and damage
the same as human beings,
which is why tree surgeons exist. If
you encounter a tree that has had its
sap bled for any reason besides maple
tapping, perform this intervention.
In a pot of water, simmer together
juniper berries, sage, and vervain. As

July 10
Sunday

 2nd ♏

Color of the day: Gold
Incense of the day: Heliotrope

Lady Godiva Day

In Coventry, England, the naked ride of Lady Godiva is enacted on this day. Godiva agreed to ride naked through town in order to dissuade her husband from levying a tax on the people of Coventry. Her act is still celebrated. I don't advocate public nudity unless you're in a safe space, but maybe you can find a suitable situation to get naked or nearly naked in a bathing suit, and partake in some reverential sunbathing. You don't need to stay in the sun long. Just ten minutes of sun, front and back, each day, helps the body to produce enough vitamin D to prevent mild depression, and it feels great. Choose a time before 11:30 am and after 2:30 pm so you're not in peak UV rays. Adequate amounts of vitamin D are also linked to the prevention of breast cancer, so be like Lady Godiva, get outside and expose yourself.

Dallas Jennifer Cobb

July 11
Monday

 2nd ♏
☽ → ♐ 5:47 am

Color of the day: White
Incense of the day: Neroli

Opportunity Spell

Cast a spell today to manifest rich opportunities to engage your passions. You will need a pen, a yellow candle, a fireproof dish, and some paper. In your ritual space, cast a circle and welcome the gods and the elements of life. Write a letter to the Universe, asking for the opportunities to unfold, whether it's opportunities to sing and dance, paint, build community, or a job. Sign it with your magical name. Lick your thumb and anoint the letter, sealing it to you. Light the candle and read the letter out loud. Focus your mind on your intention and say:

I open to opportunities.

I open to experiences.

I open to the flow of life.

My dreams shall come to be.

By the elements of life,

May it be so!

Fold the paper and light it with the candle. Scatter the ashes in the wind.

Abel R. Gomez

July 12
Tuesday

2nd ♐

Color of the day: Red
Incense of the day: Ginger

Soul of Rock 'n' Roll

One of the most accessible and powerful ways to access the unconscious mind and energetic self is through music. We all know that music sets the emotional tone in movies, can remind us vividly of times gone by, and can pick up our spirits when we're in a funk. What's your favorite kind of music? What does it evoke for you? Spend some time today really listening to it, and maybe some genres you don't normally put on. If you're a musician, play a song that tells the universe how you're feeling today. If you're not, make a rattle out of a paper cup and some dried beans, or just sing along to your favorite tunes. Dance to the music. At the end of the day, check in with how you feel. If you have more energy, and are in a good mood, then don't forget to put music in your magical toolbox!

Castiel

July 13
Wednesday

2nd ♐

☽ → ♑ 10:14 am

Color of the day: Yellow
Incense of the day: Marjoram

Spell for Success in Conflicts

In Scottish tradition there was an ancient ritual and prayer that could be used when facing a conflict such as a court case or other difficult situation. The person who performed the ritual arose very early and went to a stream or river that marked a boundary, one that did not become small in the summertime. The person dipped their face in the stream three times and then bathed their face in the nine rays of the Sun. After this, the following prayer was recited, which was said to provide complete success:

> I will go in the name of
>   the gods
> In the form of deer, in the
>   form of horse
> In the form of snake, in the
>   form of a ruler
> I am stronger than all
>   persons.
>
> The hands of the gods
>   protect me
> The strength of Spirit
>   envelops me

*The Sacred Three protecting
and helping me
The help and protection of
the Sacred Three.*

Sharynne MacLeod NicMhacha

Try to preserve their personalities.
Have yourself a Bulfinch Memory
day. It could be important to future
generations.

Paniteowl

July 14
Thursday

2nd ♑

Color of the day: Green
Incense of the day: Myrrh

Bulfinch Spell

Today is the birthday of Thomas
Bulfinch, a renowned American
mythologist. Many people have read
and appreciated his writings, and his
efforts have preserved ancient lore.
My "Bulfinch Spell" is to honor his
attempt to preserve knowledge that
may have been lost forever. For this
spell, you simply need to start a new
journal recording things about your
own life and family history. On the
front page of the journal, write the
word "Memories." Let your mind
wander over the people in your life,
and write down their habits, their
recipes, their idiosyncrasies, and note
how they have influenced your life.

July 15
Friday

2nd ♑
Full Moon 2:40 am
☽ → ♒ 4:30 pm

Color of the day: Rose
Incense of the day: Thyme

Fairy Wishes

Mix up some all natural, herbal
fairy dust for yourself and the
kids. My original recipe uses
½ cup lavender, ½ cup rose petals,
½ cup jasmine blossoms, 2 tablespoons chamomile, and about ¼ cup
star anise. It was ground in small
batches in a coffee grinder and then
combined together. We made some
the other night that substituted
½ cup oak moss and ¼ cup cedar
for the jasmine and star anise. The
result was a woodsy smell that my
daughters loved. I think I preferred

it as well. We made it in the food processor, which won't give you a powder, but does chop it up nicely. If you really need some glitz for it to be "real" fairy dust, toss in a couple teaspoons of glitter. To use for wish magic, pour some in the palm of your hand, make your wish, and then blow the dust out off your hand.

Laurel Reufner

July 16
Saturday

3rd ♒

Color of the day: Blue
Incense of the day: Patchouli

A Ward Against Set

According to Egyptian tradition, today is the birthday of Set, god of the desert. Set also oversees thunderstorms and upheavals. He stands guard over Ra's barge in the underworld. Though at times Set has been considered evil, he is more properly understood as a god of necessary challenges and hardships. In modern times, careless practices make the deserts expand. Once-fertile land shrivels into lifeless dust. When Set sees humans behaving in uncivilized ways, he moves in and claims the land as desert. He sends the thunder and lightning but withholds the rain. War and discord attract his attention. Acts of compassion and husbandry ward him off, for such is not his concern. Address Set with this prayer:

> Mighty one of the desert,
>
> Sunset-haired god of the dust,
>
> May it please you to stay out there,
>
> On the horizon, tending the barren lands,
>
> And not come here where people dwell.

Elizabeth Barrette

July 17
Sunday

 3rd ≈

Color of the day: Orange
Incense of the day: Eucalyptus

Understanding Motivations of a Troubled Person

People are complex, but the reasons for why they act as they do come down to four components, much like magical elements: pain, fear, love, and power. Everyone has a little of each in their life. If a person you encounter is a fly in your ointment and knowing where the crazy comes from might help, then take these four cards from your tarot deck: the Hanged Man, the Lovers, the Tower, and the Emperor. Swing a pendulum between the cards, eliminating one card at time. The order they fall in is the order of their most basic motivations. The Hanged Man is pain of choice (conscious or otherwise), the Lovers card is love, the Tower is fear, and the Emperor is power. The order that the pendulum gives you is how these components are ranked concerning the person you're asking about. You can then use this information to plan how to handle this individual.

Diana Rajchel

July 18
Monday

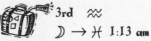 3rd ≈
☽ → ♓ 1:13 am

Color of the day: Lavender
Incense of the day: Narcissus

Journey Within

The dark Moon is, of course, associated with the Crone aspect of the Goddess, but what do you associated with the waning Moon other than working for decrease or banishing? One archetype you might try tapping into is the priestess, or shaman, guide to the inner and underworld mysteries. Make time for an internal journey this waning Moon–day. Create a quiet space. Light a dark blue or black candle and incense such as patchouli or oak moss. Close your eyes and visualize your image of priestess or shaman. Invoke your guide with the following chant:

> Great One as Priestess
> Shaman of my soul
> Guide me within to
> Where I shall be whole

Chant until you feel yourself in a trance state, and then go where this aspect of the Goddess leads you. Be sure to have paper and pen nearby to record your experiences when you return from your inner journey.

Castiel

July 19
Tuesday

3rd ♓

Color of the day: Gray
Incense of the day: Cinnamon

The Goddess Is Alive

The hummingbirds flash among the red shaggy heads of monarda, tomatoes—still green—fatten on the vine, and as the fingers of dusk glide over the hills, fireflies twinkle above the lawn. Growth and maturity are everywhere; the pace of the year begins to ease. The Goddess casts her spell over the land now as we approach the miracle of the harvest. July pulses with life. Take a break from your hectic schedule today, and be fully aware of the magic the Goddess surrounds us with at this time of year. Stand barefoot in the grass and ground yourself. Feel as if roots are growing from your feet into Mother Earth. You are now part of this season, the time of year the Old Ones called "the Ripening." In mid-July the song of summer is at its height. Look around you—the Goddess is alive and magic is afoot.

James Kambos

July 20
Wednesday

3rd ♓
☽ → ♈ 12:25 pm

Color of the day: Brown
Incense of the day: Lavender

Banish Bad Dreams

After you've cleared any clutter out of your bedroom and made sure that it has a serene and restful feeling, clap loudly in the corners and burn a stick of frankincense incense to lift and purify the vibrations. Then, construct a simple altar to Morpheus, the winged god of dreams, using a dark-blue candle, an amethyst, a small dish of valerian root mixed with 1 teaspoon sea salt, and a naturally shed feather. Right before bed, light the candle and sit comfortably with your eyes closed and your hands in prayer pose. Mentally call on Morpheus. Tell him that you've been having bad dreams lately and ask him to help you resolve whatever issue(s) are causing them so that you can sleep peacefully and awake refreshed. Repeat nightly until the New Moon. Then, bury the amethyst outside and throw the valerian mixture into a moving body of water.

Tess Whitehurst

July 21
Thursday

 3rd ♈

Color of the day: White
Incense of the day: Jasmine

Holy Fools and Divine Madness

Throughout the ages, saints, mystics, Witches, and seers have used madness or aspects of The Fool as a tool to mask their powers of prophecy, connection to the Divine, ability to alter the weather, and other such boons . . . thereby avoiding condemnation. Today, however, the invitation is to revel in the wonders of the world, letting yourself become drunk on the wine of spiritual insight without fear. Today, read tarot, draw runes, consult oracle decks, write provocative invocations, and otherwise cause sacred mischief as you tear off the veils that have obscured your deepest knowings. Be sure to share your findings with others and let in the freedom of being fully in the magic of who you are. Verbalize this affirmation:

> I am a seeker and keeper of
> Truth; let the magic of the
> Mystery flow in and through
> me, now and always.

Chandra Alexandre

July 22
Friday

 3rd ♈

Color of the day: Purple
Incense of the day: Yarrow

An Apple Spell for Beauty

The apple itself is a potent symbol, and you may already be aware that slicing an apple across the middle reveals a five-pointed star inside—another important magical symbol. Today, Freya's day, is a good day for beauty magic. Since the Moon is waning, increase beauty by dispelling something you feel is blocking your true beauty. Remember: beauty is within as well as without, and the way you feel about yourself makes you beautiful. Beauty comes from confidence and happiness. What is blocking this in your life? Would you like to start exercising to gain more energy? Whatever it is, do it today, or promise yourself to begin. Slice an apple in half horizontally to reveal the star inside. Slice a very thin circle from one half and let it dry—keep it on your altar for a while as a reminder. Visualize your goal while you eat one half of the apple; bury the other half.

Ember Grant

July 23
Saturday

3rd ♈

☉ → ♌ 12:12 am
☽ → ♉ 12:58 am
4th Quarter 1:02 am

Color of the day: Black
Incense of the day: Magnolia

Faerie Magic at Dusk

It's long been said that dawn and dusk are the times of Fey. Indeed, these two times of day are the 'tween . . . the midway points between day and night. Ever wonder why your pets are more active at that time? Dawn and dusk are the thresholds between "this" and "that," and are both enigmatic and mystical as a result. Tonight at dusk, steep a cup of thyme tea, grab a jar with milk and honey mixed together, and take yourself to a lush spot in nature. Lie on the ground and smile; feel what it's like to be a child. If you're daring, smear yourself with dirt and build little figures out of grass, branches, and leaves. Get creative and forget the worries of the day. By doing this, you are invoking the Innocent Self: something that the faerie realm values in high esteem. (In fact, the Feri Tradition of Witchcraft calls this venerated part of Self the "Black Heart of Innocence.") Anoint yourself with the thyme tea. Splash it around, drink it, and be merry. When you're ready to settle down, sit with your back against a tree (make sure you're surrounded in nature, away from traffic—human or vehicular!). Grin, and blur your vision. See what you see! Communicate to the wee folk in whatever way you deem fit. Alter your consciousness and suspend rationality. Open yourself to vision—who knows what you'll see? Keep in mind that visions and faerie sight do not strictly appear through the vision of the eyes, but through that of the third eye! When you're done playing with the Fey, bow to the area and leave your offerings of milk and honey, asking them to be kind to you and yours. Tell them your desires, wishes, and dreams. Return and repeat this working at dawn or dusk on any day the Fey beckon you to their terrain!

Raven Digitalis

July 24
Sunday

4th ♉

Color of the day: Yellow
Incense of the day: Juniper

Cauldron Spell

As with most spells, many of the same ingredients and tools are used, just not in the same measures or with the same intent. Here is a basic cauldron spell that can be adapted for many different purposes. You can use a large cauldron over an open fire, or you can use a small cauldron over small votive candle. Half fill the cauldron with pure spring water and place it over the fire. As it warms, add herbs appropriate to your intent. Stir the cauldron with a wooden branch and speak to the swirling waters as the water simmers and steam starts to rise. If you chose to use the cauldron spell for divination, add some cinnamon and pour some olive oil onto the simmering water. Douse the fire and wait for the water to cool. Gaze into the cauldron and "read" the symbols you see floating in the oily surface. Each of us has our own symbols that mean something specific. It may take awhile to discover what your personal symbols are, but the more you use this technique, the more clearly your symbols will manifest for you.

Paniteowl

July 25
Monday

4th ♉

☽ → ♊ 12:34 pm

Color of the day: Ivory
Incense of the day: Rosemary

Purifying home

Monday, governed by the Moon, is a good day for doing purification work. With the warm weather of summer upon us in the Northern Hemisphere, now is a good time for energetically cleansing and purifying your home. Start at the main entrance, and walking clockwise, open all the doors and windows wide letting the fresh air flow in and through. At the main entrance again, affirm: "I purify this home." Using a shell, or bowl, burn dried sage or sweet grass for purification and blessing, and walking clockwise, smudge each opening with the smoke of the sacred herbs. Bless it: "This home is safe, happy, healthy, and whole." Now smudge yourself, affirming: "All who live here are safe, happy, healthy, and whole." Walking widdershins (counterclockwise), close each window and door, and returning to the main entrance, incant: "All is well in this home." Purify seasonally and after anything odd or untoward has happened.

Dallas Jennifer Cobb

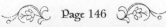

July 26
Tuesday

 4th ♊

Color of the day: Maroon

Incense of the day: Geranium

Lilith Is Fair

Need something banished from your life and can't wait until the dark of the Moon or a Saturday? Consider working banishing magic today, as Tuesday's energy and the waning Moon phase aligns perfectly with the dark goddess Lilith. Described as a darkly sexy and alluring deity with wings and the taloned feet of an owl, Lilith is quite capable of removing the negative influences that may haunt your life. Call on her tonight. Light a black and a red candle for Lilith. Then repeat the charm:

> Lilith, dark goddess, hear my cry,
>
> Aid me now under a midnight sky.
>
> Banish and remove my troubles and strife,
>
> Making room for new things to spring to life.
>
> By owl feather and taloned feet,
>
> As I will it, so shall it be.

Ellen Dugan

July 27
Wednesday

 4th ♊

☽ → ♋ 9:11 pm

Color of the day: Brown

Incense of the day: Lilac

Respectful Communication

Wednesday is Mercury's day, the Roman messenger god. Use this spell today to clear away mixed messages in your communication. Ask the help of the four winds to clarify your words and expressions and improve your listening skills. Face each direction and blow on a feather as you chant:

> Winds of the East, carry my words
> Winds of the South, let them be clear
> Winds of the West, let them be true
> Winds of the North, may I think first
>
> Winds of the East, help me to hear
> Winds of the South, may I listen with care
> Winds of the West, help me respond
> Winds of the North, let me know when to speak

Visualize being understood and understanding others. Keep the feather in a place where you can see it, remembering that words say a great deal about your character and that listening is a vital part of communication.

Ember Grant

on your altar. A money/prosperity box would be a good location. Under a prosperity-drawing gemstone is another good spot. To preserve your privacy, you might want to make sure the "check" is face down.

Laurel Reufner

July 28
Thursday

 4th ♋

Color of the day: Crimson
Incense of the day: Balsam

Check to Banish Debt

Use the energy of the coming New Moon to start decreasing your debt. Light a green candle and start some prosperity incense smoldering. Create the semblance of a check using a blank, unlined piece of paper. Decide which particular debt (if you have more than one) you wish to focus on first. How much money will you need to pay off this debt? Make the check out to yourself for that amount. Place the "check" under the candle and allow it to burn down completely. Once the incense and candle have burned themselves out, place your "check" somewhere safe

July 29
Friday

4th ♋

Color of the day: White
Incense of the day: Cypress

Banishing Spell

Draw upon the power of Saturn today to banish a person, influence, or occurrence in your life. As with any sort of serious magic, you may wish to consult your guides or divinatory oracle before proceeding. If you get a positive response, gather together three black candles, myrrh incense and oil, a pen with black ink, and three photocopies of the Tower tarot card (use three pieces of blue paper if this is unavailable to you). In your ritual space, cleanse the candles and dress them in oil. Light your incense. Charge the candles with your breath and light them. Write that which you wish to banish on the tarot cards and say a chant like:

> Leave us, leave us
>
> Your presence is enslaving
>
> Go now forever
>
> Return to love

Let the energy build and spiral out into the Universe. Allow the candles to burn out. Burn the copies of the tarot cards to complete the spell.

Abel R. Gomez

July 30
Saturday

4th ♋

☽ → ♌ 2:16 am

New Moon 2:40 am

Color of the day: Gray
Incense of the day: Rue

Dark Moon Vigil

The New (Dark) Moon rises around 6:00 am and sets around 6:00 pm. We can't see her in the night sky, but we feel her

presence. The Dark Moon is associated with a drawing in of powers and is the ideal time to work with inward-directed energies, including the keeping of vigil. The word *vigil* comes from a Latin word meaning "awake," and a vigil refers to a period of staying awake to keep watch or pray. Most vigils are kept through the night, often on a high, open spot around a vigil fire. Why keep vigil? You might perform vigil for personal empowerment or to mark a life transition. It's a wonderful way to mark initiation, new status, completion of educational goals, or the taking of a new name or spiritual identity. Keep your Dark Moon vigil at night—her energies will bathe you, even if she isn't directly overhead. Build a small fire, wear magical garb, and keep your tools and craft symbols with you. Stay silent during your vigil and fast throughout the period if you can manage it. As sunrise approaches, carry out a ceremony marking your new name or status. Break your fast, and revel in the keeping of your vigil.

Susan Pesznecker

July 31
Sunday

 1st ♌

Color of the day: Amber
Incense of the day: Hyacinth

A Flower Spell for Abundance

In July, colorful flowers are everywhere. Black-eyed Susans star the roadsides with golden yellow, and white clouds of Queen Anne's lace rise above the wild grasses along country lanes. And early goldenrod adds its sunny hue to the late-season palette. Colorful flowers can lift your spirit and help you attain your magical goals. For this spell, we'll use the flowers found in nature at this time of year to bring abundance. Upon your altar place a bouquet of the flowers I've mentioned. The black-eyed Susans will serve to strengthen the spell, Queen Anne's lace will send out positive vibrations, and goldenrod will bring prosperity and success. Next light three candles—yellow for mental sharpness, white for balance, and gold for success. Think of just enough abundance coming into your life. End the spell by laying a dollar bill in front of the flowers and candles. Allow the candles to burn down.

James Kambos

August is the eighth month of the year and is named for Augustus Caesar. Its astrological sign is Leo, the Lion (July 22–August 23), a fixed-fire sign ruled by the Sun. This is the time of "first fruits," the beginning of the harvest season. The month begins with the ancient festival of Lughnasadh, when the Irish honored Lugh, the many-skilled god, and celebrated with games and feasting. The Anglo-Saxons called this Lammas, or "loaf mass." A loaf of bread was baked with the first harvested grain and blessed at Mass. This is a good time to share a homemade loaf with family and friends. This is the midpoint of the light half of the year. In many places, August means "back to school"—time to prepare for fall and, in some cases, more work and less relaxation time. We begin to harvest our gardens now and reap what we sowed in the spring—the Full Moon of August is often called the Corn Moon. The landscape begins to hint at the autumn to come—fields and gardens turn yellow with goldenrod, sunflowers, and black-eyed Susans. Daylight wanes more quickly now, and the evening music of cicadas serenades us gently into cooler nights. We can sense that summer is drawing to a close as we prepare to enjoy a bountiful harvest.

August 1
Monday
Lammas
Ramadan begins

 1st ♌

☽ → ♍ 4:41 am

Color of the day: Gray
Incense of the day: Clary sage

The First harvest

After the Sun God's triumph at Litha, he begins to wane and transfer all of his strength into the food we will harvest to keep us alive through the winter. This food is gathered in stages, and so the Sun God dies in stages. Ancient people took this very seriously, and no one wanted to be the one to "kill" the God by cutting the last of the harvest. They would take turns throwing scythes at the last standing sheaf of grain so the whole community would share the responsibility. A safe and fun way to incorporate this tradition into your own celebration is to get or make a piñata shaped like the Sun. Fill it with candy or with birdseed, dried corn, and grass seed if you're going to be out in a yard or field. Dance around the piñata to bless it as the image of the Sun God and honor him. Then have everyone in your party take turns whacking, and when your piñata is finally broken, let the bounty of the Sun wash over you. Share a feast of late-summer fruits like tomatoes, peaches, corn, and peppers, and leave some fresh produce as an offering.

Castiel

Holiday lore: Lammas is a bittersweet holiday, mingling joy at the current high season's harvest with the knowledge that summer is soon at an end. Many cultures have "first fruit" rituals on this day—the Celt's version is called Lughnasadh; the Anglo-Saxon version called Hlaf-masse. In the Middle Ages, the holiday settled on August 1, taking its current form for the most part, with sheaves of wheat and corn blessed on this day.

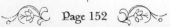

August 2
Tuesday

1st ♏

Color of the day: White
Incense of the day: Ylang-ylang

Celtic Reaping Blessing

After the symbolic acts of reaping that took place at Lammas, people watched their fields for signs that the entire crop was ready for harvest. In Scotland, the harvest ritual was performed by a male head of household, who faced east and made the first sacred cut:

> On the day of the feast, at the
> rising of the Sun
> With the back of the ear of
> grain to the east
>
> I go forth, with my sickle
> under my arm
> And I reap the first cut
>
> I will let my sickle down
> While the fruitful grain is in
> my hand
>
> I will raise my eyes upwards
> And turn on my heel swiftly
>
> Turning right, as the Sun
> also travels
> From east to west, and from
> north to south
>
> I give thanks for the growing
> crops upon the ground

> Bless each ear and handful in
> the sheaf.

Sharynne MacLeod NicMhacha

August 3
Wednesday

1st ♏
☽ → ♎ 6:04 am

Color of the day: White
Incense of the day: Lilac

Drimes (Greek)

The first three days of August in Greece are called Drimes. A change of season is in the air and certain activities are avoided, such as chopping wood, swimming in the sea, and washing hair. People also abstain from eating meat until August 15. This is a time of transition. Expressions of this season of abundance include leaping over bonfires shouting "figs and walnuts!" and celebrating all night in vineyards. The weather on this day is said to predict the weather for the next three months. To celebrate the upcoming harvest season, enjoy foods today such as grapes, figs, and walnuts.

Light candles to symbolize a bonfire and raise a toast to the harvest season. Invite abundance into your life with these words:

> Harvest time is drawing near,
>
> May I reap from work this year.
>
> May fruit be heavy on the vine –
>
> Abundance flow to me like wine.

Ember Grant

with golden sparkles coming down through the crown of your head, into your heart, and out through the palms of your hands to fill the water. Say:

> Lakshmi, goddess of abundance, I call on you!
>
> Please infuse this water with vibrations of harmony and financial abundance!
>
> May I be surrounded by luxury, attract luxury, and be a magnet for luxury.
>
> Thank you, thank you, thank you! Blessed be. And so it is.

Soak in the water for at least forty minutes. After you dry off, write down everything you can think of that you're grateful for, and then write a thank-you note to the universe.

Tess Whitehurst

August 4
Thursday

 1st ♎

Color of the day: Turquoise
Incense of the day: Carnation

The Financial harmony Bath

Slice an orange into thin wedges and throw it in your bath water along with the petals of one red rose, one yellow rose, and one pink rose. Light a green candle and cinnamon incense. Hold your hands over the bath and visualize bright white light

 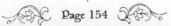

August 5
Friday

1st ♊
☽ → ♏ 7:57 am

Color of the day: White
Incense of the day: Orchid

Calendula Blessings

August is also known as *wyrt*, or green plant Moon. It is a time for celebrating health and vitality, family, and friends. *Calendula officinalis*, also known as 'Pot Marigold' or 'Scotch Marigold,' is abundant in August, with bright orange and yellow blossoms shaped like the summer sun. Known for its high levels of antioxidants that fight cancer-causing free radicals, calendula is also known to brighten the spirit and ward off depression. It also has anti-inflammatory, antiseptic, and bactericide qualities. An edible flower, it is great in summer salads and dishes, celebrating health and vitality. Invite friends and family to a potluck celebration. Encourage dishes that come from their gardens, their ovens, or their hands. Make a huge green salad with summer seasonal veggies, and adorn it with bright, edible calendula petals. As the sun shines upon you, soak in the radiant energy of friends, family, and healing calendula.

Dallas Jennifer Cobb

August 6
Saturday

1st ♏
2nd Quarter 7:08 am

Color of the day: Black
Incense of the day: Sandalwood

Calm Your Mind, Gather Your Thoughts

It's easy to get overwhelmed with the energies of the day. If you've recently been through an emotionally draining experience, a highly Gnostic/mystic spiritual communion, a mind-warping drug trip, or any other occurrence that's left you a bit shaken or overwhelmed, a spell like this is ideal. Gather a sprig of rowan (ruby) berries and/or leaves. Grab a pad of paper and a pen, and lay outside on the grass (nighttime is best). Close your eyes and slip into a meditative state of mind, placing the sprig of rowan on your brow (Ajna) chakra. Start thinking about the event or day you experienced, slowly playing it out in your mind from start to finish, and backwards from finish to start. Continue this for a while: this helps your mind assimilate, organize, and make sense of one's experiences. When you're ready, sit up and write out the events in sequence. For example:

*Woke up, Took a shower,
Tripped over the cat, Broke
the coffee pot, Fell asleep on
the couch and was late for
work, etc.*

Once organized in a tidy list, place
the paper and the rowan on your
altar. After "sleeping on it," you'll
find that your mind is in a more
refreshed, balanced state.

Raven Digitalis

Historical fact: Today commemorates the day the atomic
bomb Little Boy fell, in 1945, on the
city of Hiroshima in Japan. Within
a few minutes, some 75,000 people
perished in the shock waves and fires
that swept through the city. Tens
of thousands more died of radiation
sickness afterward. On this day, the
people of Hiroshima celebrate a peace
ceremony in memory of the dead.
You may also take today to offer a
silent prayer vigil chanting: "Never
again, never again."

August 7
Sunday

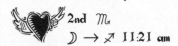

2nd ♏

☽ → ♐ 11:21 am

Color of the day: Yellow
Incense of the day: Heliotrope

A healing Love Spell

Today marks the Adonia ritual in
ancient Greece commemorat-
ing the death of Aphrodite's lover,
Adonis. We can heal our heart of
a romantic relationship through
magic, whether it ended with death
or simply because it was not recipro-
cal. This is especially good to heal a
crush. Gather two white candles, a
toothpick, scissors, and pink string.
In your ritual space, cleanse your
candle with your breath and charge a
candle to represent you and the other
to represent your former lover. With
the toothpick, carve your name on
one and your former lover's name on
another. Light them. Tie the string
around the candles and say:

This is the love I knew.

Cut the string, imagining the connection between the two of you becoming weak. Affirm:

May my heart be full of love.

*May your heart be full of
love.*

I am healed and whole.

May the love we had shared
spiral out

And bless all the worlds.

So mote it be.

Bury the candles in opposite directions.

Abel R. Gomez

water and rinse the teapot with the boiled water before adding your tea and filling the teapot with the rest of the boiling water. Let the tea steep for at least six minutes. If you have a tea cozy, use it! If not, wrap the teapot in a warm towel while the tea steeps. Pour the brewed tea into a favored cup that you use only for spellworking. Take three deep cleansing breaths and inhale the fumes of the tea before drinking it. Feel the heat of the tea seeping into your body. Relax. The more you use this ritual, the quicker and stronger your sense of serenity will come to you.

Paniteowl

August 8
Monday

2nd ♐

Color of the day: Silver
Incense of the day: Narcissus

Serenity Spell

We are so fortunate in today's world to be able to go to the grocery store and buy blended teas for many purposes. Some people think they have to grow their own in order to create an effective spell, but that is not necessary. How you prepare the tea is the secret to spellcasting, for YOU are the ingredient that is not in the bag! Choose a tea that is blended to calm and comfort you. Use a china teapot you have specifically dedicated to your spellworking. Boil spring

August 9
Tuesday

2nd ♐
☽ → ♑ 4:38 pm

Color of the day: Maroon
Incense of the day: Cinnamon

Harvest Your Dreams

The first harvest of the season has begun in rural areas around the world. But what about your own personal harvest? Have your dreams come true? Are you any closer to achieving your goals? This spell will help get you headed in the right direction. Begin by looking through old magazines and cut out photos representing your goal—the picture could be of a new house, a new car, or it could be a photo depicting someone working in a job you'd like to have. Spread the photos out in front of you. Have an attractive box on hand decorated any way you wish. Look at the photos and say,

> *These are my dreams. These are my wishes. Bring them to me in the most positive way.*

Now reach out with your power hand; draw each picture toward you, one by one. Put them in your box and forget about them for a while. Wait and see what happens.

James Kambos

August 10
Wednesday

 2nd ♑

Color of the day: Yellow
Incense of the day: Bay laurel

Wisdom Walk

Let's face it: most of us live with our harshest critics 24/7. That inner voice can very difficult to quiet. I've found that a good walk usually does the trick better than anything else. As an added bonus, it's often a good way to recharge my inner batteries and get my thinking focused and back to working toward my goals. You don't need to go anywhere special for this exercise, as long as you have room to walk. Outdoors is preferable, since it seems easier to gather the wisdom inherent in nature when out in it. Listen to your inner voices. Carry on a conversation with yourself. Every time that inner critic chimes in with something you know is unfounded, question it. Point out to yourself the flaws and embrace the positives. Mull over possible solutions to roadblocks holding you back from your goals. Return renewed in spirit and with the beginnings of a plan to move forward in your life.

Laurel Reufner

August 11
Thursday

 2nd ♑
☽ → ♒ 11:47 pm

Color of the day: White
Incense of the day: Apricot

The Smooth Traffic Spell

If you commute to work, you likely get stuck in traffic. This isn't always bad—sometimes those mysterious traffic slow-downs save you from being in the wrong place at the wrong time. Still, until you can choose mass transit, you might want to try this technique to get from point A to point B more smoothly: Find some classical music or trance/techno on your car radio (or load some onto your iPod.) It's important that the music not have lyrics. Pay close attention to the traffic surrounding you, and visualize the musical composition worming its way into the waves of traffic you travel, anchoring itself on a building or other structure that symbolizes "arriving home," whether that's your apartment, a flagpole, or even the big star at a Texaco station. Drive safely, and feel the waves of the music deliver you to your goal.

Diana Rajchel

Holiday lore: King Puck is a virile old goat who presides over the fair in Killorglin in Ireland. He watches the proceedings from a platform built in town, wearing a shiny gold crown and purple robes. Among the activities: gathering day, which includes a parade; fair day itself, and the buying and selling of livestock; and scattering day, when the goat is disrobed, dethroned, and sent back into the field at sunset.

August 12
Friday

 2nd ≈

Color of the day: Purple
Incense of the day: Violet

Inner Beauty

The energies of Venus and a waxing Moon phase are ours to work today. Take this opportunity to work for inner beauty—the sort of loveliness that shines through. You will need the following for this Friday spell: a pink candle, a coordinating holder, a fresh, pink rose in a vase, and a few rose quartz stones—the ultimate warm fuzzy stone. Arrange the components of the spell on a safe, flat surface any way you like, then repeat the charm three times.

> Friday is devoted to Venus
> the goddess of love,
>
> Lady, hear my call for help,
> answer from above.
>
> A pink rose for affection and
> to brighten my day,
>
> The rose quartz stones will
> bring joy and confidence my
> way.
>
> May my inner beauty spell
> shine true, for all to see,
>
> With harm to none, as I will
> it, then so shall it be.

Ellen Dugan

August 13
Saturday

 2nd ≈
Full Moon 2:58 pm

Color of the day: Gray
Incense of the day: Magnolia

Carry a Torch for Diana

Ancient Romans celebrated Nemoralia, Festival of Torches, from August 13 to 15 (or the Full Moon). This holiday honored Diana, the Moon goddess. Hunting or killing of animals was forbidden. For this occasion, women should take a ceremonial bath, then dress their hair with seasonal flowers. If Diana has granted a prayer of yours, carry a torch or candle to a lake or other body of water (or a cauldron of water) and speak your thanks. To make a prayer, write your request on a ribbon and tie it to the altar. People in need of healing may make a figure of clay or bread in the shape of the body part to be healed. Serve a feast of fruits and vegetables. Dance and sing in honor of Diana:

> Maiden of the silver Moon,
>
> Flash your mirror in the
> lake.
>
> Lend us magic in our rite,
>
> Torch and water, hound and
> snake.

Elizabeth Barrette

August 14
Sunday

 3rd ♒︎

☽ → ♓︎ 8:54 am

Color of the day: Amber
Incense of the day: Juniper

Port-O-Pagan

My good friend Rainmaker is known for the Port-O-Pagan she keeps with her at all times. It's a small velveteen bag containing a set of items designed for magical readiness—magic on the go! You can put together your own Port-O-Pagan. Begin with a zippered or drawstring bag and fill it with a number of items for every magical eventuality. I use the following:

A 9-foot cotton cord, knotted every 12 inches
White chalk
Kosher salt
Smudge stick
Candle
Matches
Small plastic glass
Pocketknife
Washable altar cloth
Quartz crystal
Obsidian
Small bell
Your favorite divination tool

Bless your Port-O-Pagan kit and keep it handy for quick use. With the above materials, you can cleanse, consecrate, or bless items; perform divination; scry; meditate; mark sacred space; or hold a simple ritual. You'll be prepared!

Susan Pesznecker

August 15
Monday

 3rd ♓︎

Color of the day: White
Incense of the day: Lily

Feast Day of the Queen of Heaven

Light candles today in blue (firmament), green (Earth), and white (underworld), honoring the power of Goddess in the three realms. Sacred especially to those goddesses who travel among the worlds—such as Hecate, Shekinah, Sophia, Persephone, Chalchiuhtlique, Yemaya, Isis, Kali, and Inanna—use the energy of this time to consecrate images, statues, and symbols of the Divine Female. Anoint your object with oil of rose, lily, wisteria, gardenia, or hyacinth, and speak a blessing of dedication as you touch Her feet,

womb, heart, throat, hands, third
eye, and crown:

> *Oh, Goddess, Mother, Sister,*
> *Lover, Friend, Fierce One*
> *and Extoller of Virtues! I sing*
> *your praises with my every*
> *breath and welcome you to*
> *dance in my rites. I bless and*
> *consecrate this image (statue/*
> *symbol) in your name and for*
> *your work that you may guide*
> *me, offer your boons, and*
> *grant me your lessons. I am*
> *ready and hail you.*

Chandra Alexandre

August 16
Tuesday

3rd ♓︎
☽ → ♈︎ 8:01 pm

Color of the day: Gray
Incense of the day: Basil

Break Attachments, Invoke Recovery

This is the time of harvest! If
they're natural in your area,
scout out a rowan tree—look for the
bright orange clusters of berries! If
you have permission from the land-
owner (unless it's public land, which
is even better), go to the tree and
leave an offering of a crystal, corn-
meal, or natural fertilizer (manure).
Thank the tree for its generosity.
Cultivate a good amount of rowan
berries and return to your "spellcrafting headquarters." Using a needle
and thread, string a large necklace
of rowan berries. Hang this garland
in an auspicious spot to let it dry.
This can be used for two significant
things: protection and recuperation
(or recovery)—just wear it around
your neck any time. All of us have
an Achilles heel: dependencies to
thoughts, substances, negative modes
of behavior, habits, and so on. As
you take the steps in "everyday life"
to break your attachment to the chosen ailment, you can deepen the process through magic. Whenever the
craving or tendency arises, sprinkle
dried rue around yourself or take a
bath with the herb steeped as a "tub
tea." Rue is said to "break attachments to anything." Once finished
using the rue, wear the garland of
rowan berries to ensure that you're
protected from the negativity, that
you're kept on track, and are stable
on the road to balance.

Raven Digitalis

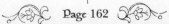

August 17
Wednesday

 3rd ♈

Color of the day: Topaz
Incense of the day: Honeysuckle

Celtic Prayer for Ritual Bathing of a Child

This lovely traditional prayer was used in a folk ritual to bless a child. It could be used at home with a vessel of consecrated water, or done at the edge of a shallow body of water. The person officiating at the ritual takes small handfuls of water and pours them gently on the child while reciting the following words:

A palmful for your age
A palmful for your growth
A palmful for your appetite

For your share of the bounty,
*   honey and warm milk*
For your share of the feast,
*   with gifts and with*
*   tribute*
For your share of the
*   treasure, my love and my*
*   joy*

For your share of palaces, in
*   the courts of kings*
For your share of the
*   Summerland, with its*
*   goodness and peace*

The three palmfuls of the
*   Secret Three*

To guard you from every ill
The Sacred Three of
*   Blessings*

So may it be!

Sharynne MacLeod NicMhacha

August 18
Thursday

 3rd ♈

Color of the day: Green
Incense of the day: Nutmeg

Dog Days Spell

All of us have those times when we feel drained and have little energy to spare. Well, here's a shocking thought . . . honor that feeling! Instead of pushing yourself to accomplish something, take a rest and let yourself "hibernate" for a bit during the hot days of August! You'll need a comfortable place to lie down and stretch out. Place a fan near you so the air will flow over your body as you rest. Drink an 8-ounce glass of water before lying down. Play soothing music, or listen to a meditation tape at a low volume. As you relax, chant this mantra:

*Soft summer air, come to me
. . . warm summer waters
cradle me . . . peace and rest
will comfort me . . . refresh
my soul, so mote it be!*

You may drift off to sleep, that's quite all right. When you awake, or feel you need to move, get up on you hands and knees and shake yourself like a dog shedding water. Stand up slowly, and drink more water. Take three deep, cleansing breaths and let your body come fully awake. Enjoy the rest of your day.

Paniteowl

August 19
Friday

 3rd ♈︎
𝄐 ☽ → ♉︎ 8:36 am

Color of the day: Rose
Incense of the day: Alder

Simple Money Spell

Sometimes the best spells are the most simple. We don't always have the time or money to get the exotic magical supplies when a need arises. Try this simple candle spell to attract money into your life. You'll need a green votive candle, olive oil, a pinch of basil, and a toothpick. In your ritual space, cleanse your candle with your breath and charge it with the intention of attracting money. Use the toothpick to carve money signs or any symbol that represents abundance to you onto the candle. Carve your initials at the bottom to draw the abundance to you. Dress your candle with oil and basil and light it on your altar. As you do so, visualize yourself having all that you need. Begin chanting something like:

> *Money come
> Money grow
> Money come
> Money flow*

Allow the candle to burn out completely. The abundance you need will come to you.

Abel R. Gomez

August 20
Saturday

3rd ♉

Color of the day: Indigo
Incense of the day: Ivy

Father Time

Saturday is named for the Roman god Saturn, god of agriculture, structure, and order. His image is the basis for the figure of Father Time, reminding us of the passing of the years. Today, with the Moon in a waning phase, is a good time to ponder the passage of time and meditate on how we spend our precious time. Perhaps you need to organize certain areas of your life, work on time management, or dedicate more free time to enjoy life's pleasures. To remind yourself of your goal, meditate on an hourglass. Some measure shorter lengths of time than a full hour, so find one of these if you wish. Focus on the sand pouring through it. Visualize an hourglass if you can't find one. Listen to music of drums or other rhythmic sounds. Remember that time is passing, and make the most of every moment you have.

Ember Grant

August 21
Sunday

3rd ♉
4th Quarter 5:54 pm
☽ → ♊ 8:53 pm

Color of the day: Gold
Incense of the day: Frankincense

Change Your Style

The wheel of the year is turning, and autumn is on the horizon. As fall approaches, this is a good time of year to change your personal style. This could be anything—a new wardrobe, hair, makeup, diet, or anything else you wish to change. Write this list on an index card using a pencil. Place this card in your pocket or purse and carry it with you wherever you go to make your transformation. This could include the salon, department store, gym, etc. As you complete a goal on your list, erase that item off your index card. Continue carrying your card until you feel your goals have been met. If you need to boost your confidence during this spell, light an orange candle in a spicy scent. Gaze at its flame and "see" the new you as you wish to be. Have fun!

James Kambos

August 22
Monday

 4th ♊

Color of the day: Gray
Incense of the day: Neroli

Clearing the Air

Clear the air after a particularly unpleasant visitor leaves by sprinkling salt water on any doorways they may have passed through. Also lightly sprinkle anywhere they may have been sitting. Follow the salt water with a flourish of lavender incense. Visualize all of that unpleasant energy dissipating as though zapped by small electrical charges as you work. Allow the incense to finish burning itself out.

Laurel Reufner

August 23
Tuesday

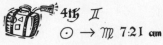 4th ♊

☉ → ♍ 7:21 am

Color of the day: Red
Incense of the day: Cedar

Charm for Safe Travel

When we wish each other "safe travel" or say, "have a good trip," we're actually administering a magical invocation of protection and safety. You can add to this effect with a travel charm. Cut a six- to eight-inch circle of blue cloth. In the center of the cloth, sprinkle a bit of lavender or sage and add small pieces of citrine, lapis, jade, and/or quartz. On a small piece of paper, inscribe the following:

> I fill the bag for travel safe,
>
> May magical powers guide you.
>
> Journey smoothly to your place,
>
> The Goddess' arms around you.

Read the charm aloud as you write, then fold the paper three times and add it to the bag. Tie the bag with a gold cord, closing it with a square knot to invoke four-sided elemental protection. Have the traveler keep the charmed amulet with them throughout their journey.

Susan Pesznecker

August 24
Wednesday

 4th ♊
) → ♋ 6:31 am

Color of the day: White
Incense of the day: Lavender

Feeding the Ancestors

In ancient Rome, today marked the opening of the portal connecting Hades' underworld abode via a labyrinth to Ceres (Demeter), goddess of grain, vegetation, and the harvest. No longer closed, this allowed the spirits of the dead to walk among the living for a day. Offerings of fruits and special foods were placed at the entranceway to create harmony and pay homage to Ceres, who also presides over liminality, that in-between state marked by a temenos, or sacred boundary. Today then is a day for trance drumming, focused meditation, dancing, and other ritual activities that take you more deeply into liminal consciousness. From here, gather the wisdom of the ancients and be sure to feed those who have guided and nurtured your spiritual journey. Leave figs, nuts, berries, sweets, or honey water at a crossroads or an opening into the ground to honor those who walk among us.

Chandra Alexandre

August 25
Thursday

 4th ♋

Color of the day: Purple
Incense of the day: Clove

An Opulent Celebration

Historically, today was Opiconsivia, a Roman festival in honor of Ops. She represents an aspect of the Great Mother Goddess, the Earth as source of crops and life. Her festival included a chariot race and horse parades. To celebrate this holiday, the presiding priestess should wear a white robe and a white veil. Lavish jewelry is also appropriate, since Ops is the goddess of opulence and treasure. Set the altar with flowers, figures of horses, vegetables and grains, stones, and other Earth symbols. Let the celebrants chant:

> Praise be to Ops, goddess of
>   Earth,
> Who brings the crops and
>   herds to birth!
> Come forth, Ops, from ripen
>   ing land,
> And spill your blessings from
>   your hand!

The priestess dispenses gold-foiled chocolate coins, saying:

> Treasure I give, to have and
>   hold,
> But know that not all
>   treasure's gold:

*Knowledge I give, for
 wisdom's rich,
And the Wise Ones know
 which is which.*

Elizabeth Barrette

*I ask you to bless me with
 beauty and confidence
 today.
By the powers of the oceans
 and seas,
As I do will it, so shall it be.*

Now towel dry off and apply your favorite lotions or perfumes and pamper yourself! The rest of the night is up to you.

Ellen Dugan

August 26
Friday

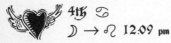

4th ♋
☽ → ♌ 12:09 pm

Color of the day: Coral
Incense of the day: Mint

Bless Your Inner Sexy Witch

How about a Friday night bathtime beauty ritual? Let's call on Aphrodite, she who rose newly born from the sea foam, and see what we can conjure up. Toss a handful of sea salt in your bath water, then mix it up to soften the water and to simulate the ocean. Light some fragrant ocean-scented candles, then indulge in a nice soak. As you prepare to rise from your bath, call on Aphrodite to bless you with beauty and to increase your inner sexy Witch.

*Aphrodite, you who rose
 from the sea foam,*

August 27
Saturday

4th ♌

Color of the day: Blue
Incense of the day: Pine

Volturnalia

Volturnalia is the Roman festival celebrating Volturnus, god of fountains and flowing waters. He was originally a tribal river god, and the Volturnus River in southern Italy is named for him. Do a spell today calling on Volturnus to wash away something that is troubling you. You will need a piece of white cloth, an eyeliner pencil or piece of colored chalk, a basin full of water, and some baking soda. Create your sacred space and focus on what you wish to wash away. Draw a symbol of it on the cloth. Hold it in both hands and say:

> Flowing, rushing, cleansing
>
> Volturnus take _____
> from me
>
> Wash away, wash away,
> wash away
>
> Now I am free.

Submerge the cloth in the basin and use the baking soda to scrub the cloth clean (continue chanting while you scrub if you like). Leave the cloth to dry and pour the water into running water. Draw a representation of yourself on the dry cloth as free of your affliction to carry as a talisman.

Castiel

August 28
Sunday

4th ♌
☽ → ♍ 2:13 pm
New Moon 11:04 pm

Color of the day: Gold
Incense of the day: Marigold

Prayer to the Virgin Goddess
With the Sun and Moon both in Virgo today, there couldn't be a better day to pay tribute to the Virgin Goddess while infusing yourself with her wonderful attributes. (Please note that "virgin" originally meant "independent/complete in oneself," and didn't indicate sexual inexperience.) Light a white or off-white soy candle. Sit comfortably, breathe deeply, and relax. When you feel ready, say:

> Virgin Goddess,
> Goddess of the Earth,
> Goddess of the Sun and
> Moon,
> I summon you.
>
> Divine Mother,
> Huntress,
> Enchantress,
> Maiden,
> Protectress,
> You of many names and
> many incarnations,
> (Among them Artemis,
> Diana, Mary, and Bast,)
> I call upon you now.

Fill me with your bright
*   spirit.*
Infuse me with your
*   confidence.*
Share with me your beauty
*   and your power.*
Instill in me the infinite
*   measure of your strength.*

Like you, may I know myself
*   as perfect and complete in*
*   myself.*
Let this wisdom bless and
*   balance my relationships,*
As you teach me to honor
*   and respect myself in all*
*   ways,*
To speak my truth,
And to stand by what I have
*   spoken, what I believe,*
*   and what I know I must*
*   do.*

Anoint your forehead, throat, and heart with frankincense oil. Continue meditating for as long as you wish.

Tess Whitehurst

August 29
Monday

 1st ♍

Color of the day: Ivory
Incense of the day: Hyssop

Sunflower Protection

August has ripened, and in many gardens you can see those watchful giants, *Helianthus annus*, the sunflower. Named after Helios, the Sun god, the sunflower head turns its face from east to west throughout the day, adoring the Sun as it progresses across the sky. Appearing to watch everything, the spritiual energies of the sunflower includes protection, flexibility, faith and good luck. Given as a gift, the sunflower symbolizes the gift of safety and happiness in the hearth and home. Today, look for a sunflower, or be like the sunflower. Turn your face toward the Sun, close your eyes momentarily and soak in the blessings of Helios. As the radiance soaks into you, breathe deeply, absorbing abundance, longevity, and prosperity. With your face turned toward the Sun, shine like the sunflower, in radiant happiness. Know that you are protected. If you find a sunflower plant today, pick one small mature seed from it, and place it in your pocket, knowing that it will point you in the right direction spiritually, and bless you with protection.

Dallas Jennifer Cobb

August 30
Tuesday
Ramadan ends

 1st ♍
☽ → ♎ 2:25 pm

Color of the day: Black
Incense of the day: Ginger

To Make a Bad Neighbor Move
There's no shame in wanting the crack dealer or wife beater elsewhere. Since tar and feathering is prohibited, try a more subtle approach. Find something that you know your neighbor stepped on—a leaf, twig, or pebble will do, although if you can lift an entire footprint out of the ground, it's ideal—and put it in a bowl or cauldron. Mix the item in with any hot-and-burning spices you can: peppers, cinnamon, cloves, garlic. Take the bowl outside, and over top of it, light a dried chili pepper (be careful not to inhale the fumes, and wear gloves!). Mix the ashes into the mix in the bowl, while repeating:

> By the power of Mars, I
> speed you on your way.

Scatter the ashes in your neighbor's path or by his/her car, and cleanse your bowl with salt and water when you've emptied the contents. Repeat, and call the police as needed.

Diana Rajchel

August 31
Wednesday

 1st ♎

Color of the day: Yellow
Incense of the day: Marjoram

Neutralizing Energy
If a location seems to have a buildup of energy, it's a good idea to neutralize the energy and start fresh. However, there are a few things to take into consideration: if the location (be it a house, a room, an area of land, or somewhere else) seems to be absolutely looming with darkness, is there a possibility that it's haunted? If so, this working may not be enough. Additionally, it's good to consider whether the energy buildup in the location is beneficial. For example, if you're on sacred land (including a cemetery), consider that the energy may serve a positive purpose. Counteract energy with this spell only if you know the buildup should be energetically neutralized.
Simply go to the area with sea salt, purified water, a quartz crystal, a matchbook, and a wand of dried sage. Ignite the sage with a number of matches (the sulfur helps chase away energy) and allow the smoke to billow. As you walk around the location in a widdershins (counterclockwise) direction, chant the word "Dismissed!" over and over. Next, sprinkle half of the sea salt as

you did before, but this time chant "Dissolved!" on repeat. Add the rest of the sea salt to the water, swirl it around, and visualize the water glowing in a soft, white light. Asperge the consecrated water around the area, chanting "Neutralized!" over and over. Finish by placing the quartz crystal in the central point of the location and declare, "So mote it be!"

Raven Digitalis

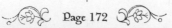

September is the ninth month of the year. Its name is derived from the Latin word *septum*, which means "seventh," as it was the seventh month of the Roman calendar. Its astrological sign is Virgo, the Maiden (August 23–September 23), a mutable-earth sign ruled by Mercury. This is the month autumn begins. Change is in the air—first noticed by the slanting angle of sunlight. We return now to a time of balance, the equinox, when day and night are equal in length. The days will soon begin to get noticeably shorter and, by the end of the month, temperatures start to cool. Chrysanthemums in every color begin blooming in neighborhoods and fall colors just begin to hint at their arrival. At the Fall Equinox, also called Mabon, we celebrate the second harvest as we enter the dark half of the year. Decorate your home and altar with clusters of grapes, apples, pumpkins, and acorns. Wine and cider are in season now and birds and butterflies begin to migrate. Woodland creatures begin storing food and preparing their nests for the winter—look for squirrels and chipmunks hiding nuts and seeds. Watch for monarch butterflies as they embark on their long journey south. The magnificent Harvest Moon is the Full Moon of September.

September 1
Thursday

1st ♎

☽ → ♏ 2:48 pm

Color of the day: Green
Incense of the day: Mulberry

Prosperity and Good Fortune

Thursday is associated with the planet Jupiter, prosperity, and good fortune. We also have a waxing Moon to help pull positive things toward us when we work magic. So, let's conjure up a good-luck spell today. You will need one of these prosperity-inducing herbs—clover, honeysuckle, or mint. (You may use all three herbs if you wish.) If you can find a four-leafed clover, all the better. Light a green votive candle and surround the outside of the candle cup with your chosen herb. Then repeat the charm:

> Good luck these fresh herbs
> will bring to me,
>
> May they increase my
> prosperity,
>
> Good luck and good fortune
> shall rule my days,
>
> I'll be blessed in many
> positive ways.

Allow the spell candle to burn in a safe place until it goes out on its own.

Ellen Dugan

Holiday lore: Many Greeks consider this their New Year's Day. This day marks the beginning of the sowing season, a time of promise and hope. On this day, people fashion wreaths of pomegranates, quinces, grapes, and garlic bulbs—all traditional symbols of abundance. Just before dawn on September 1, children submerge the wreaths in the ocean waters for luck. They carry seawater and pebbles home with them in small jars to serve as protection in the coming year. Tradition calls for them to gather exactly forty pebbles and water from exactly forty waves.

September 2
Friday

1st ♏

Color of the day: White
Incense of the day: Mint

Rune Cookies

September ushers in the harvest and the autumn season. The grain is reaped and the vegetables are gathered. Now is a good time to work magic related to home and hearth, abundance and prosperity.

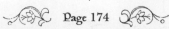

This spell uses runes from the Elder Futhark. You will need a batch of sugar cookies and some red frosting. Frost each cookie with a rune, such as:

Fehu: wealth, fruition, plenty. (ᚠ)
Uruz: health and strength. (ᚢ)
Gebo: gifts and generosity. (ᚷ)
Wunjo: joy and comfort. (ᚹ)
Jera: a good harvest, hopes
      rewarded. (ᛃ)
Sowilo: success, goals met, honor. (ᛋ)
Berkano: fertility and personal
      growth. (ᛒ)
Ingwaz: family, hearth and home,
      domestic bliss. (ᛜ)

Serve the cookies in a baking pan held high, so that each person chooses without being able to see them. The rune on your cookie represents how the bounty of this year's harvest time will manifest for you. Eating the cookie internalizes the rune's energy and blessing.

                    Elizabeth Barrette

September 3
Saturday

 1st ♏

    ☽ → ♐ 5:03 pm

Color of the day: Black
Incense of the day: Rue

Bringing in the Elements

As the Earth turns on the cusp of autumn, it's a fine time to work with the elements.

Earth grounds us and gives us our center. Bring earth into your space with natural stoneware or earthenware. Set stones, rocks, and crystals around your home. Use natural sea salt in your kitchen.

Air is energizing and improves the mind's clarity. Open the windows. Burn candles, incense, or essential oils. Hang wind chimes and banners outside your windows and mobiles inside your home.

Fire is energy in its purest form. To bring in fire, burn candles and incense. If you have a fireplace, use it for companionable fires and as a point of gathering and meditation. Hang prismatic crystals in your windows. Cook with fiery spices and peppers.

Water calms, soothes, and heals. Set up a small, bubbling tabletop fountain. Put out a bowl of water, with flower petals or floating candles on its surface.

                    Susan Pesznecker

September 4
Sunday

 1st ♐
2nd Quarter 1:39 pm

Color of the day: Orange
Incense of the day: Frankincense

Shrunken head Spell

Sometimes there are people in our lives whose main job in life seems be to tell us what to do . . . constantly! I'm not talking about teachers or bosses, whose job it is to do just that, but those people who seem to think we can't think for ourselves. September is a great time to use the abundance of the season to create our own shrunken-head spell! All you need is a ripe, juicy apple and a sharp knife. Carve a face into the apple. As you carve the eyes, say:

> These are _____'s eyes.

Then the nose, saying:

> This is _____'s nose.

Then carve the mouth, the ears, and even the chin. You get the idea! You don't have to be a great artist to do this sculpture. Place the sculpted apple on a small plate and put it a window that gets the most light. Look closely at the apple and say:

> Busybodies have no place
> intruding in my personal
> space. Find some other to
> annoy, I'll watch you fade
> with so much joy.

The apple will dry and shrink while still retaining the semblance of a face. Each day you see the "shrinking skull" you'll be reminded to not let this person butt into your personal business. When the spell is complete, toss the apple into a wooded area where it will be a treat for the animals.

Paniteowl

September 5
Monday
Labor Day

 2nd ♐
☽ → ♑ 10:03 pm

Color of the day: Lavender
Incense of the day: Clary sage

Jade Tree Success Blessing

If you're already working at a job you love, this ritual can make it even better. Otherwise, it can help you to discover and acquire a position that brings you prosperity and joy. Cleanse nine moonstones by running them under cold water. Hold them in both hands and mentally empower them with your intention to be happy and prosperous at work. Place them in a clear glass jar. Fill the jar with water and put a cutting of jade into the jar. Place the jar near your front door (inside the house). Over the next weeks and months, the cutting will grow roots. When enough roots have grown, plant the jade in a pot with the moonstones at the bottom. Place the plant near your workspace or the area where you look for work. Water it no more than once a week. (Please note: jade usually does well anywhere indoors.)

Tess Whitehurst

to better mix the herbs and their scents. Hold the mortar in your hands and visualize a soft, protective white light emanating from the bowl. Place in a small drawstring bag. Either hang from your rearview mirror or tuck into the glove box or under a seat. When doing so, visualize that same protective light of the herbs extending out to surround your vehicle, keeping it safe and snug. You might want to renew the herbs every three to six months.

Laurel Reufner

September 6
Tuesday

2nd ♑

Color of the day: Gray
Incense of the day: Ginger

Aromatic Car Protection Charm

Add some extra protection to your ride when driving, especially in treacherous weather, with this car protection charm bag. Take 1 tablespoon fennel, 1 tablespoon anise, and 1 teaspoon wormwood. Lightly grind in a mortar and pestle

September 7
Wednesday

2nd ♑

Color of the day: Brown
Incense of the day: Lavender

Safe Travel Spell

We have a waxing Moon phase occurring on a Mercury day today. Here is the perfect opportunity to work a spell for safe travel. Whether that travel is a trip for business, pleasure, or just the commute to work each day, Mercury will guide you and protect you on your travels. Engrave an orange candle with a winged foot (the symbol of the god Mercury). As you light the spell candle, focus your intention on safely traveling and arriving at your destination on time and with no fuss. Repeat the spell:

> Mercury guard me well, as I travel today,
>
> I will arrive safely and on time, come what may.
>
> By plane, boat, train, or car, please watch over me,
>
> Answer my request with all possible speed.
>
> By Wednesday's magic this spell is spun,
>
> For the good of all, bringing harm to none.

Ellen Dugan

September 8
Thursday

2nd ♑
☽ → ♒ 5:42 am

Color of the day: Turquoise
Incense of the day: Apricot

Remove Negativity

This spell uses the purifying and magical qualities of cider to remove negativity from the home. This very old spell might help to cleanse your home of any unwanted energy. In an old saucepan combine one cup of cider, a pinch of clove, a dash of salt, and one rusty nail. Bring the mixture to a boil and simmer a few minutes as you stir it with a cinnamon stick. Visualize all negativity being drawn into this brew. Remove the pan from the heat and let cool. Set the nail aside, but pour the liquid and the cinnamon stick outside away from your home. The earth will neutralize its negativity. Take the nail to a secluded area and bury it as you say:

> Nail of rust, dissolve to dust.
> My home is now protected
> from all harm, and so I end
> this charm.

Leave the nail undisturbed.

James Kambos

September 9
Friday

2nd ♒

Color of the day: Purple
Incense of the day: Rose

Have You Acted Justly?

Unfortunate situations happen, and you may have to make a decision where you're not sure if you've acted fairly to everyone involved. If you've made your decision but aren't sure it was the right one—and still have time to change your course—take the Justice and Judgement cards out of a tarot deck and place them next to each other. Place a red or blue seven-day jar candle between them and allow it to burn, making sure you trim the wick once a day. If black soot appears around the edge of the candle, you have been unjust. If the candle burns clean, you have acted fairly. If you find black soot, snuff the candle out and do what you can to correct your mistake. You may need to do a tarot reading to find out what you missed about the issue. Apologies are a powerful healing magic.

Diana Rajchel

September 10
Saturday

2nd ♒

☽ → ♓ 3:26 pm

Color of the day: Brown
Incense of the day: Sage

Laundry Spell

Some days are more difficult than others. In addition to cleansing yourself and your home, magically cleanse your clothes from unpleasant vibrations. Go into a light meditative state and begin placing your clothes in the washer. You may wish to add a few drops of lavender, rosemary, or sage essential oil. As you place your clothes in the washing machine, say something like this:

> Magic machine, cleaner of clothes,
>
> Banish the harm, wherever it shows.
>
> Clean all the dirty, musty, and old,
>
> Destroy dense vibrations, the gross and the bold.

Enchant and empower your clothes as they go in the dryer. Imbue them with a special magical intent. For example, if you wanted to boost confidence you might say:

> Enchant these garments, may confidence grow,

No longer in fear, my true
self will show.

When I wear these clothes,
proud I will be,

I will truly open to the most
beautiful me.

Abel R. Gomez

filling you with strong, healing light.
Imagine channeling this glorious
light out into the world. Chant the
following:

Sunlight heal,
Sunlight shine,
Send your strength
To me and mine.

Repeat the chant as many times as
you like. After the candles burn out,
keep the herbs and flowers on your
altar for a while, then return them to
the earth with a blessing, envisioning
them transferring healing strength to
soil, which spreads throughout the
land.

Ember Grant

September 11
Sunday

 2nd ♓

Color of the day: Yellow
Incense of the day: Juniper

healing Strength

Many people will remember
today as the tragic anniversary
of the attack on the World Trade
Center. You can use this ritual to
send healing strength into the world,
as well as for your own personal
healing. Sunday is a day of empowerment. Decorate your altar or other
special place with yellow and white
candles, rosemary, and marigold flowers. Burn frankincense. As you light
your candles, visualize the radiant
light of the Sun flowing through you,

September 12
Monday

 2nd ♓
Full Moon 5:27 am

Color of the day: Gray
Incense of the day: Hyssop

A Purifying Moon Bath

Nearly all Witches observe the
Full Moon in one way or another. Some choose to perform elaborate
ceremonies or work with their coven.

Others meditate or ritualize solitarily, while others simply reflect on the energy throughout the day, perhaps leaving offerings under the moon-light. Whatever your practice, it's a great idea to incorporate a cleansing Full Moon bath into your "moonly" regime. Lemons represent the light of the Moon, just as oranges represent the Sun. For the cleansing bath, get a full, fresh, organic lemon, slice it in half, and squeeze all the juice into the bath water. Let the rinds float in the tub, and add a good handful of sea salt. Sea salt is used to connect to the ocean, whose tides are dic-tated by the lunar cycle and thus the energy of the Great Goddess. If you can, turn off all the lights and ignite a white tealight candle in the room. If you have any seashells, throw 'em in the tub as well. When you get into the bath, completely submerge and cleanse yourself. Visualize your energy body becoming cleansed and purified, focusing on the healing and cleansing waters of life. Whether you're male, female, or somewhere in between, the nurturing and purify-ing energy of the Goddess can help invigorate the soul and align you to your destined path.

Raven Digitalis

September 13
Tuesday

 3rd ♓
☽ → ♈ 2:49 am

Color of the day: Black
Incense of the day: Ylang-ylang

Bittersweet Blessing

Today is the birthday of Milton Hershey, a great entrepreneur who made milk chocolate widely available to Americans. Many favor-ite foods and beverages—including chocolate, but also vanilla and cof-fee—are actually exotic imports, though today they're commonplace. Now is a good time to honor our ancestors, their delicious discover-ies, and the lands of origin. Decorate your altar in brown and white. Add photos of cocoa plants, vanilla orchids, and coffee bushes, plus pic-tures of people associated with them. For "cakes and ale" choose from milk chocolate truffles, vanilla-flavored white chocolate, chocolate-covered espresso beans, hot chocolate, coffee, etc. Say:

> Blessed be the ones who went before,
>
> And for the future laid a treasure store.
>
> Blessed be the lands beyond the seas,

*Where marvels grow beneath
the mighty trees.*

*Blessed be the bitter and the
sweet,*

*In every corner of the Earth,
a treat.*

Eat, drink, and give thanks!
                Elizabeth Barrette

to move into a season of focused learning and accomplishment. A "to do" list is a powerful tool. It creates accountability and stimulates success—we all love to check stuff off our lists. Identify what you want to learn, issues that need resolving, and what new endeavors you want to initiate. Set yourself in motion to accomplish what you want to this fall, and enjoy placing those check marks.

                Dallas Jennifer Cobb

September 14
Wednesday

 3rd ♈

Color of the day: White
Incense of the day: Marjoram

Back to School

September is when many North American children go back to school. No matter your age, you probably still feel that little rush of excitement and anticipation in early September, looking forward to a new teacher, new classes, new friends, and new learning. Because Wednesday governs communication, education, and writing, today is a great time to write down your little list of seasonal "to do's." While we are not yet into autumn, the school cycle urges us

September 15
Thursday

 3rd ♈
    ☽ → ♉ 3:25 pm

Color of the day: Purple
Incense of the day: Balsam

Gathering of Initiates
(First Day of the Great Eleusinian Mysteries)

Have you been through trials and ordeals, but still chosen the spiritual path? Then you are an initiate, one who accepts the paradoxical truth that order and chaos, creation and destruction, the One and the many, simultaneously make up this divine reality. Take a moment today for a simple visualization. Imagine yourself in an open, natural setting. Slowly, throngs of people begin to appear on the horizon. As they approach, you begin to see faces, and you recognize sister and brother spiritual seekers. Other faces you have yet to know, but you intuit that they too are part of your clan wave, your sacred lineage. You welcome them to circle with you, and you are greeted with smiles of recognition. Take in the warmth of the moment, knowing that today, you have encountered the fullness of those who stand with you on the road less traveled.

Chandra Alexandre

Holiday lore: Keirou no Hi, or Respect for the Aged Day, has been a national holiday in Japan since 1966. On this day, the Japanese show respect to elderly citizens, celebrate their longevity, and pray for their health. Although there are no traditional customs specifically associated with this day, cultural programs are usually held in various communities. Schoolchildren draw pictures or make handicraft gifts

for their grandparents and elderly family friends or neighbors. Some groups visit retirement or nursing homes to present gifts to residents.

September 16
Friday

3rd ♉

Color of the day: Pink
Incense of the day: Violet

Beneficial Cutbacks

For full magical potency, it is usually best to gather herbs during the Full Moon since the gravitational pull of the Moon draws the sap of plants up out of their roots and into their leaves. But cutting plants during the waning Moon also has its advantages, since it can signal to a plant to start to diminish instead of flourish, which in this waning time of year is beneficial. Go out today and do some pruning. The cuttings that you take at this time are best added to compost, or perhaps used only in spells for sending things away. As

 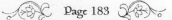

you work in your garden, repeat this chant to communicate your intent to your plants:

> Grow you have done
> Grow you may
> In the bright sun
> Of the day
>
> Time to slumber
> Time to sleep
> Autumn's coming
> Close you keep
>
> Now to draw back
> Go within
> Later come back
> When spring begins

Castiel

September 17
Saturday

 3rd ♉

Color of the day: Black
Incense of the day: Ivy

Celtic Love Spell

There are many love spells and charms in the Celtic folk tradition. Here is a particularly magical spell from Scotland, which requires the use of many difficult-to-obtain items:

> It is not knowledge of love
> To draw water through a
> reed,
> But the love of the one you
> choose
> And their warmth you draw
> to you.
>
> Arise early on the day of the
> Sun
> And go to the flat, broad
> stone.
> Take with you foxglove
> And the blossom of
> butterbur.
>
> Lift these on your shoulder
> In a wooden shovel
> Obtain nine stems of ferns
> Cut with an axe
>
> Take three bones of an old
> man
> That have been taken from
> the grave.
> Burn them on a fire of wood
> And make them into ashes
>
> Shake this in front of the
> breast of your intended
> While standing in the sharp
> north wind
> And I pledge and warrant
> That she (he) will never leave
> you.

Sharynne MacLeod NicMhacha

September 18
Sunday

3rd ♉

☽ → ♊ 4:06 am

Color of the day: Gold
Incense of the day: Almond

Notice the Work Around You

If the noise in your head becomes so loud that you often walk into telephone poles or friends yank you back from curbsides lest you meet doom, then you definitely need a little help joining us in the present. Practice this centering technique to help you focus your attention on what's at hand (and take any medication you are prescribed, as well). Place one finger above your navel, and one on your forehead/third eye chakra. Take four deep breaths, picturing an electric conduit between them. Switch hands and repeat. Burst the energy you've built through the crown of your head and the soles of your feet. If you are in a meeting or any other situation where you find yourself losing focus, tap yourself again on the forehead or above the navel, sending a "burst" up and down your body. You can pass off the technique as a passing gesture.

Diana Rajchel

September 19
Monday

3rd ♊

Color of the day: Silver
Incense of the day: Neroli

Embracing Possibility

Autumn is back-to-school time, and nothing suggests "possibility" like a clean stack of school supplies. Visit your local office-supply store and indulge yourself in a set of new tablets or notebooks; a fresh box of wax-scented crayons in brilliant colors; a bouquet of golden pencils; a package of multicolored gel pens; a sketchpad; scrapbooking papers; and, of course, a Pink Pearl eraser. Consider that these school supplies represent a blank slate—a fresh start as you prepare for the Autumnal Equinox. Use the tablet and sketchbook to plot out projects and ideas for the coming months. You might start a new Book of Shadows or a new journal; try using different colors of inks for different themes. Work early in the day to harness the gathering energies of the Sun and choose Wednesday—ruled by Odin—to stimulate your creative juices and firm your efforts. Say the word aloud: possibility. Possibility!

Susan Pesznecker

September 20
Tuesday

 3rd ♊
4th Quarter 9:39 am
☽ → ♋ 2:53 pm

Color of the day: White
Incense of the day: Geranium

Boudoir Boost

Looking to improve things in the bedroom? Give this a try for increasing the passion. If need be, clean the room. It's hard for any energy to get flowing if there is a lot of clutter around. Next, light a red candle and burn some incense. Jasmine, cinnamon, and patchouli are all good choices to cleanse and protect this special space. While the candle burns, call on the favors of Aphrodite, Freya, and Hathor, asking for their blessings. Add some special touches for each goddess around the room, such as shells for Aphrodite, gold for Freya, and music for Hathor.

Laurel Reufner

September 21
Wednesday

UN International Day of Peace

 4th ♋

Color of the day: Yellow
Incense of the day: Bay laurel

Get Rid of a Lover Spell

Most love spells are concerned with attracting a romantic partner into your life, but let's face it, there are times when you want to get rid of a lover. If you're sure you want to remove your lover from your life, try this spell. Take a blemished apple and rub it with a rag you've soaked with vinegar or lemon juice. Then peel the apple and visualize yourself free of your lover. As you're peeling your apple, say:

You once turned my head,
now you're the one I dread.

Let the peel fall on the floor. Bury the peel, or toss it onto the compost pile. Take the peeled apple and throw it into a muddy river or stream and walk away.

James Kambos

September 22
Thursday

 4th ♋
☽ → ♌ 9:55 pm

Color of the day: White
Incense of the day: Clove

Calling helpful Spirits to an Area

Native cultures have long held the notion of spirit and ancestral summoning in high esteem. If there's an area that you feel could benefit from the aid of good spirits, a ceremony such as this can help. At daybreak, go to the area you wish to consecrate or dedicate to the spirits and ancestors. This can be a house, a room, an area of land, a ritual space, or another sacred area. Offer a bit of pure tobacco to the spirits by placing it on the ground or in the four directions. Light a bundle of sweet grass and say the following in the form of a song—just create your own tune!

Spirits of Air, come to me . . . bless this place, so shall it be . . .

Spirits of Fire, come to me . . . bless this place, so shall it be . . .

Spirits of Water, come to me . . . bless this place, so shall it be . . .

Spirits of Earth, come to me . . . bless this place, so shall it be . . .

Spirits of Sky, come to me . . . bless this place, so shall it be . . .

Spirits of Land, come to me . . . bless this place, so shall it be . . .

Spirits of Space, come to me . . . bless this place, so shall it be . . .

Spirits of Time, come to me . . . bless this place, so shall it be.

Raven Digitalis

September 23
Friday

Mabon – Fall Equinox

 4th ♌

☉ → ♎ 5:05 am

Color of the day: Rose
Incense of the day: Orchid

An Apple Ritual

The Autumnal Equinox, when the forces of light and darkness are equal, is affectionately known as the Witches' Thanksgiving, when we give thanks to the gods and the ancestors for all they have blessed us with. Perform a simple apple ritual today to show your gratitude. Take a freshly washed apple to your ritual space and hold it to your heart. Reflect on the journey the apple seed has gone through, from seed through soil, to tree, and finally fruit. Reflect on how it has come to you from a store, a farmers' market, or your own backyard. Finally, reflect on the origin of this fruit from the very first apple growers and say:

> Behold the gifts of the
> ancestors. Their work is
> my blessing.

Take a bite of the apple, savoring its sweet juices and crunchy flesh. On your next bite, contemplate a blessing in your life. Speak it and take another bite to seal it. Do this until the entire apple is consumed. End by saying:

For the nameless wonders of this sweet life, I give gratitude. And so the wheel of the year turns once again, within me and around me. Blessed be.

Abel R. Gomez

September 24
Saturday

 4th ♌

Color of the day: Gray
Incense of the day: Pine

Changing Leaves Spell

This time of year it's obvious that change is happening on the Earth. The vibrant colors of the leaves are truly their last spurt of energy before they go dormant. If you find yourself in need of changes in your life, then find some time to walk through the woods or a park and gather as many of the fallen leaves that still show some color. Take them home and tie the leaves with orange ribbon, making a rough bouquet. Place the bouquet in a basket on your dining table and take note each day as they wither and fall to pieces. When the leaves are totally dry, crush them to a fine powder and save the powder in a paper bag. Often there are public bonfires happening at this time of year. You can cast the bag of powder into one of those fires, or build a small fire in your own backyard. Watch the fire for a bit and locate an area that seems "open." Say these words before you burn the bag:

> Fire burn and light my way,
>
> Make my thoughts as clear as day.
>
> Cleanse my fear of change to come,
>
> And strengthen who I will become.

> Paniteowl

September 25
Sunday

 4th ♌
D → ♍ 12:49 am

Color of the day: Orange
Incense of the day: Eucalyptus

Scottish Morning Prayer

We can make each moment of every day sacred, whether or not it is a special holiday or feast day. This was the practice of the ancestors who found ways to ritualize and make sacred very act they undertook. Here is an excerpt from a Scottish prayer that was recited upon arising each morning:

> Bless my body and my soul
> Bless my heart and my speech
> Bless my belief and my path
>
> Strength and business of
> morning
> Force and wisdom of thought
> Bless my path 'til I sleep this
> night
>
> Bless each thing I see and
> hear
> Bless each ray that guides
> my way
> Each thing that I pursue
>
> I offer you love with my
> whole devotion
> I offer you affection with all
> of my senses

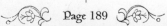

*I offer you worship with my
whole life*

*May I walk this day with
Spirit
Shielded from ill, shielded
from harm
Blessed by the Sacred Three.*

Sharynne MacLeod NicMhacha

and enlist the help of Forseti, the
Norse god of justice, by saying:

> *Forseti, I call on you!*
>
> *Please bring a swift and fair
> resolution to this dispute.*
>
> *Let justice prevail!*

Anoint the charm with olive oil and
keep it near your court documents
until the dispute has been resolved.
Then bury it at the base of a tree, in
a hole that's at least a foot deep.

Tess Whitehurst

September 26
Monday

 4th ♍

Color of the day: Silver
Incense of the day: Rosemary

Swift Justice Ritual

Legal troubles? Today's a great day
to do some magic to help resolve
them once and for all. But consider
yourself warned: this ritual will bring
about the fairest possible outcome,
whatever that may be. Cleanse a
hematite by bathing it in sunlight
for at least ten minutes. With hemp
twine, tie the hematite into a piece of
white or natural-colored flannel along
with two sprigs of fresh rosemary
and a tablespoon of dried elecampane
root. Hold the bundle in both hands

September 27
Tuesday

 4th ♍
☽ → ♎ 12:51 am
New Moon 7:09 am

Color of the day: Maroon
Incense of the day: Cedar

Change and New Tasks

The New Moon is traditionally a
time of new beginnings. Think
of something you'd like to start, or
a change you would like to make in
your life. Write this on a piece of

paper. Find a black plate or other dish and place your paper on it. On a black (or white) candle, carve either the word *begin* or the word *change* on the outside of the candle, depending on your need. Place the candle on top of your paper. Ideally, as the candle burns, wax will spill down to cover the paper. As you light the candle, visualize the change or new beginning you seek. Recite the following chant:

> New Moon candle, as you burn,
>
> Help me with this task.
>
> Soon your bright light will return,
>
> Bringing what I ask.

Allow the candle to burn until it's finished—this may take several days of re-lighting, depending on how much time you have. When it's complete, free the candle from the plate and break off the hardened puddle of wax and your paper. Bury these if you have a place to do so, or discard.

Ember Grant

September 28
Wednesday

 1st ♎

Color of the day: Topaz
Incense of the day: Lilac

Autumn Festival of the Great Goddess (Navaratri)

Today, the Hindu lunar calendar welcomes in autumn, and with this auspicious occasion, we greet the Mother of the Universe, Maa Durga. Called the Inaccessible One, she stands outside of time and space, fighting evil in the cosmic realm on our behalf. Traditionally, devotees light lamps and fast, opening their hearts through song and prayer, pouring out their love and appreciation to Her in all forms seen and unseen. Today, celebrate the gifts of Her grace through good thought, right action, and appropriate speech. Utter Her mantra,

> OM DUM DURGAYAI NAMAH

in four parts: first out loud, then whispered, then internally, then in complete silence, just allowing it to settle into the psychic fabric and matter of your beingness. In this way, you perform both an honoring and a prayer that takes you more deeply into resonance with the Divine Will.

Chandra Alexandre

 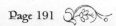

September 29
Thursday
Rosh hashanah

 1st ♎

☽ → ♏ 12:05 am

Color of the day: Crimson
Incense of the day: Nutmeg

hecate's house

Rosh Hashanah, the Jewish New Year, is a time of introspection and prayer, repentance, and spiritual renewal. It is also a time for putting your spiritual house in order. Call upon Hecate, goddess of the Dark Moon, the Crone of Greek mythology, for help. Hecate is the beginning and the end. Invoke her energy to help let go of outdated patterns, and to help establish new, healthy habits. Draw a house. Inside the house, write things that support you spiritually: helpful habits, routines, allies, and practices. Outside the house, list what is spiritually destructive. Say:

> Hecate be with me
> As I put my house in order,
> My spirit is strong and
> shining bright
> Help me to make what is
> wrong now right,
> Hecate be with me always.

Keep the list on your altar, review it frequently, and make conscious effort to keep your spiritual house in order.

Dallas Jennifer Cobb

September 30
Friday

 1st ♏

Color of the day: Purple
Incense of the day: Cypress

As Fate Would have It

As practitioners of magic, we certainly have a hand in our own destiny, but it pays to honor the forces beyond us that shape our lives. Perform a ritual to the Fates, Norns, and other weavers of the greater tapestry. Gather together the Wheel of Fortune card from your tarot deck or the Jera rune (ᛃ), gold and silver candles, white and black cords, and frankincense incense. Lay the card/rune on your altar and light the candles on either side. Hold the cords in your hands and say:

> Workers and weavers of life,
> I honor you this day.

Close your eyes and focus on the things in your life that have shaped who you are. As you do so, twist the cords together. When you are finished, knot the ends together and lay it on the altar. Close your ritual by thanking the Fates, requesting aid for any changes you'd like to make, extinguishing the candles, and burying your cords.

Castiel

October is the tenth month of the year. Its name is derived from the Latin word *octo*, meaning "eight," as it was the eighth month of the Roman calendar. Its astrological sign is Libra, the Scales (September 23–October 23), a cardinal-air sign ruled by Venus. October is autumn's promise fulfilled. The resplendent colored leaves dazzle us in hues of gold, crimson, and orange, blazing throughout forests and neighborhoods. This is truly a magical month, with its climactic major holiday, Samhain (which means "summer's end") on the 31st. This is the last harvest festival of the year, the night when it's said the veil between the worlds is thin—a night to honor our ancestors and the souls of the departed. This night came to be called All Hallows Eve since the Christians named the next day All Saints' Day—this is the origin of the name Halloween. Decorations for this night abound on nearly every doorstep. Jack-o'-lanterns light the darkness, and the crisp, cool air seems filled with enchantment. Leave an apple outside for wandering spirits and light a candle in the window to guide them on their journey. October's Full Moon is called the Blood Moon in honor of the sacrificed livestock that would feed families through the winter.

October 1
Saturday

1st ♏

☽ → ♐ 12:42 am

Color of the day: Blue
Incense of the day: Pine

Sending Magic with Candle Stubs

Most Witches and magical practitioners save the ends of their candles after they've burned down completely. Additionally, many people store dripped wax from candles used in magical ceremonies. Sometimes these candles are only those that had specific spells and prayers enchanted in them (which are usually first anointed and carved with symbols), but you can also save the wax from any candle that's been used in sacred space (such as those used on altars, or those that illuminate nighttime circles). If you've stored up an abundance of wax, you've basically got a spell on your hands! Make use of the wax by completely melting it in a pot on a double-boiler (this is essential, so the wax doesn't burn or destroy the pot). Pour the wax into a mason jar, putting a candlewick in the center and suspending the top of it with a chopstick (so the wick stays perfectly straight). Once completely cooled, ignite the candle and, keeping an eye on it, allow it to burn to the base. If you wish, add some energy to the candle by visualizing the vaporized wax sending its pent-up energy up to the cosmos. Once burnt out, sprinkle a bit of water and sea salt in the jar and toss it in the trash!

Raven Digitalis

Holiday lore: According to Shinto belief, during the month of October the gods gather to hold their annual convention. All of the *kami* converge on the great temple of Isumo in western Honshu, and there they relax, compare notes on crucial god business, and make decisions about humankind. At the end of this month, all over Japan, people make visits to their local Shinto shrines to welcome the regular resident gods back home. But until then, all through the month, the gods are missing—as a Japanese poet once wrote:

> The god is absent;
> the dead leaves are
> piling up,
> and all is deserted.

October 2
Sunday

1st ♐

Color of the day: Yellow
Incense of the day: Heliotrope

Dream a Journey with the Tarot

One of the reasons that famed psychiatrist Carl Jung was fond of tarot was because the images are nearly universal in the Western world. Empresses and priests all figure into tales that many of us grew up with, and those tales have formed assigned meanings. All you need to do to experience those archetypes face to face is to see them and loan them a bit of your will. You can have a tarot adventure in your personal dreamland by pulling the Fool out of the tarot deck and then by choosing the other cards you want to explore, whether that's the Eight of Cups or the Tower, right before bedtime. Spend twenty minutes before you go to sleep picturing yourself as the Fool leaping into the other cards. Carry these imaginings in your mind as you go to sleep. This may take several tries before the imagery builds in your deepest mind.

Diana Rajchel

October 3
Monday

1st ♐
☽ → ♑ 4:16 am
2nd Quarter 11:15 pm

Color of the day: White
Incense of the day: Lily

Sacred Devotions

In the Hindu traditions, the path of Bhakti, or devotion, is one of the quickest and most heart-opening paths to illumination. Through Bhakti we open to love, engage in love, and connect to the original whim of God to love Herself in all Her parts. This is the love that embraces the fullness of life, the love that kisses the Infinite. What in you connects to the fabric of love that flows through all things? Offer some of that love today to the Earth and to the gods. At your altar, leave a token of your love to feed the gods. Offer song, food, poetry, anything that your heart longs to offer. Allow yourself to breathe deep in the moment. Make your offering a spell that ripples through all the worlds bringing healing and connection to all beings. From love all things arose, to love we will return. Blessed be.

Abel R. Gomez

October 4
Tuesday

2nd ♑

Color of the day: Gray
Incense of the day: Basil

Catching the Rain

In many parts of the world, autumn brings the replenishing rains after the hot dry summer. Now is a good time to install a rain catchment system. It can be as simple as a single rain barrel connected to a downspout from your existing roof gutters. You can then use stored rainwater for irrigating your garden or lawn. Here is a blessing for your rain barrel:

> *Save up for a sunny day*
> *The abundance of the rain*
> *That thunderstorms send*
>   *my way*
> *For the clouds' loss is my*
>   *gain.*
> *Store water like hidden seed*
> *In a barrel fat and round*
> *Fast against a future need –*
> *Then I'll pour it on the*
>   *ground.*
> *Store abundance here as well*
> *Gathered from the fertile land*
> *Strengthened by this magic*
>   *spell*
> *'Til I call it to my hand.*

Elizabeth Barrette

October 5
Wednesday

2nd ♑

☽ → ♒ 11:18 am

Color of the day: Topaz
Incense of the day: Bay laurel

Tasseomancy

Tasseomancy (tasseography) is divination accomplished by reading tea leaves. To try it, you'll need loose tea or dried herbs, a teacup with a plain white interior, and a saucer. Place one teaspoon dried herbs or loose tea into the teacup. Fill the cup with freshly boiled water, top with the saucer, and steep for five minutes. Remove the saucer and enjoy the tea, leaving a bit of liquid in the bottom of the cup. Now is the time to pause and "ask" the tea leaves a silent question about what you'd like them to reveal. Cover the tea cup with your hand and swirl it deosil (sunwise) several times. Remove your hand and allow the marc—the wet leaf material—to settle. Observe it carefully. Are any shapes, patterns, or images (animals, trees, etc.) clearly apparent? Does the marc create any impressions or insights? Have you received an answer to your question?

Susan Pesznecker

October 6
Thursday

 2nd ≈≈

Color of the day: White
Incense of the day: Balsam

Day of Protection and Inner Guidance

Invoke the presence of the goddess Tara, Protector and Compassionate One, today when you awake and again before you go to sleep. She is the Star goddess who will help guide you out of unconscious realms wisely during your day and into them wisely as you sleep. During the day, be on the lookout for signs and synchronicities that will help lead you toward the best choices and outcomes. Tara will help keep you clear of ego, attachments, and other worldly or emotional entanglements as you come to each challenge or crossroads. At night, pay attention to your dreams and their special message to you, asking Her to help reveal the meaning of your visions. You may wish to chant Tara's special activating mantra,

*OM STRIM TARAYAI
SVAHA*

as you put your sacred intentions out into the world.

Chandra Alexandre

October 7
Friday

 2nd ≈≈

☽ → ♓ 9:13 pm

Color of the day: Pink
Incense of the day: Yarrow

Love Apples

This is a simple spell to bring you closer to your lover. Light a red candle. Take an apple, preferable a juicy red one, and cut it in half across the middle, revealing the seeds within. Carefully use the tip of the knife to remove the seeds. On an unlined piece of paper, and using red ink, write one attribute you look for in a significant other (or, if you're already in a stable relationship, write one attribute that you find attractive in your partner). Wrap the seeds in the paper and burn them in a fireproof dish, watching until it is all reduced to ashes. If you wish, allow the candle to burn a bit longer before blowing it out. It is done.

Laurel Reufner

October 8
Saturday

Yom Kippur

 2nd ♓

Color of the day: Brown
Incense of the day: Patchouli

Celtic Prayer for Sleep

Many traditional prayers were recited in Celtic countries throughout the day to give thanks for meals, to protect one during a journey, and to bless work and daily activities. There were also prayers for safe and restful sleep, such as this prayer from Scottish folk tradition. (Note: You may wish to invoke specific gods, goddesses, or other spiritual allies in the second verse.)

> May the gods protect the
> house, the fire, and the
> cattle
> Every one who dwells within
> tonight
> Shield me and my beloved
> group
> Preserve us from violence and
> harm
>
> The gods shall be at my feet
> The gods shall be at my back
> The gods shall be at my head
> The gods shall be at my side
>
> Preserve us and keep us this
> night in this place

> And in every place in which
> we dwell
> On this night and every
> night
> This night, and every night.

Sharynne MacLeod NicMhacha

October 9
Sunday

 2nd ♓

Color of the day: Amber
Incense of the day: Juniper

Prosperity Knot Spell

Sunday is a good day for doing manifestation work because Sunday governs success, prosperity, confidence, and hope. Harness these energies with this simple knot spell for manifesting or bringing something into your life. Use a red or gold cord for luck or prosperity. Hold it and envision clearly what you want to manifest. Nine is the number for renewal and new beginnings, so tie the cord nine times, with each knot binding your magical energy to what you want to create. Incant your intentions:

Knot one, the spell's begun

Knot two, I know what to do

Knot three, it will come to be,

Knot four, what I wish and more,

Knot five, my vision's alive,

Knot six, in the material world it's fixed,

Knot seven, tie earth to heaven,

Knot eight, influence fate,

Knot nine, now is the time,

I bind the mundane and divine.

And make what I wish, mine.

Dallas Jennifer Cobb

October 10
Monday
Columbus Day (observed)

 2nd ♓

☽ → ♈ 8:57 am

Color of the day: Lavender
Incense of the day: Clary sage

Explorer's Talisman Spell

Columbus Day reminds us of the great things that come when people have the courage to explore their world and make a difference for the future. Talismans have always been used to remind us of specific people, places, things, or feelings, and today would be a good day to select a talisman to help you explore your own world and encourage bravery in yourself to accomplish goals and dreams. Read about Christopher Columbus and think about how his life was a series of adventures and exploration. Chose a charm that would represent a significant aware-ness you get from reading about him, perhaps a ship in full sale to express adventure and seeking new lands. Perhaps an anchor would represent finding land and exploring the inte-rior. Each of these could represent your own feelings of reaching beyond yourself, or seeking within to explore your own ego.

Paniteowl

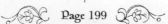

October 11
Tuesday

 2nd ♈
Full Moon 10:06 pm

Color of the day: White
Incense of the day: Cinnamon

happy hunting

Today is the Hunter's Moon. This Full Moon received its name for obvious reasons, the crops are in now and the hunting season has begun. What are you hunting for at this time of your life? A new job, a new home, or a new love? During this October Full Moon, why not tap into that "hunting" vibe and work a little Full Moon magic so you can find whatever it is you are hunting for. To begin take red or deep orange candle and engrave it with a Moon symbol. Then fix it securely in its holder. Allow it to burn in a safe place. Go outdoors and watch that Hunter's Moon rise tonight. Meditate on what it is that you wish to accomplish with the magic.

> As the Hunter's Moon lights up the night,
>
> May my goals and dreams all come to light.
>
> That which I am seeking, may I quickly find,
>
> I close up this spell with the sound of a rhyme.

By the full October Moon this hunting spell is now spun,

For the good of all, so mote it be and let it harm none.

Ellen Dugan

October 12
Wednesday

 3rd ♈
☽ → ♉ 9:35 pm

Color of the day: Brown
Incense of the day: Honeysuckle

Truth and Justice

On this day in 1692, the governor of Massachusetts sent the letter that ended the Salem Witch trials. In this season of remembering our ancestors, take time at your altar to light two candles—one white and one black. Light the white one for the victims of persecution, both those falsely accused and those hunted for their beliefs. Light the black one as a statement against intolerance, injustice, and violence. Obtain a list of the names of those persecuted and executed during the Salem Witch trials, the European Witch trials, and add names of people you know who have been discriminated against because they practice magic or are Wiccan, Asatru, Romani, Pagan, or even Jewish or Christian. Remember the many nameless victims being falsely accused of witchcraft even today in Africa, the Middle East, and India. Look at your list and light your candles every day between now and Samhain.

Castiel

October 13
Thursday
Sukkot begins

 3rd ♉

Color of the day: Crimson
Incense of the day: Jasmine

A healing Water Ritual

Since ancient times, societies have worshipped and celebrated water with festivals and magical rites. On this day in ancient Rome, a festival known as Fontinalia honored fountains and fresh drinking water. Remnants of Pagan water worship can be found today in the form of holy springs and wells throughout Europe. Many of these sites are reported to have water that contains healing properties. To create your own water ritual, cover a table or altar with a blue cloth and in the center place a clear glass or crystal bowl. Fill with bottled spring water, then add a few pink rose petals and a tablespoon of rose water. Gently stir the water with your finger in a clockwise direction. Relax, and feel all the negative feelings you've had recently being absorbed by the loving vibrations of this healing water. Leave the water undisturbed overnight. The next day sprinkle the water about your yard, or gently pour it onto a grassy area.

James Kambos

 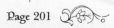

October 14
Friday

 3rd ♉

Color of the day: White
Incense of the day: Rose

Banish Leftover Negativity from Past Romance(s)

If you're having trouble manifest-ing a relationship, or manifesting a positive relationship, the problem might be that you're carrying around some leftover energy from a past rela-tionship or two. This energy can take many forms: cords of attachment to the old flame(s), outmoded patterns or limiting beliefs about yourself or romance in general, and/or lingering fears or wounds. Here's a ritual to help clear away this energy and create the space for beautiful new romantic conditions. (Before you begin, make sure you've let go of old gifts, letters, pictures, and other reminders of the old flame(s), as these will hold the old energy in place.) Smudge yourself with white sage smoke and say:

*Freya, love goddess, beautiful
and bold:*

*Please cleanse me and release
me from the old.*

Now light a white candle and soak in a sea salt bath into which you've strewn the petals of six white roses.

Tess Whitehurst

October 15
Saturday

 3rd ♉
☽ → ♊ 10:15 am

Color of the day: Gray
Incense of the day: Rue

A Binding Spell

Today is a good day for magic to dispel negativity or to get rid of an unwanted presence in your life—this includes any bad habits you wish to break. On a piece of paper, write down what you wish to bind. When you bind something you immobilize it, stop it in its tracks. Remember, you should never do a binding spell to cause harm to anyone or manipu-late another person. Roll your paper and tie a piece of ribbon or string around it, clinching it tight. Tie three knots and, for each knot, say the fol-lowing words:

*Bind this tight, hold it fast,
mind my words, make it last.
Let no harm come to me, for
the good of all so mote it be.*

Visualize your bad habit ending, or the bothersome person keeping his or her distance. Bury the paper outside in a place where it won't be disturbed.

Ember Grant

October 16
Sunday

3rd ♊

Color of the day: Amber
Incense of the day: Eucalyptus

Eat Mindfully

We all know the saying, "You are what you eat." Modern life makes it challenging to eat a healthy, balanced diet consisting entirely of natural and wholesome foods. Almost everything on grocery store shelves contains substances that seem appealing, but aren't really good for the human body. However, every little step helps move in the direction of healthy eating. For this spell, prepare one meal with all organic ingredients. As you shop, say:

> All this is the sort
> Of food I support.

As you cook your meal, say:

> Mix, measure, and make,
> Beat, batter, and bake:
> By my work and hands,
> So my conscience stands.

As grace before eating, say:

> We are what we eat,
> And so are complete.
> May we be as pure,
> As rich and secure,
> As all this good food.
> We give gratitude!

Elizabeth Barrette

October 17
Monday

3rd ♊
☽ → ♋ 9:38 pm

Color of the day: Ivory
Incense of the day: Rosemary

The Scrying Mirror

When we scry, we gaze into a reflective surface and open our "mind's eye," ready to receive information or visions. The scrying mirror is an ancient tool used by many of the old mystery schools. Scrying mirrors can be purchased, but they're simple to make.

An easy approach to creating a scrying mirror is with a medium-size photo frame. Clean the glass surface thoroughly and charge the framed glass with the four elements by sprinkling with salt water and passing through the smoke of a burning smudge. Dry carefully, then paint the glass with glossy black paint. Allow to dry well. To charge your mirror, expose it to the light of the Full Moon overnight. Once charged, wrap it in a black cloth. Use it only at night and never let sunlight touch the glass. To use, unwrap and gaze deeply into the mirror. What do you see?

Susan Pesznecker

October 18
Tuesday

 3rd ♋

Color of the day: Red
Incense of the day: Bayberry

Face Your Fears

In the darkness of mid-October, invoke Kali, the Hindu Triple Goddess of creation, preservation, and destruction. With her insatiable hunger, she births then devours. As the seasons slide toward death, now is time to face the fears that devour you. And Tuesday, ruled by Mars, is a day for courage. Sit quietly with your fears. Do not run, but turn to face them. Entertain worst-case scenarios; imagine yourself with cancer, poverty, or madness. Look deep into the face of fear, and see Kali, the Dark Mother. And remember, out of the darkness must come light. Now ask Kali to walk by your side, as you travel through the wheel of the seasons, journeying within to face your fear.

Abide with me Kali, and walk through my fires of fear. Be near in darkness, so that my fear may be revealed to light.

Dallas Jennifer Cobb

October 19
Wednesday

Sukkot ends

 3rd ♋
4th Quarter 11:30 pm

Color of the day: Yellow
Incense of the day: Lavender

Bettara-Ichi Day (Japanese Festival of Good Fortune)

Let Ebisu, Japanese god of luck and prosperity, inspire you to create a talisman. Begin by meditating upon the specific qualities of good fortune you seek to attract. For example, do you want a new job? Do you seek a lucky charm? Do you desire a bountiful crop or success on an exam? Now, choose a meaningful object to become the talisman and, holding it at your heart, direct this guiding intention to it with your mind. Breathe three times onto the object. Next, imbue it with the energies of the four elements, from earth to water to fire to air. You can do this using ritual tools or simply through visualization techniques. Finally, return it again to your heart and breathe with conscious intention another three times. Seal the rite with consecrating oil or a kiss. Your talisman is now ready to wear or place upon your altar. Good luck!

Chandra Alexandre

October 20
Thursday

 4th ♋
))→ ♌ 6:06 am

Color of the day: Green
Incense of the day: Nutmeg

Pinning It Down

This is a spell to pin down career goals, literally and figuratively. On a piece of paper, write down one goal you really need or want to achieve at work. On the other side of the paper, write down three to five steps for achieving that goal. Finally, fasten the paper, goal-side out, to a nearby corkboard where you can easily see it. When your goal has been realized, finish the spell by burning the paper. As you watch it burn, thank the universe for its assistance. (This spell would also work for a student.)

Laurel Reufner

October 21
Friday

 4th ♌

Color of the day: Pink
Incense of the day: Mint

Averting the Evil Eye

The "evil eye" has long been a term denoting negative energy being sent from one person onto another. The term carries the notion of covetousness, envy, and wishes of destruction—in other words, it's a curse. If you believe the "covetous gaze" might be put on you, consider a quick banishing ritual such as this. Also, be sure not to finger-point! It's much more productive to protect yourself, regardless of the source. Before you go to sleep for the night, go outside and construct a large eye shape on the patio just outside the door. Do this by pouring black pepper in an artistic formation. (To make lines with pepper, just use the "pour" side of a store-bought pepper container.) Once you've made this eye (even very simple one), do the same at all other doorways leading outside of the house. When you wake up in the morning, go outside and blow the eyes away using forceful breaths. Conclude by saying:

> Evil eye, you must flee! Leave
> this place, so mote it be!

Raven Digitalis

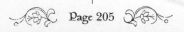

October 22
Saturday

 4th ♌
☽ → ♍ 10:40 am

Color of the day: Blue
Incense of the day: Sandalwood

Celebrate Astarte

Today is thought to be the festival day of Astarte, a Phoenician goddess of sexuality and of war. She is honored with the Festival of Willows. I find this to be highly appropriate, as the willow is associated with the Divine Feminine, the element of water, and has the astrological correspondence of the Moon. Today, gather some small supple branches from a willow tree and create a garland. Wear the willow in your hair, and meditate on Astarte and get to know this deity. See what she teaches you.

> Astarte, ancient goddess, I call upon you,
>
> I ask you, great Lady, to please grant me a boon.
>
> By the power of willow and the waning Moon,
>
> May I be blessed with enchantment and wisdom true.
>
> By the waning Moon this meditation is begun,

> May enlightenment, wisdom, hope, and peace, surely come.

Ellen Dugan

October 23
Sunday

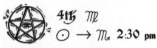 4th ♍
☉ → ♏ 2:30 pm

Color of the day: Gold
Incense of the day: Marigold

To help Someone Feel Safe

After suffering serious violence, a person may have trouble sleeping, finding peace of mind, or even breathing regularly. While only time and professional treatment will heal all the wounds that caused this state of fear, you can create a place that holds a mood of comfort and safety if that person lives with you or comes into a space you have regular control over. Place amethysts in each corner of a room, and spray a tea made from hops flower, valerian, and cinnamon in the space. Stand in the center of the room and chant:

> Here you are safe, in protected space.
>
> In this place, dwell in grace.

Repeat this spell frequently and charge the amethysts under the sun once a month. Encourage this person to seek help with the situation that has him/her living in fear, and be as compassionate and empowering as you can.

Diana Rajchel

October 24
Monday

4th ♏
☽ → ♎ 11:49 am

Color of the day: Lavender
Incense of the day: Neroli

House Blessing

Celebrate a new home or apartment with a house blessing. You'll need a new broom, a protective smudge (cedar and sage are good choices), bread, wine, and salt. Light the smudge and walk the grounds, moving around the property's perimeter sunwise (deosil). At each cardinal point (north, east, south, west), pause and acknowledge the guardian of that direction and ask for benevolent protection. Next, take the salt, bread, and wine and stand at the main entrance. Repeat the following, handing each item to the homeowner:

> *Bless this home and all who enter!*
>
> *Here is bread, that you never hunger.*
>
> *Here is wine, that you never thirst.*
>
> *Here is salt, that your life always be well seasoned!*

Enter through the front door, sharing hugs and handshakes. Move through the house deosil, smudging it. As each room is smudged, the homeowner should use the broom to sweep old, stale energies toward and out of the front door. Blessed be!

Susan Pesznecker

October 25
Tuesday

4th ♎

Color of the day: Black
Incense of the day: Ylang-ylang

Let Go of Guilt

Holding on to guilt doesn't do anyone any good. And everyone makes mistakes! Today's a great day to forgive yourself for yours so that you can move forward into a beautiful future. Start with three white candles. Relax and let your mind move to the reason(s) for your guilt. Light one candle and say:

I am willing to let go of guilt.

Now gently conjure up a feeling of love in your heart. Surround the situation with this feeling of love, then light the second candle and say:

I am willing to transform guilt.

Inhale, close your eyes tightly and tense up every muscle in your body, and then fully release all the tension. Light the third candle as you say:

I now choose to forgive myself completely. I now surrender to the perfection of the present moment.

Allow the candles to burn for at least forty minutes, and then extinguish.

Tess Whitehurst

October 26
Wednesday

4th ♎
☽ → ♏ 11:08 am
New Moon 3:56 pm

Color of the day: White
Incense of the day: Lilac

Potion Party

There is sometime special about the Halloween season. Our beloved dead walk among us and the entire world is immersed in magic and mystery. Even the most skeptical are willing to at least try something magical. So how can you engage even the most skeptical of your friends and still do some magic? Throw a potion party, of course! The magic of the Mysterious Ones flows through all things. Herbs, crystals, news clippings, candles, paint, even the food we eat all have the potential to spin spells in motion and manifest our wills. Food can be particularly powerful because it is something we have every day. Gather a group of friends, magical or otherwise, for an evening of magical and edible potion making. Everyone can bring a different beverage and fruit. Once everyone has arrived, lay the fruit and beverages out and invite guests to intuitively pick fruits. If they're having trouble, you can always keep a copy of *Cunningham's Encyclopedia of Wicca in the Kitchen* by Scott Cunningham out as a resource. Once everyone has made their own brew, guide them in charging them with intention. Then, let the party begin as the beverages are passed around and the energy of the potion changes people. Who says magic can't be fun?

Abel R. Gomez

halves together with the cord—white for any purpose, black for protection, red for love, green for money, blue for healing—and make sure to leave ends at the top about six inches each. Tie the apple spell to a tree limb and walk backwards for five steps, keeping your eyes on it. Before you turn away say:

> As you return to earth and Sun, let my magical will be done.

Castiel

October 27
Thursday

1st ♏

Color of the day: White
Incense of the day: Jasmine

An Apple a Day

Here is a quick and easy spell formula that you can adapt to almost any situation. All you need is an apple, an herb, and a colored cord corresponding to your purpose. Cut the apple in half crosswise, so that you can see the five-pointed star within. On one half, place the herb that you have chosen—bay leaf for protection, basil for love, mint for money, lavender for healing—and then place the other half on top. Focusing on your purpose, bind the

October 28
Friday

1st ♏
☽ → ♐ 10:45 am

Color of the day: Coral
Incense of the day: Thyme

A Black Candle Spell

Now the Earth retreats into darkness as we enter the dark half of the year. The darkness has a special energy of its own which aids in magical work. This spell draws upon the subtle energies found in darkness, which propel magic into the unseen realm more quickly. After sunset, preferably well after dark, cast a circle or say a protective prayer. Walk clockwise around your space as you carry a black candle, but do not light it. Speak Words of Power and announce your desire, whatever it might be. Rub the candle to charge it. Feel your magic being absorbed by the candle. As you near the end of your spell, put the candle down in a safe place and light it. The flame is now releasing your need into the cosmos. Let the candle burn out. Your wish will be fulfilled. So mote it be.

James Kambos

October 29
Saturday

1st ♐

Color of the day: Indigo
Incense of the day: Sage

harvest home Wreath

Now is the time to prepare for the coming winter. A house blessing can easily be put together to encourage health, wealth, and comfort through the cold months to come. You'll need:

Grapevines for wreath (if you can find the vine and weave the wreath yourself, so much the better)
Dried pumpkin seeds threaded on cotton thread, NOT polyester!
Holly berries threaded on cotton thread
Dried slices of apple and oranges laced with cotton thread
Small balls of suet rolled in birdseed and laced with cotton thread
Three ears of Indian corn

Tie the three ears of corn together to form a trine. Tie the corns to the wreath. Weave the strings of berries, fruits, and seeded suet around and through the ears of corn. Place the wreath near the door to your home you use most often. This is not just for decoration, but also to help sustain the life around you, as you ask for your own life to be sustained and nurtured through the winter. Sympathetic magic works!

Paniteowl

Holiday lore: Many villages in the English countryside share the tradition of "lost-in-the-dark bells." Legend tells of a person lost in the dark or fog, heading for disaster, who at the last moment was guided to safety by the sound of church bells. The lucky and grateful survivor always leaves money in his or her will for the preservation of the bells. This day commemorates one particular such case, a man named Pecket in the village of Kidderminster, in Worcestershire, who was saved from plummeting over a ravine by the bells of the local church of St. Mary's. In honor of this event, the bells still ring every October 29.

October 30
Sunday

1st ♐
☽ → ♑ 12:39 pm

Color of the day: Orange
Incense of the day: Eucalyptus

Prayer for a Blessed Passing
In Celtic tradition, it was believed that good weather at the time of death heralded a peaceful passing, and people wished a *bas sóna* ("happy death") would be the fate of each

and every person. Here are some traditional prayers recited for a sacred passing:

*You go home tonight to your
home of winter
To your home of autumn,
and spring, and summer
You go home this night to
your eternal home.*

*Sleep now, sleep, and away
with your sorrow
The sleep of the seven lights
be yours, beloved
The sleep of the seven joys be
yours, beloved.*

*Death without fear, with joy
and forgiveness
As the Sun of the skies pours
its love on your body
As you travel to the dwelling
place of peace.*

*Sleep now, sleep, and away
with your sorrow
A death of peace and
tranquility
This night the brightness
and summertime shall
come!*

Sharynne MacLeod NicMhacha

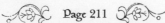

·October 31
Monday
halloween – Samhain

 1st ♑

Color of the day: White
Incense of the day: Narcissus

A Light to Guide the Spirits

Tonight is often called the Witches' New Year, a night of celebration, when the veil between the worlds is thin. Samhain (Summer's End) is the ancient Celtic festival at the root of our modern Halloween. Traditionally, ancestors were honored tonight and candles were placed in windows to guide their spirits. For this spell, you can use your Halloween jack-o'-lantern or create a special one carved with celestial symbols. Place a candle inside the pumpkin and set it in a place of prominence in your home or on your porch. To personalize the candle to honor a specific person who has passed, carve their name in the candle. Bless it with the following chant:

> On this night, a hallowed
>   eve,
> Spirits walking, roaming free,
> Guide them with this
>   glowing light,
> They have no need to bring
>   us fright.

Ember Grant

 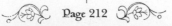

November 2
Wednesday

 1st ♒︎
2nd Quarter 12:38 pm

Color of the day: Yellow
Incense of the day: Lavender

Woden's Wild horses

This is the Festival of Woden. In AD 998 it became a Christian festival, All Souls' Day, drawing inspiration from the original heathen one. Asatruar celebrated Woden as god of the dead. They paraded the Hodening "wild horse," also known as the winter mare of Cailleach. They dressed in costumes for sacred theater, presenting plays that revealed the cycle of life, death, and rebirth. Women baked "soul cakes" for living and dead alike, another custom that survived into later versions of this holiday. Chances are, you just honored the dead on Samhain, so let's do something different for Woden's festival. Honor the wild horses. They symbolize liberty and independence; it uplifts even the most downtrodden spirit to see wild horses running free over open ground. Visit their sanctuaries, read about them, or make a donation to help ensure that there will always be wild horses in the world.

Elizabeth Barrette

November 3
Thursday

 2nd ♒︎

Color of the day: Crimson
Incense of the day: Clove

Thor's Day, Protect and Prosper

Today we have the planetary association of Jupiter and a waxing Moon phase. This is most auspicious for prosperity and protective spells. Also, Thursday is Thor's day. This day of the week was literally named after him. This Norse god was called the god of the people. He is the everyman's god. He represented the farmer as well as the warrior. Thor is associated with rain and crops, and his hammer is both a protective and a fertility symbol. You may call on Thor for protection and prosperity magic. Light a green candle and repeat the following charm.

> By the light of a waxing
>   Moon,
> May the god Thor grant me
>   a boon
> Send protection and
>   prosperity to me,
> Please grant my request with .
>   all possible speed.
> By Thursday's magic this
>   spell is spun,
> For the good of all, bringing
>   harm to none.

Ellen Dugan

 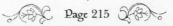

November 4
Friday

2nd ≈

☽ → ♓ 3:18 am

Color of the day: Coral
Incense of the day: Cypress

See the history of an Object

If you find an object that seems to carry a story, try to scry the tale. With the object in your hand, sit in front of a mirror in a darkened room. Have a friend light a candle behind you. Close your eyes, count from ten to one, and then open them and look at the object in the mirror with your eyes slightly unfocused. Tell your friend the impressions coming to mind or that you glimpse in the mirror—colors, shapes, people, faces. If you're losing the thread and think about other things, count from ten to one and repeat the exercise. Keep going until the images and concepts begin repeating. When finished, turn on the light and see what you have found out. If you can, do some library research on the object and see how it might match what you found out with the mirror divination.

Diana Rajchel

November 5
Saturday

2nd ♓

Color of the day: Blue
Incense of the day: Patchouli

Wail and Moan Spell

During the month of the Mourning Moon, let Demeter walk with you. Her daughter Persephone, the light of Demeter's life, was stolen away. And Demeter mourned. As the seasons change, let your unexpressed grief arise and be felt. As the days grow short, mourn for the loss of the sun. As the nights grow long, cry for the passing of summer. As the wheel of the year turns, wail for your lost youth, the failures of your body, the growing frailties of age. In a dark and quiet space, let your grief rise up, a tide that overflows your eyes and your throat. Wail, moan, scream, and cry like Mother Demeter mourning the loss of "the light of your life." Grief is part of life. Just as spring is followed by summer, autumn, and winter, buds go to flower, fruit, and seed, so life leads to loss, death, and later, rebirth.

Dallas Jennifer Cobb

November 6
Sunday

Daylight Saving Time ends 2 am

 2nd ♓

☽ → ♈ 2:02 pm

Color of the day: Gold
Incense of the day: Almond

Autumn's End
(Northern hemisphere)

This is a time when we begin to move from metaphysical inner world attentiveness to deeper transformational soul work. In the Southern Hemisphere, we go from relationship to pursuit of our individual dreams. But, we must consider the chains that bind. Where are you stuck? Light a black candle anointed with sandalwood or geranium oil, having carved on it a word or representation of whatever you wish to release. Do a focused meditation by gazing at the candle flame, unblinking, for as long as possible. Remember to breathe into your belly fully, exhaling by forcing air through your throat to produce an oceanlike sound. During the spell, first activate and then sever associations with your word or image. You are done when your inscription has melted—or you feel the work completed. Allow the candle to burn all the way down, or keep it for other similar spells.

Chandra Alexandre

November 7
Monday

 2nd ♈

Color of the day: White
Incense of the day: Neroli

Remove a Curse Spell

If you feel you're the victim of a curse or any negative magic, this spell will remove all negativity. For this spell you'll need a piece of paper, a craft pen with brown ink, and three small hawthorn branches with the thorns intact. Begin by making a quick sketch on the paper of a house. This could resemble your house or the kind of house you'd like to have. It doesn't need to be fancy. Around your sketch draw a circle. What you're doing is surrounding your home space with protective brown earth energy. Beneath your sketch write out why you think you've been cursed. Next, in your cauldron or fireplace ignite the hawthorn branches and burn the paper in this ritual fire as you say:

> Curse be burned, curse be
> turned. Curse be gone, with
> harm to none!

After the ashes cool, scatter them randomly outdoors. Like the ashes you've scattered, the curse's power will also break down.

James Kambos

 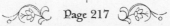

November 8
Tuesday
Election Day

 2nd ♈

Color of the day: Red
Incense of the day: Ginger

Leadership Enhancement

It's interesting that Election Days fall on Tuesdays, the day of Mars, the warrior god. The influence of this day includes strength, action, leadership, protection, and politics. No matter what your part is in today's Election Day, it's a good day to work magic for leadership ability, or to send that energy to aid world leaders in their decisions. Focus either on yourself or on wishing strong leadership for the good of all. Light a red or white candle, and sprinkle the area around it with dried basil. Visualize yourself (or others) as a successful leader, guiding others with love, compassion, and respect. Light the candle and use the following chant:

> Lead with love and guide
> with care,
>
> Empower people everywhere.
>
> Understanding is the key,
>
> For good of all, so mote it be.

Use this chant for yourself any time you are in a leadership role and need a boost of confidence.

Ember Grant

November 9
Wednesday

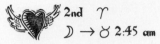 2nd ♈
☽ → ♉ 2:45 am

Color of the day: White
Incense of the day: Lilac

Healing Conflict

Even the best of friends sometimes find themselves in conflict. It's part of life. If you find yourself in a situation that you are ready to heal, light a blue candle in your ritual space or in an area where you will not be disturbed. Take a breath and speak to the other person's higher self, apologizing for your role in the conflict. Breathe some love to this person. If the person is attacking you or causing unnecessary drama, create an energetic boundary between you and this person. Visualize a strong, white barrier surrounding you and say:

> I block all harm in my
> direction.
>
> I reflect love and healing to
> you.
>
> May I be forgiven for my
> deeds.
>
> I forgive you, too.

Repeat the spell for seven days. Spend some time thinking about the situation and your role. What in the conflict is your doing? Be willing to look within to heal. Approach the situation with love in your heart and you can do no wrong.

Abel R. Gomez

November 10
Thursday

 2nd ♉
☽ Full Moon 3:16 pm

Color of the day: Turquoise
Incense of the day: Carnation

Full Moon Elemental Spell

Build a fire outside. This can be in your yard, or in a small cauldron on a porch, or simply an arrangement of candles on your windowsill. When the Full Moon is visible, set a shallow bowl of water in front of your fire positioned in such a way so that the Moon and the flames are reflected in the surface of the water. Sprinkle ground cinnamon on the surface of the water, and light incense of dragon's blood. Fan the incense across the water in your bowl so the images ripple, saying:

Mother Moon hear my call

Elementals one and all

Hear the spell I cast tonight

*While bathed in Mother
  Moon's pure light*

Then state your desire clearly. Be very sure you know exactly what you want. Wait at least a quarter of an hour before snuffing your candles and emptying the bowl.

Paniteowl

November 11
Friday
Veterans Day

 3rd ♉

☽ → ♊ 3:10 pm

Color of the day: Purple
Incense of the day: Violet

The Ancestors

Most magical traditions provide some way to honor their ancestors—those who have gone before. Here are some ways to honor your dear departed:

1. Set up an ancestor altar. Place pictures of your departed loved ones. Use colors and decor that would have been pleasing to them, and add reminiscent artifacts. I regularly leave a shot of good scotch when thinking about my Uncle Jim, while reflections on my beloved grandmother involve her small iron cauldron or her rolling pin.

2. Honor them at special meals by setting them a place at the table. You might even cook up one of their favorite dishes. Don't forget to offer them a toast!

3. Use scrying tools (mirrors, crystal balls, fire) or other divination tools to speak with or consult your ancestors. Remember: they still love you, and they're still watching over and are available to you—their influences are a strong part of your everyday life.

Susan Pesznecker

Historical lore: Veterans Day commemorates the armistice that ended the Great War in 1918. Oddly, this war ended on this day, November 11, at 11 am (the 11th hour of the 11th day of the 11th month). Though Congress changed Veterans Day to another date in October at one point during this century, in 1968 they returned the holiday to November 11, where it stands today. The number 11 is significant. In numerology, it is one of the master numbers that cannot be reduced. The number 11 life path has the connotation of illumination and is associated with spiritual awareness and idealism—particularly regarding humanity. It makes sense then that this collection of 11s commemorates the end of an event that was hoped to be the War to End All Wars. Unfortunately, it wasn't the last such great war, but we can at least set aside this day to ruminate on notions of peace to humankind.

November 12
Saturday

3rd ♊

Color of the day: Black
Incense of the day: Pine

Clear the Energy in Your home

A perfect day for a space clearing! Begin by clapping loudly around the perimeter of each area of your home, paying special attention to corners and anywhere else you imagine stagnant energy might be hiding. This will begin to lift and loosen negative energy. Open the windows if weather permits and burn a bundle of dried white sage so that it's smoking like incense. (Carry a dish underneath it to catch the embers.) Move the smoke around the perimeter of each area. Attune the energy to a high vibration in each area by ringing a chime or bell. Add a touch of sweetness by misting each area with rose water. Finally, stand in a central location with your hands in prayer pose. Close your eyes and verbally affirm the conditions you'd like to experience in your home, such as "harmony," "abundance," and "peace."

Tess Whitehurst

November 13
Sunday

3rd ♊

Color of the day: Yellow
Incense of the day: Frankincense

Purging Parasitic Energies

If there's any chance you have parasitic energies attached to your person, consider this spell. First, think of any possible reason you might feel this way. (Remember that it's good to contemplate, but not good to play the blame-game.) Could another person be unconsciously draining your energy? Is it possible that you have astral "floaters" or leeches attached to your energy sphere? Could it be a harmful spirit of some variety? Is there something else that's sucking your life force? Is it your job, an unhealthy relationship, or discontent in another situation? Look for a practical solution. In addition to these "real-life" steps, you can incorporate magic by using the herb wormwood. Wormwood has long been used medicinally to purge internal parasites from the digestive tract. Similarly, it can be used energetically to purge parasitic energies. To perform a spell of this nature, construct a ritual space as you normally would. Think of a word or a phrase to repeat as a mantra, such as:

> Flee from me, parasitic
> energy. So mote it be!

Work yourself into an "ecstatic" state—one that allows for personal freedom and experimental magical action. As you chant your mantra, surround yourself in wormwood by throwing the dried herb around you, rolling around in it, burning it and smudging yourself with its smoke, and drinking some wormwood tea. (Please keep in mind that wormwood can be toxic in large doses, so don't drink more than a small cup's worth.) After you've surrounded yourself in the essence of wormwood, visualize yourself as cleansed and purified, thank the spirits, and close the circle.

Raven Digitalis

November 14
Monday

 3rd ♊

☽ → ♋ 2:19 am

Color of the day: Silver
Incense of the day: Lily

Spell Against the Evil Eye

There were many spells and charms in Scotland to cure the effects of the evil eye. The formula was only effective if passed down from man to woman, and from woman to man. It was used in conjunction with water from a stream over which both the living and the dead passed.

> I trample upon the evil eye
> As the horse upon the plain
> and the swan upon the water
>
> Power of wind I have over it
> Power of fire I have over it
> Power of thunder and
>   lightning
>
> Power of storms I have over it
> Power of Moon I have over it
> Power of Sun and of stars
>
> A part of it upon the grey
>   stones
> A part of it upon the steep
>   hills
> And a portion of it upon the
>   swift waterfalls

*A part of it upon the great,
salt sea*
*She herself is the best
instrument to carry it*
The great, salt sea.

*In the name of the Sacred
Three*
*In the name of all the Secret
Ones*
*And of the powers all
together.*

Sharynne MacLeod NicMhacha

the wolf, for the greater good. Tyr, or Tiw, is a good deity to call on for integrity, fair play, and justice. Be warned that if you invoke Tyr in legal matters, such as a court case, you should be absolutely sure that you are the one in the right, or the magic could backfire on you.

*Tyr, Tuesday is devoted to
you,*

*Bring your wisdom and
justice true,*

*Help me to defend that which
is mine,*

*Grant me your protection for
all time.*

Ellen Dugan

November 15
Tuesday

3rd ♋

Color of the day: White
Incense of the day: Basil

Integrity and Justice

The day gets its name from the Norse god Tyr. You may also see his name spelled as Tiw, or Tiu. This day of the week was called Tiwesdaeg by the Anglo-Saxons. Tyr is the Norse god of justice and legal matters. He is associated with the sword and the spear, and he sacrificed his one arm restraining Fenrir

November 16
Wednesday

 3rd ♋

☽ → ♌ 11:17 am

Color of the day: Brown
Incense of the day: Bay laurel

Contact Your Ancestors Spell

In November the spirit realm is closer to us; this is a perfect time to contact your loved ones who've passed over to the other side. For this ritual you'll need to use a magic mirror. Cover your altar with black fabric and place the magic mirror upon your altar. Light a black candle, and in front of the candle place a photo of the deceased relative you wish to contact. Begin gazing into the mirror. You may call upon your ancestor or ask them a question. The mirror will mist over, then the face of your relative will appear. They'll probably look younger than you remember them. They may speak to you or convey their answer by a gesture. Each of us will see things differently. Expect your session to last about fifteen minutes. Thank your ancestor and ground yourself by eating a small snack.

James Kambos

November 17
Thursday

 3rd ♌

Color of the day: Green
Incense of the day: Apricot

When Faith Falters

There's much more in the world to lose faith in than just God(s). You can find your trust in your partner wavering, or your belief that the people around you have good intentions. When this happens, it is not a time to be silent, but a time when you need to make it known that you need reason for hope and trust. While asking for a sign too often might wind up with an unfortunate lightning strike, you can gently ask for a little help with this method: Every time you feel completely overwhelmed by despair, write down what grieves you on a slip of paper and place it in a bowl or jar. Once a month, take these slips of paper out, read them aloud and burn them— you are telling the divine that these are the things you need help with. Always ask that divine assistance help gently.

Diana Rajchel

November 18
Friday

3rd ♌
4th Quarter 10:09 am
☽ → ♍ 5:19 pm

Color of the day: White
Incense of the day: Vanilla

Anise Friendship Cookies

Cream together 1 cup softened butter with 1 granulated cup sugar and 1 cup packed brown sugar. Beat in 1 egg. Mix together 2½ cups flour with 1 teaspoon baking soda, and ½ teaspoon each salt, cinnamon, and cloves. Stir in ½ cup chopped pecans (I always consider nuts optional.)and 1 tablespoon anise. Shape into two rolls measuring 10 inches long. Wrap in plastic wrap and refrigerate for at least 4 hours. Cut into ¼-inch thick slices. Bake about 2 inches apart on ungreased baking sheets at 375 degrees F for 8 to 10 minutes. Share with friends and loved ones.

Laurel Reufner

November 19
Saturday

4th ♍

Color of the day: Indigo
Incense of the day: Sage

Protection Charm

According to folk customs, today is Warlock Day, when strangers in black should be avoided. Most Witches adore black clothing and meeting magic workers of any tradition. Even so, it's always good to have a little protection charm with you. Gather together a small black cloth, string, a small pentacle charm, and dried garlic, rosemary, and bay. Place the ingredients on the black cloth and tie a string around the edges to create a pouch. Hold the charm between your hands and visualize the charm emanating protective purple like. Say something like:

> By Sun and Moon,
> by Earth and Sea
> This magical bag
> shall protect me.

Seal the spell by saying something like:

> For the good of all
> And the harm of none
> I spin this spell
> So shall it be done.

Carry the charm with you to protect you from any harm.

Abel R. Gomez

November 20
Sunday

 4th ♏
)→ ♎ 8:16 pm

Color of the day: Amber
Incense of the day: Eucalyptus

health and Energy

Sunday is a good day for magic concerning health. Since the Moon is in a waning phase today, focus on removing bad habits or barriers to your well-being. Would you like to quit smoking? Are you making excuses to avoid exercise? Do you eat too much junk food? Sprinkle a pinch of ground cinnamon on a plate. Put some citrus juice in a glass, set it in the center of the plate, and then put yellow or white candles around it. Use at least three candles and carve words or symbols that represent your goal into each one. As you light the candles, visualize their positive energy infusing the juice. Know that as the candles burn they will transform the negativity and bad habits. Chant three times:

> Sun and Fire, give to me,
> health and vital energy.

After ten minutes, drink the juice. Let the candles burn out.

Ember Grant

November 21
Monday

 4th ♎

Color of the day: Ivory
Incense of the day: Hyssop

Friendship Spell

Although we may have many acquaintances in our lives, a true friend is a treasure we should honor and respect. Sometimes we take our friends for granted and forget to tell them how much their friendship enhances our life. Here is an easy spell to encourage the friendship to grow and last forever.
Take a picture of your friend and hold it in your hand. Look closely and think about the things you know will give your friend pleasure. Next, get a basket and fill it with things your friend will like. You might add fresh herbs or essential oils. You might include a gift certificate to a day spa or an oil change for a car. Yes, add gourmet coffee blends or specialty teas, as well as homemade cookies or chocolate truffles.
Write a note stating:

> Thank you for being my
> friend

. . . and that's all you need to say.

Paniteowl

 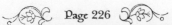

November 22
Tuesday

 4th ♎
☉ → ♐ 11:08 am
☽ → ♏ 8:58 pm

Color of the day: Gray
Incense of the day: Ginger

Weirding Stones

Weirding stones are used for divination. They provide a simple Yes-No system that's easy to make and fun to use. You'll need three stones of about the same size and shape. One should be red, one whitish, and one dark. Here are some possible choices:

Red: bloodstone, garnet, red agate, ruby, cinnabar, red fluorite
White: moonstone, opal, milky quartz, white marble
Black or gray: obsidian and snowflake obsidian, onyx, hematite

Once you've gathered the stones, store them in a small bag (yellow or indigo for psychic powers) and keep them with you—day and night—for seven days. This will allow the stones to bond with you, making them receptive to your questions and intuition. To use the weirding stones, visualize your question, then toss them onto a flat surface. The white stone indicates "yes" and the black stone "no." The red stone is the marker; whichever stone falls closest to it holds the answer to your question.

Susan Pesznecker

November 23
Wednesday

 4th ♏

Color of the day: Brown
Incense of the day: Marjoram

Uncover a Secret, Solve a Mystery

Do you suspect your partner is having an affair? Or do you need to find out who keeps stealing your mail? If you're ready to get to the bottom of something, this spell might be just the thing. But take note: it will only work to reveal dishonesties and/or unravel mysteries in a fair and just way. In other words, it won't work just to find dirt on someone, or if your motivation is otherwise in the slightest bit impure. Just before midnight, take your household broom to an out-of-the-way three-way crossroads. (Ideally, no cars will pass during the spell.) If it's too dark to see, light a black

 Page 227

candle or oil lantern. Sweep the area in the middle of the crossroads as you chant:

> Hecate, Hecate, goddess of night,
>
> Reveal the secrets, make everything right.

Leave three heads of garlic at the crossroads as an offering to Hecate.

Tess Whitehurst

November 24
Thursday

Thanksgiving Day

 4th ♏

☽ → ♐ 8:57 pm

Color of the day: White
Incense of the day: Mulberry

Giving Thanks for Peace

Many of us have given thanks for the Earth's bounty at our Mabon feast but will still gather with family and friends today for Thanksgiving, and such gatherings can be stressful. Make up a sachet to carry with you to dispel stress wherever you go today. In a white spell

bag place a piece of hematite, a piece of rose quartz, lavender, chamomile, rosemary, and yarrow. Take the sachet with you to a place where you feel safe and at peace, and hold it to your heart. Say the following chant to charge it:

> Flowing waves of serenity
>
> Wash over me, wash over me
>
> I breathe in peace, it fills me
>
> Serenity, wash over me

Carry your sachet on your person, and hold it in your hand when you are feeling particularly frazzled. Take a deep breath, and maybe repeat the chant again in your head. May your Turkey Day be stress-free!

Castiel

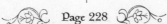

November 25
Friday

 4th ♐
New Moon 1:10 am

Color of the day: Rose
Incense of the day: Orchid

A highland Prayer for the New Moon

In Scotland, the New Moon was honored as the start of a new cycle, and people kept a silver coin in their pocket that they turned three times when they first saw the new crescent Moon, known as *Rioghainn na h-oidhche*, "Queen of the Night." Here are some traditional Celtic verses which were recited upon first seeing the New Moon:

> Hail to you, New Moon
> Beautiful Guiding One of
> the Sky
> Hail to you, New Moon,
> Beautiful Loved One of my
> Heart!
>
> I am bending my knee to you
> I am giving you my hand
> I am lifting my eye to you
> New Moon of the Seasons!
>
> You are traveling in your
> path
> You are steering the full tides
> You are illuminating your
> face to us
> New Moon of the Seasons!

> Holy be each thing
> Which she illuminates
> Fragrant be every night
> On which she shines!

Sharynne MacLeod NicMhacha

November 26
Saturday
Islamic New Year

 1st ♐
☽ → ♑ 10:05 pm

Color of the day: Gray
Incense of the day: Ivy

Increasing happiness

Numerous studies have been done with the herb Saint John's wort. While the FDA won't attest to its effectiveness in balancing the mind and increasing happiness, numerous people swear by it. If you haven't tried Saint John's wort for issues of depression, you may wish to research it a little more and give it a shot. (However, consult your health-care practitioner before incorporating any medicines into your system, herbal or synthetic.) In the meantime, or in conjunction with interna

Saint John's wort treatments, you can perform this working every morning when you wake up. Gather a handful of the dried herb and find a comfortable spot outside of your home. If you are taking a tincture or capsules of Saint John's wort, bring them outside with you with a glass of water. Hold the herb up to the Sun (cupped in your hands) and say:

> Holy John, Holy Sun,
> increase my wellness and
> bring me joy.

Envision the herbs surrounded in glowing sunlight, filling them with the light of the cosmos and the light of hope. Once you've meditated for a few minutes, swallow the capsules or tincture with water (if you are taking it internally), and sprinkle the dried herb around you in a clockwise circle. Sit there for a moment and soak up the vibrations, also envisioning the rays of the Sun illuminating the herbal circle and entering the brow of your head. Assure yourself that you're filled with additional sunlight and the medicine of Saint John's wort, and be sure to tackle the day with a smile.

Raven Digitalis

November 27
Sunday

 1st ♍

Color of the day: Orange
Incense of the day: Heliotrope

helpful horus

Sunday governs health and healing, and is a good day for protective magic. Invoke the Egyptian god Horus, the god of light and healing. Horus appears with the head of a falcon and the body of a man. The Eye of Horus, or the all-seeing eye, is a symbol used in many cultures to ward off evil. Invoke Horus to enlighten you and aid you in times of illness, injury, and recovery, but also call on Horus to protect you. Light a white candle, and looking into the bright flame, invoke Horus.

> Horus heal me, keep me safe,
> Protect my mind, body, and
> spirit.
> Watch over my home, my
> family, and friends,
> Keep us safe, healthy, and
> light.
> Protect my car, my yard, my
> community
> Be with me as I travel.
> Horus, heal me, make me
> whole, keep me filled with
> light and life.
> Brighten me, and keep away
> evil.

Dallas Jennifer Cobb

 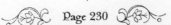

November 28
Monday

1st ♑

Color of the day: Lavender
Incense of the day: Narcissus

The Serpent of Sustainability

As Pagans, we draw inspiration from the world around us. Nature functions in cycles, where the waste output by one system becomes the nutrient input to the next system, all fitting together to form a worldwide ecosystem. We call this "sustainable" because it can keep going indefinitely. Human systems aren't all sustainable, but we are working in that direction. For this spell, you need a wide beeswax candle and an image of Ouroboros, the snake swallowing its own tail. Inscribe a copy of Ouroboros onto the candle and onto all your sustainability efforts (your recycling bin, etc.). Light the candle, saying:

> As the great serpent
> Ouroboros
> Turns to swallow its tail,
> The Earth and I sustain each
>   other,
> Forever, without fail.

Meditate on sustainability and how to achieve it at least once a month. When the candle is down to a stub, use it to light your next candle.

Elizabeth Barrette

November 29
Tuesday

1st ♑
☽ → ♒ 2:02 am

Color of the day: Black
Incense of the day: Cedar

honor Local Traditions

Many Pagans and Witches have adopted practices that were and are traditional for the Native American Indians, such as smudging, drumming, and totem animals. But there is a fine line to walk between honoring and appropriating. It does well to remember that many Native American Indians today live on reservations with substandard housing, poor health care, and limited education, fearing their culture is disappearing. Do some research today into what tribe once lived (or still lives) in your area. If they were pushed out, make an appropriate offering in remembrance of those who were driven away. If the tribe is still present, find a way to contribute to the preservation of their culture—perhaps their tribe has a museum you can visit where you can make a donation. Find a way to tell the spirits passed how grateful you are for what their culture has given you.

Castiel

November 30
Wednesday

1st ♒

Color of the day: White
Incense of the day: Honeysuckle

**Day of hecate/
Feast of Saint Andrew**

The last day of each month is sacred to Hecate. Today, also the Feast Day of Saint Andrew, is a perfect time to combine the goddess's bent for justice with the saint's blessing on legal documents, contracts, proposals, and other sorts of written agreements. Even if you have nothing official that needs to be signed, you may wish to use this opportunity to draw up a paper enumerating your personal commitment to practice, devotion, and the magical arts. Begin with a meditation on your spiritual path and the ways in which you would like to see it grow. Centered in your heartspace and grounded in your belly, begin writing your sacred contract—one that joins mind, body, and spirit. When finished, sign with an "X," speak your promise to Hecate that what you have written is something bold and true, and offer a kiss on your sign to seal the oath.

Chandra Alexandre

December is the twelfth month of the year, its name derived from the Latin *decem*, meaning "ten," as it was the tenth month of the Roman calendar. Its astrological sign is Sagittarius, the Archer (November 23–December 22), a mutable-fire sign ruled by Jupiter. Winter settles in, with this month being cold, yet filled with mirth. Although the Winter Solstice is the official start of the season, it also marks the return of the Sun and, even though we won't notice it for a few months, the days are growing longer. In many cultures, this has traditionally been a time for celebrating with friends and family, enjoying music and giving gifts. The Romans celebrated Saturnalia during this month, one of the origins of Christmas. Other winter holidays such as Hanukkah and Kwanzaa are celebrated with feasts, candles, and other bright decorations that remind us of the continuing cycle of life—the great wheel of the year keeps turning. Yuletide evergreens, such as pine trees, and garlands and wreaths of holly, symbolize that despite the bleak appearance outside, the land is only sleeping and will return with vigor in spring. Stars are used to symbolize the divine spirit and also to represent the Sun—whose glowing gift of light gives us life. As one year ends, so another begins, amid a sparkling and icy winter landscape. December's Full Moon is called the Snow Moon

December 1
Thursday

 1st ≋
) → ⟊ 9:45 am

Color of the day: Purple
Incense of the day: Balsam

A Teatime Spell

The making and drinking of tea is a ritual enjoyed worldwide. And on this day the Japanese celebrate the tea ceremony. This teatime spell will help alleviate stress. If you can, brew loose tea for this ritual. Select a tea suitable for your magical purpose. Here are some examples: Black tea will attract prosperity. Jasmine will draw love or prophetic dreams. Masala chai will aid in protection. Choose a time when you won't be disturbed and brew your tea according to the directions. Use a pretty cup and a nice napkin. Serve cookies if you wish. Above all, make it a special time of day. As you pour your tea, savor the aroma. As you sip your tea, feel your spirit absorbing its magical energy. Let the warmth of the tea melt away your worries. Now your spirit is magically charged.

James Kambos

December 2
Friday

 1st ⟊
2nd Quarter 4:52 am

Color of the day: White
Incense of the day: Vanilla

Find a Solution

Let's say you're stuck in a tricky interpersonal situation, or you're stuck in a project and don't really know what needs to happen next. In either case, you need to think "outside the box." This lateral thinking is a special state not easily achieved, so try this spell to get there: At sunset or dawn, find a bridge to cross or "build" one with construction paper on your floor. Light a white candle, and stepping slowly and deliberately, state each character involved with the problem. At the other end of the bridge, turn slowly first right and then left. On the way out, say:

> With each step my world
> expands, each drop of rain,
> each grain of sand paves new
> crossroads at which I stand.

Cross the bridge again, blow out the candle, and bury the wax. A new solution will reveal itself to you shortly.

Diana Rajchel

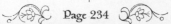

December 3
Saturday

 2nd ♓
☽ → ♈ 8:51 pm

Color of the day: Gray
Incense of the day: Ivy

Travel Spell

As we pack for a trip, we get so caught up in having the right clothes or making sure our reservations are confirmed that we often forget to "insure" our trip will be a safe one. Travel insurance is a good idea, but a magical "insurance plan" doesn't hurt, given the difficulties with all types of travel in our world today. Lavender has been used for years as a calming herb to help comfort and encourage rest. Simply place a few sprigs of lavender in your suitcase and travel bag. Put a lavender soap in your carry-on bag or purse so that you can have a quick "aromatherapy" moment if your stress levels rise. Give yourself a breath of lavender air to help overcome anxiety, and you will have a better travel experience whether you are in a car, on a plane, or on a train.

Paniteowl

December 4
Sunday

 2nd ♈

Color of the day: Amber
Incense of the day: Frankincense

Cookie Magic

However you celebrate the winter season of light and greenery, it's a great time to work some cookie magic! Prepare your favorite roll-out cookie dough (or buy a tube of dough in the grocery case). Work in allspice for prosperity, cinnamon or ginger for success, or walnuts to see wishes come true. Roll out and cut with cookie cutters, or use a table knife to cut your own shapes. Decorate before baking with silver dragées, decorative sprinkles, and sanding sugars, using them to create astrological, runic, or other symbols. Apply colored icings after the cookies are baked and cooled. A sandwich bag with the corner snipped off makes a cheap and disposable icing bag. Use colored icings for color magic: green for prosperity, blue for peace, yellow for happiness and light, and red for family power. Share the cookies with your family and visualize them feasting on the magics within!

Susan Pesznecker

December 5
Monday

2nd ♈

Color of the day: White
Incense of the day: Narcissus

Anglo-Saxon Winter Wisdom

In many ancient European traditions, winter was the proper time to gather inside for the recitation of sacred tales, poems, legends, and lore. Some were intended to make the listener think about the sacred images and ideas encoded within them. Here is an example of a gnomic poem from Anglo-Saxon tradition which talks about the meaning of winter:

> It is for frost to freeze
> For fire to consume wood
> For the earth to grow
> For the ice to make a bridge
> And for the water to bear a
> covering
> Wondrously to shut in
> The seeds of the earth
>
> The gods alone unbind the
> fetters of frost
> The winter sea is unquiet
> The warm season returns
> Summer is brilliantly hot
> The sea is unquiet
>
> The somber path of the dead
> is longest secret
> It is for holly to be in the fire
> For the possessions of a dead
> man

To be divided up
Glory is the best reward.

Sharynne MacLeod NicMhacha

December 6
Tuesday

2nd ♈
☽ → ♉ 9:34 am

Color of the day: Gray
Incense of the day: Geranium

Earth's Treasures

The holiday season is a time of abundance and generosity. By exchanging gifts, we share energy, which moves throughout the community. These gifts symbolize the treasures of the Earth, given to us so that we may survive and thrive. For this spell, you need a green bowl and some chocolate coins covered in gold foil. Decorate your altar with earth symbols. Put the coins in the bowl and the bowl on your altar. Hold your hands over the bowl, saying:

> Bowl of the Earth
> And coins of gold
> Give abundance
> For us to hold.

Pour the energy of abundance through your hands. Repeat this process on the next three nights. Then hand out the gold coins to your friends and family, saying (silently if they are not also Pagans):

> All that I give returns to me times three.

Elizabeth Barrette

pose. Today, take stock of your reactions to events and people, noticing your tendencies and patterns. Pause to honor those you have inadvertently hurt or disappointed in the past, and rededicate yourself to the project of spiritual awakening. To seal this commitment, blend together cinnamon and honey, close your eyes, and taste the nectar. Finish by offering some rolled in a small piece of white cloth beneath a tree to sweeten your future impacts and outcomes.

Chandra Alexandre

December 7
Wednesday

 2nd ♉

Color of the day: Topaz
Incense of the day: Marjoram

Remembrance Day

In the United States, today is a day many still recall with shock and horror, for the bombing of Pearl Harbor came as quite a surprise. As magic workers, we may use the events of history to gain knowledge of human nature and the ways we engage our fears, attachments, pains, and joys. Knowing this, we may perhaps make better choices, lead lives more in tune with our soul's pur-

December 8
Thursday

 2nd ♉
☽ → ♊ 9:52 pm

Color of the day: Green
Incense of the day: Mulberry

Prosperity Prayer

With the holiday season upon us, many of us feel the pressure to buy and give gifts. Sometimes we don't have enough money, and sometimes we feel "poor" of spirit. Thursday is a good day for working spells for good fortune, material and financial wealth, so take some time to say a prosperity prayer. Enrich your spirit, and remember where the real riches are.

> I am rich with the gifts of the earth, stability and longevity.
>
> I am blessed by the presents of air, inspiration and communication.
>
> I am wealthy with the offerings of fire, the spark of passion and spirit.
>
> I am filled with the gifts of water, creativity and emotion.
>
> I am rich beyond my dreams, wealthy and fabulously taken care of.
>
> I am loved and cherished, good enough as I am.

Holiday lore: Cultures around the world have shared a penchant for the ritual burning of scapegoats, enemies, and devils. There's something primal about the roar of a large bonfire and its ability to bring purging light to a community. Today is such a day in the highland towns of Guatemala. Men dress in devil costumes during the season leading up to Christmas, and children chase the men through the streets. On December 7, people light bonfires in front of their homes, and into the fires they toss garbage and other debris to purify their lives. At night, fireworks fill the air.

*The Goddess loves me and
will provide for me. All is
well in my world.*

Dallas Jennifer Cobb

December 9
Friday

 2nd ♊

Color of the day: Purple
Incense of the day: Rose

Parking Spell

Every good Witch knows a parking spell. Part of the training many of us go through during our first few years in the occult arts is how to bring magic into everyday life. Parking spells are a great example of this, especially if they are short and rhythmic. That way they are easier to chant, allowing your mind to focus more deeply on your magical intent. When you arrive to your destination and begin looking for parking, visualize an available spot near the door. As you do this, chant:

*Goddess and God of love and
grace,*

*Help me find a parking
space.*

It's important you visualize your car driving into this spot. You don't want someone else driving into your spot! Be sure to offer some gratitude for your parking. You may wish to say something like:

*Thank you for this parking
spot,*

*Within my heart, I forget
you not.*

Abel R. Gomez

December 10
Saturday

 2nd ♊
Full Moon 9:36 am

Color of the day: Blue
Incense of the day: Rue

Mighty Mother

The Full Moon before Yule is a potent, deeply powerful time. The Mother is heavily pregnant with the young Sun God, and she shines with brilliant glory in the winter's night sky. Drape your altar in white and silver, and have a silver candle, a dish of water, and a moonstone or hand for a ritual to tap into tonight's special energy. In a pinch bowl, mix three drops of jasmine oil, lemon oil, and rose oil with half a teaspoon of almond oil. Use the oil to anoint the silver candle, the moonstone, and your third eye and heart chakra. Light the candle and place the moonstone in the water before it. Repeat the following chant:

> *Waters of life*
>
> *Shining bright*
>
> *Full of power*
>
> *Full of light*
>
> *Mighty mother*
>
> *Bless me tonight*

As you chant, visualize the white and silver light of the Moon shining from behind your navel, and then spiraling larger and larger until it fills your entire body. When you feel full of the power of the Goddess, channel that energy in your own working for healing, creativity, prosperity, etc. When you close your ritual, be sure to thank the Goddess specifically in her Mother aspect.

Castiel

December 11
Sunday

 3rd ♊
☽ → ♋ 8:26 am

Color of the day: Orange
Incense of the day: Almond

Deck the halls!

Even though the Full Moon was yesterday, those magical energies are still with us. Add today's astrological association of the Sun and you've got yourself the perfect combination to empower and protect your home for the upcoming sabbat. It's time to break out the holiday decorations and to deck the halls! Here is a fabulous opportunity to bless your Yuletide decorations. The following candle spell uses both color magic and aromatherapy. Burn a red cinnamon-scented candle and a green pine-scented candle to put yourself in a festive mood. As you go to decorate your house for the Yule sabbat, repeat this simple charm:

> *The colors of green and red do symbolize the Lord and Lady,*
>
> *While the scents of cinnamon and pine bring cheer and prosperity.*
>
> *Now waft around us with your magical aromatherapy,*

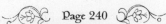

Bless our home as we "deck the halls" for Yuletide's season of peace.

Ellen Dugan

which is a powerful step toward inner peace. Find a picture or statue of Mother Mary and set it next to a clear glass bowl filled with water. Put a floating candle into the water along with the petals from a pink rose. Light the candle and say:

Mother Mary, please heal my heart.

Tess Whitehurst

December 12
Monday

 3rd ♋

Color of the day: Silver
Incense of the day: Rosemary

Mother Mary Spell for Mothers

Having or being a mother can be a tricky thing. Mothers and children alike tend to hold such high standards for motherhood that they can rarely (if ever) be reached. This can lead to many challenges, including feelings of guilt, low self-esteem, anger, abandonment, and resentment. Not only that, but if you're harboring negative feelings about your mother, and you're female, you're definitely harboring negative feelings about yourself, because "the mother" is an archetype that resides within you, whether you have children or not. This is a ritual to help heal mother issues on all levels,

December 13
Tuesday

 3rd ♋
☽ → ♌ 4:48 pm

Color of the day: Black
Incense of the day: Cinnamon

Lucia

The actual Saint Lucy was Italian, but somehow she became part of a Swedish festival. She is represented by a girl in a white gown crowned with candles, bearing coffee and sweet treats or mulled wine, walking through her family's home just before dawn. This is a celebration of light—the real Saint Lucy blinded herself because her beautiful eyes attracted too much attention.

Bake sweet treats today and create a centerpiece for your altar or table by lighting as many candles as you wish in a circle. Cut out paper stars and place them on the table and under the candles. Put your plate of treats and a cup of coffee or wine in the center of the circle and bless them with the following words:

> Lucy's light, dispel the dark, bless this food, with all your heart.

> As I drink, and as I eat, I honor you—thanks for this feast.

Ember Grant

December 14
Wednesday

 3rd ♌

Color of the day: Yellow
Incense of the day: Bay laurel

Mistletoe for Prophetic & Intuitive Dreaming

At this time of year, mistletoe tends to be available in most grocery stores—usually fresh! While this plant is renowned for increasing love between two people, its usage is actually more varied. Mistletoe has long been renowned as an herb of protection (of all kinds), animal magic (including hunting), longevity, and anti-evil. For our purposes, let's utilize its energies both of sleep and dream magic, and of revealing hidden things. Dreams can give us symbolic answers to numerous questions. Prophetic dreaming is actually a relatively common occurrence; it's only a matter of choosing to listen to the subconscious messages our mind gives every night, and how deep we delve into those transmissions! Hang a sprig mistletoe above your bed (or tack a sachet of sifted mistletoe to the wall above the bed). When you lie down for sleep, gaze at the mistletoe and say:

> Holly King, Jack Frost, the Reaper, and the Dreamer: hear my prayers! Rush upon me this night. Illuminate

my vision, let me see deeper
truth. May insight and
knowledge permeate my
dreams! As I will, so mote
it be.

Raven Digitalis

the fabric. Hold your hands over the
spices as you say:

*Spices three, protect my
home, my family, and me.*

Tie up the corners of the cloth, then
tie them together with a blue ribbon
or piece of yarn. Squeeze the bag gently to release its scent. Keep the mojo
bag in a kitchen cupboard and renew
this spell occasionally.

James Kambos

December 15
Thursday

 3rd ♌
☽ → ♍ 10:58 pm

Color of the day: White
Incense of the day: Carnation

A Mojo Bag for Protection

At this time of year, kitchens
everywhere are filled with the
spicy fragrance of holiday cookies and
pastries baking. Many of the spices
used in holiday baking make powerful ingredients for mojo bags that are
used for protection. Work this spell
to bring more protection into your
life. Blend a teaspoon each of cinnamon, ground clove, and nutmeg.
Take a square piece of white cotton,
or a cotton handkerchief, and lay it
flat. Place the spices in the center of

December 16
Friday

3rd ♍

Color of the day: Rose
Incense of the day: Thyme

Car Protection Spell

Nearly everyone travels in cars
these days. Why not protect
your car with a little knot magic?
Simple and powerful, knot magic
allows us to focus our magical intention by tying knots on a consecrated
cord. You'll need a thirteen-inch
black cord and a silver pentacle. Tie
the pentacle in the final knot to seal
the spell. Carry the cord in your car
as a protective charm.

Knot one,
I call to the power of the
eternal sun.

Knot two,
By the holy moonlight
shining through.

Knot three,
To protect from any harm
there may be.

Knot four,
Shielding the roof, windows,
and doors.

Knot five,
By my Will, it comes alive.

Knot six,
This cord I do bewitch.

Knot seven,
By the light of starry heaven.

Knot eight,
By the elements mighty and
great

Knot nine,
The magic now is mine.

So mote it be.

Abel R. Gomez

December 17
Saturday

 3rd ♏
4th Quarter 7:48 pm

Color of the day: Brown
Incense of the day: Sandalwood

Cookie Therapy

The holidays can easily be frustrating, overwhelming, and depressing. Try a little cookie therapy with these Oatmeal Raisin Spice cookies, where the mixing is a meditation and the smell of them baking works some aromatherapy to help lift your spirits. Begin by combining 1 cup flour, 1 teaspoon cinnamon, ½ teaspoon nutmeg, 1 teaspoon baking soda, and ½ teaspoon salt. Add in ¾ cup brown sugar, ½ cup white sugar, ¾ cup raisins, and 2 cups rolled oats. Use your hands to mix the ingredients thoroughly. Now add 1 beaten egg and ¾ cup softened butter. Mix well using either your hands or the back of a spoon. Refrigerate for about half an hour to make the dough easier to handle, then form into ping-pong sized balls and place on a greased cookie sheet about 2 inches apart. Bake at 350 degrees F for 11 to 13 minutes or until edges are browned. For extra added benefit, share with friends or neighbors.

Laurel Reufner

December 18
Sunday

4th ♏

☽ → ♎ 3:06 am

Color of the day: Yellow
Incense of the day: Eucalyptus

Holiday lore: Saturnalia was the Roman midwinter celebration of the solstice, and the greatest of the Roman festivals. It was traditional to decorate halls with laurels, green trees, lamps, and candles. These symbols of life and light were intended to dispel the darkness of the season of cold. The festival began with the cry of "Io Saturnalia!" Young pigs were sacrificed at the temple of Saturn and then were served the next day. Masters gave slaves the day off and waited on them for dinner. Merry-making followed as wine flowed and horseplay commenced. Dice were used to select one diner as the honorary "Saturnalian King." Merrymakers obeyed absurd commands to dance, sing, and perform ridiculous feats. It was also a tradition to carry gifts of clay dolls and symbolic candles on one's person to give to friends met on the streets.

Epona

Today is the Feast of Epona, an earth mother goddess who became the much-beloved Celto-Roman goddess of horses. You may not have access to horses, but you can meet the goddess of these sacred animals in an astral journey. Create an altar with a picture of Epona or a white horse, and surround it with apples and roses. Sit or lie down before it and close your eyes. Breathing steadily, imagine yourself standing in an open field of long, swaying grass. Repeat Epona's name to focus your intent and invoke the Goddess. She may appear as a white mare or as a woman with flowing hair sitting horseback. Offer her an apple, or a garland of roses, and ask for her blessing. Make note of what she tells you, and thank her before she gallops away and you return from your journey. Leave the apples and roses from your altar outside to return to nature.

Castiel

December 19
Monday

4th ♎
Color of the day: Gray
Incense of the day: Lily

Welcome the Gods of Winter

In Celtic countries, many ritual processions took place in the weeks leading up to the solstice and Christmas season. Many had very ancient Pagan origins. In remote areas, songs were sung by groups of men who went from house to house. One of the men wore a bull's hide and led the procession around the house in a sunwise direction. The leader shook the horns and hooves of the hide, while the other men beat on it with sticks. These are some of the words to their ancient winter processionals:

Hey the gift, ho the gift,
Hey the gift on the living!

I see on the hills, I see on the
shore
I see the host upon the land

Since the poet must not tarry,
Arise and open the door to
me

Prosperity be upon this house
And all you have heard and
seen

Ho! Hail! Let there be joy!

Sharynne MacLeod NicMhacha

December 20
Tuesday

4th ♎
☽ → ♏ 5:33 am

Color of the day: Scarlet
Incense of the day: Ylang-ylang

Winter Insights

Winter—the season when the land darkens and sleeps—is also a potent time to work with spirit and insight. The long, dark months provide time to wind down, reflect on the past months, and prepare for spring's bounty. On each night between now and the New Year, turn out the lights and light a purple candle (for insight and destiny). Repeat the following charm:

As the Earth sleeps deep

and prepares to burst forth

with life anew,

may I use this time

for renewal,

gathering energy

for my rebirth

in the spring.

Look into the flame, scrying for insights and contemplating your relationship to nature, magic, and those you love. When finished, settle down with paper and pencil and do some planning. What project would you like to undertake in the months to come? How will you begin? What do you need to see your ideas take root and burst into bloom?

Susan Pesznecker

how the energy of life shines even beneath the snows of winter. Build a ring of eight snow lanterns: a hollow dome of snow with a smoke hole and a lit tealight inside. The candlelight shines through the snow, reminding us of the sleeping seeds below. For us, the eight snow lanterns represent the quarter days and crossquarter days of the wheel of the year. We are also reminded to interact peacefully with people of other faiths.

Elizabeth Barrette

December 21
Wednesday
hanukkah begins

  4ħ ♏

Color of the day: White
Incense of the day: Lilac

Eight Guiding Lights

Hanukkah begins today, the Jewish Festival of Lights. People light candles, one per night, until all eight candles on the menorah are aglow. This commemorates a historic miracle in which a small container of oil kept temple lamps lit for eight nights until fresh oil could be obtained. The Festival of Lights celebrates spirituality, community, and the divine light that shines through cold dark times. From a Pagan perspective, we may consider

December 22
Thursday

Yule – Winter Solstice

4th ♏

☉ → ♑ 12:30 am

☽ → ♐ 7:03 am

Color of the day: Turquoise
Incense of the day: Nutmeg

Bring Out the Love in Your Food

Family reunions and holidays can be tough, but if you come from one of those families where you bring a dish to a celebration, you can use this bit of magic to ease the holiday tension: Choose a dish where you spend time mixing, stirring, or sifting. As you do so, conjure your hopes for a peaceful family gathering. Have a home video with happy memories or some cheerful music playing while you create. If all your memories are just too harsh, watch something that makes you laugh while you cook. Take the happiness you're feeling and watch it streaming from you into what you're cooking. Chant as you cook:

Over and in, I stir love in.

Up and out, the love bakes throughout.

The food will take the love you're putting into it, and anyone who consumes it will feel that love and laughter that you've put in.

Diana Rajchel

Holiday lore: The Yule season is a festival of lights and a solar festival, and it is celebrated by fire in the form of the Yule log—a log decorated with fir needles, yew needles, birch branches, holly sprigs, and trailing vines of ivy. Back porches are stacked with firewood for burning, and the air is scented with pine and wood smoke. When the Yule log has burned out, save a piece for use as a powerful amulet of protection through the new year. Now is a good time to light your oven for baking bread and confections to serve around a decorated table; sweets have an ancient history. They are made and eaten to ensure that one would have "sweetness" in the coming year. Along these lines, mistletoe hangs over doorways to ensure a year of love. Kissing under the mistletoe is a tradition that comes down from the Druids, who considered the plant sacred. They gathered mistletoe from the high branches of sacred oak with golden sickles. It is no coincidence that Christians chose this month to celebrate the birth of their savior Jesus. Now is the time when the waxing Sun overcomes the waning Sun, and days finally begin to grow longer again. In some Pagan traditions, this struggle is symbolized by the Oak King overcoming the Holly King—that is, rebirth once again triumphing over death. And so the holly tree has come to be seen as a symbol of the season. It is used in many Yuletide decorations. For instance, wreaths are made of holly, the circle of which symbolized the wheel of the year—and the completed cycle. (*Yule* means "wheel" in old Anglo-Saxon.)

peace and healing, green for friendship and happiness, yellow for communication, purple for inspiration, and combine colors to suit you—use a rainbow to make chakra balancing beads. Get beads in different shapes and sizes for visual interest. Twist the end of the wire through and around one large bead so the bead becomes a stopper at the end of the wire. Thread the other beads onto the wire while concentrating on the effect you want them to have. When you are satisfied, make a loop at the end of the wire for hanging. Hang them in the window and enjoy the sparkle they bring to your life.

Castiel

December 23
Friday

4th ♐

Color of the day: Coral
Incense of the day: Yarrow

Let a Little Light In

Nothing brightens a window like colored glass, and light streaming through color is a great way to subtly influence the energy of a room. You can achieve this effect quickly and cheaply with glass beads and beading wire. Use blue beads for

December 24
Saturday
Christmas Eve

 4th ♐
♌ → ♑ 8:47 am
New Moon 1:06 pm

Color of the day: Indigo
Incense of the day: Patchouli

Modresnach (The Mothers' Night)

A Pagan celebration particularly important in Britain, many symbols and aspects of this festival dedicated to mothers (notably those long dead) were assimilated into Christmastide. One aspect not typically remembered nowadays, however, is the oracular properties of dreams bestowed upon dreamers this night. To tap into knowledge about events in the coming year, place basil, mugwort, and valerian under your pillow or make a delicate tea of these herbs to ingest just before bedtime. Create an intention for this work, knowing that your dreams will be especially potent and you may experience lucidity, especially if you are already a solid dreamer. This year, as the New Moon energies combine with the wisdom of the ancient ones, you are in for a real power boost in the dream world. Be sure to have a journal near your bedside on which to record thoughts and remembrances upon waking. And do leave food offerings to thank the spirits of all mothers, preferably placing them under a tree (symbolic of potent life-force energy and the coming together of seen and unseen realms).

Chandra Alexandre

December 25
Sunday
Christmas Day

 1st ♑

Color of the day: Orange
Incense of the day: Marigold

Rich in Spirit

In Jamaica, Christmas is celebrated with gifts of food and drink, and household visiting. Most Jamaicans make a rich dark Christmas cake laden with fruit, port and over-proof rum, and either ginger or sorrel wine. It is common to give a piece of your cake and a bottle of your wine as a gift for family, friends and neighbors. If you celebrate Christmas, take a lesson from the Jamaican tradition and make gifts for your family, friends, and neighbors, instead of buying them. Don't succumb to the pressure to run out and purchase more meaningless "stuff," give the gift of your time, energy, and care. And as you soak the fruitcake with alcohol, know that you also infuse it with your spirit. So when you give these traditional gifts of wine and cakes to those you love, you gift them with a sacred part of you: Spirit.

Dallas Jennifer Cobb

December 26
Monday
Kwanzaa begins

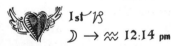 1st ♑

☽ → ♒ 12:14 pm

Color of the day: Lavender
Incense of the day: Clary sage

A Family Unity Spell

Today the African American community begins the celebration of Kwanzaa. One of this weeklong holiday's principles is unity. The holiday season is a very important time for our communities and families—and friends we love as family, even if they aren't relatives.

Create a unity altar with pictures and mementoes of your loved ones—family, friends, anyone dear to you. You can include pets, too. In the center of the altar, place a white candle. If you don't have images or symbols for everyone, write their names on pieces of paper. If you don't have a white candle on hand, use a decorative bowl, and place a stone or other item in the bowl for each person you wish to include. Speak this chant over the altar:

Family, friends, near and far,

Love unites our hearts.

Keep our bond both true and strong

When we're together or apart.

Ember Grant

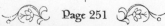

December 27
Tuesday

1st ♒

Color of the day: Red
Incense of the day: Bayberry

On Building Community

As our calendar year comes to a close, take a moment to light a white candle and to reflect on all of the lessons that you have acquired. Ask the Lord and Lady for illumination and wisdom to help guide your footsteps in the coming year. Meditate on how one tiny candle flame has the ability to add light into a dark night. Now imagine what would happen if all of the Witches and Pagans banded together. If all of us were represented by our own light, think about how much illumination would truly be out there. Instead of bickering among ourselves about traditions and community politics, let's work together and make a stronger, richer, and more diverse community.

By the light of a candle flame,

God and Goddess, I call your names.

Now spread illumination in the community

For the good of all of us, so shall it be.

Ellen Dugan

December 28
Wednesday

hanukkah ends

1st ♒

☽ → ♓ 6:45 pm

Color of the day: Brown
Incense of the day: Honeysuckle

Call in More Work

Are you working hard, or hardly working? If it's the latter, and you'd rather it be the former, this spell should do the trick. With the waxing Moon and the Sun in Capricorn (especially on a Wednesday), it's also a great day to manifest plenty of joyful work in the year ahead. Write your full name on a small square of paper. Pour a quarter-size dollop of honey on the center of a plate. Stick the paper to the honey, writing-side up. Then cover the top of the paper with honey as well. Hold a big red candle in both hands, close your eyes, and visualize/ feel what it will be like to be happily hard at work, getting paid for something you enjoy. Place the candle on top of the honey and paper and surround it with shiny coins. Light the candle as you say:

Abundance is everywhere and life is sweet.

Tess Whitehurst

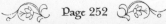

December 29
Thursday

 1st ♓

Color of the day: Purple
Incense of the day: Myrrh

horseshoe Spell

Most people know that a horseshoe nailed up over a doorway is supposed to bring good luck. However, the position should be with the open heel at the top to hold the luck. Heels down is said to let the luck spill out and is a sign of disrespect. It's best to find a used horseshoe that has been pulled by a farrier, NOT a shoe that has been thrown by a horse. Try finding a stable in your local area and ask if they have any used horseshoes, or if they will give you the name of a farrier. If you can't locate a source for used shoes, you can use a new shoe, but be sure to rub it on the ground and get it good and soiled. Set it out for a full Moon cycle, just as you would a crystal or other magical tool. Rinse the shoe in a moving body of water . . . a lake, a stream, or the ocean. Hang the shoe with heels up over your front door and ask it to bring luck to your home.

Paniteowl

December 30
Friday

 1st ♓

Color of the day: White
Incense of the day: Mint

Combat Depression and Stagnation

If you've been feeling particularly depressed or unmotivated lately—and you're not alone after the holiday season—it's a good idea to proactively combat this stagnant energy. A magical root that has long withstood the test of time (and the workings of numerous hoodooists, Witches, and magicians!) is High John the Conqueror. Legend has it that a slave named John was so skilled in manipulation and persuasion that he never became submissive as a slave. Instead, he outwitted and conquered every threatening situation around him. As a result, the root given his name is said to hold an unbeatable amount of potency and magical power. Procure a full, unbroken High John root. Size is unimportant as long as the root's circular form is intact. Empower the root by anointing it with a pleasant essential oil (like frankincense or lavender), and by loudly chanting your wishes into it over and over (such as "Freedom! Happiness! Success!"). Carry the root in your pocket until it gets lost on its own. Recharge the root as frequently as you'd like! There truly is no other energy medicine like High John the Conqueror root.

Raven Digitalis

evening. Use them over the course of the week when making purchases with the goal of them returning to you multiplied.

Laurel Reufner

December 31
Saturday
New Year's Eve

1st ♓

☽ → ♈ 4:48 am

Color of the day: Gray
Incense of the day: Magnolia

New Year's Prosperity

First of all, let me wish you a Happy New Year! May it be healthy, prosperous, and wonderful. Many cultures around the world have special rituals and celebrations to help ensure a great New Year. One such custom holds that placing coins on your windowsills at night on New Year's Eve will draw more prosperity your way in the coming year. Charge some coins for the job and place one on each windowsill in your home. Personally, I love the idea of using dollar coins for this task. Remember to collect them up the following

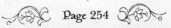

A Guide to Witches' Spell-A-Day Icons

 New Moon Spells

 New Year's Eve, Day

 Imbolc

 Valentine's Day

 Ostara, Easter

 April Fool's Day

 Earth Day, Earth Spells

 Beltane

 Mother's Day

 Father's Day

 Litha

 Lammas

 Full Moon Spells

 Mabon

 Samhain, Halloween

 Thanksgiving

 Yule, Christmas

 Health Spells

 Home and Garden Spells

 Protection Spells

 Travel and Communication Spells

 Money and Success Spells

 Love and Relationship Spells

 Grab Bag of Spells

Daily Magical Influences

Each day is ruled by a planet that possesses specific magical influences:

Monday (Moon): peace, healing, caring, psychic awareness, and purification.

Tuesday (Mars): passion, sex, courage, aggression, and protection.

Wednesday (Mercury): conscious mind, study, travel, divination, and wisdom.

Thursday (Jupiter): expansion, money, prosperity, and generosity.

Friday (Venus): love, friendship, reconciliation, and beauty.

Saturday (Saturn): longevity, exorcism, endings, homes, and houses.

Sunday (Sun): healing, spirituality, success, strength, and protection.

Lunar Phases

The lunar phase is important in determining best times for magic.

The waxing Moon (from the New Moon to the Full Moon) is the ideal time for magic to draw things toward you.

The Full Moon is the time of greatest power.

The waning Moon (from the Full Moon to the New Moon) is a time for study, meditation, and little magical work (except magic designed to banish harmful energies).

Astrological Symbols

The Sun	☉	Aries	♈
The Moon	☽	Taurus	♉
Mercury	☿	Gemini	♊
Venus	♀	Cancer	♋
Mars	♂	Leo	♌
Jupiter	♃	Virgo	♍
Saturn	♄	Libra	♎
Uranus	♅	Scorpio	♏
Neptune	♆	Sagittarius	♐
Pluto	♇	Capricorn	♑
		Aquarius	♒
		Pisces	♓

The Moon's Sign

The Moon's sign is a traditional consideration for astrologers. The Moon continuously moves through each sign in the zodiac, from Aries to Pisces. The Moon influences the sign it inhabits, creating different energies that affect our daily lives.

Aries: Good for starting things, but lacks staying power. Things occur rapidly, but quickly pass. People tend to be argumentative and assertive.

Taurus: Things begun now do last, tend to increase in value, and become hard to alter. Brings out an appreciation for beauty and sensory experience.

Gemini: Things begun now are easily changed by outside influence. Time for shortcuts, communications, games, and fun.

Cancer: Stimulates emotional rapport between people. Pinpoints need, supports growth and nurturance. Tend to domestic concerns.

Leo: Draws emphasis to the self, to central ideas or institutions, away from connections with others and emotional needs. People tend to be melodramatic.

Virgo: Favors accomplishment of details and commands from higher up. Focus on health, hygiene, and daily schedules.

Libra: Favors cooperation, compromise, social activities, beautification of surroundings, balance, and partnership.

Scorpio: Increases awareness of psychic power. Precipitates psychic crises and ends connections thoroughly. People tend to brood and become secretive under this Moon sign.

Sagittarius: Encourages flights of imagination and confidence. This Moon sign is adventurous, philosophical, and athletic. Favors expansion and growth.

Capricorn: Develops strong structure. Focus on traditions, responsibilities, and obligations. A good time to set boundaries and rules.

Aquarius: Rebellious energy. Time to break habits and make abrupt change. Personal freedom and individuality is the focus.

Pisces: The focus is on dreaming, nostalgia, intuition, and psychic impressions. A good time for spiritual or philanthropic activities.

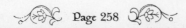

Glossary of Magical Terms

Altar: a low table that holds magical tools as a focus for spell workings.

Athame: a ritual knife used to direct personal power during workings or to symbolically draw diagrams in a spell. It is rarely, if ever, used for actual physical cutting.

Aura: an invisible energy field surrounding a person. The aura can change color depending upon the state of the individual.

Balefire: a fire lit for magical purposes, usually outdoors.

Casting a circle: the process of drawing a circle around oneself to seal out unfriendly influences and raise magical power. It is the first step in a spell.

Censer: an incense burner. Traditionally, a censer is a metal container, filled with incense, that is swung on the end of a chain.

Censing: the process of burning incense to spiritually cleanse an object.

Centering yourself: to prepare for a magical rite by calming and centering all of your personal energy.

Chakra: one of the seven centers of spiritual energy in the human body, according to the philosophy of yoga.

Charging: to infuse an object with magical power.

Circle of protection: a circle cast to protect oneself from unfriendly influences.

Crystals: quartz or other stones that store cleansing or protective energies.

Deosil: clockwise movement, symbolic of life and positive energies.

Deva: a divine being according to Hindu beliefs; a devil or evil spirit according to Zoroastrianism.

Direct/Retrograde: refers to the motions of the planets when seen from the Earth. A planet is "direct" when it appears to be moving forward from the point of view of a person on the Earth. It is "retrograde" when it appears to be moving backward.

Dowsing: to use a divining rod to search for a thing, usually water or minerals.

Dowsing pendulum: a long cord with a coin or gem at one end. The pattern of its swing is used to predict the future.

Dryad: a tree spirit or forest guardian.

Fey: an archaic term for a magical spirit or a fairylike being.

Gris-gris: a small bag containing charms, herbs, stones, and other items to draw energy, luck, love, or prosperity to the wearer.

Mantra: a sacred chant used in Hindu tradition to embody the divinity invoked; it is said to possess deep magical power.

Needfire: a ceremonial fire kindled at dawn on major Wiccan holidays. It was traditionally used to light all other household fires.

Pentagram: a symbolically protective five-pointed star with one point upward.

Power hand: the dominant hand, the hand used most often.

Scry: to predict the future by gazing at or into an object such as a crystal ball or pool of water.

Second sight: the psychic power or ability to foresee the future.

Sigil: a personal seal or symbol.

Smudge/Smudge stick: to spiritually cleanse an object by waving incense over and around it. A smudge stick is a bundle of several incense sticks.

Wand: a stick or rod used for casting circles and as a focus for magical power.

Widdershins: counterclockwise movement, symbolic of negative magical purposes, sometimes used to disperse negative energies.

TELL US WHAT YOU THINK!

At Llewellyn our aim is to keep pace with your passion for lifelong learning and magical living. Please help us to understand and serve you better by taking our short survey (approx. 5 minutes).

Please go to

http://www.llewellyn.com/surveys.php

to complete the online questionnaire and let your voice be heard.

Thanks in advance for your feedback!

GET SOCIAL WITH LLEWELLYN

Find us on **facebook** • Follow us on **twitter**

www.Facebook.com/LlewellynBooks • www.Twitter.com/Llewellynbooks

GET MORE AT LLEWELLYN.COM

Visit us online to browse hundreds of our books and decks, plus sign up to receive our e-newsletters and exclusive online offers.

- **Free tarot readings • Spell-a-Day • Moon phases**
- **Recipes, spells, and tips • Blogs • Encyclopedia**
- **Author interviews, articles, and upcoming events**

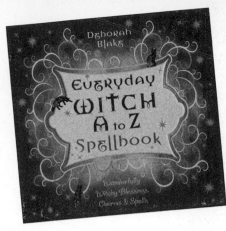